# JOURNEY OF FIVE CAPUCHIN NUNS

*The Other Voice in Early Modern Europe:*
*The Toronto Series, 1*

# Journey of Five Capuchin Nuns

MADRE MARÍA ROSA

~

*Edited and translated by*

SARAH E. OWENS

Iter Inc.
Centre for Reformation and Renaissance Studies
Toronto
2009

Iter: Gateway to the Middle Ages and Renaissance
Tel: 416/978–7074    Email: iter@utoronto.ca
Fax: 416/978–1668    Web: www.itergateway.org

Centre for Reformation and Renaissance Studies
Victoria University in the University of Toronto
Tel: 416/585–4465    Email: crrs.publications@utoronto.ca
Fax: 416/585–4430    Web: www.crrs.ca

We thank the Gladys Krieble Delmas Foundation for a generous grant of start-up funds for
The Other Voice in Early Modern Europe: The Toronto Series, a portion of which supports
the publication of this volume.

**Library and Archives Canada Cataloguing in Publication**
María Rosa, Madre, 1660–1716
Journey of five Capuchin nuns / edited and translated by Sarah E. Owens.

(The other voice in early modern Europe : Toronto series ; 1)
Co-published by: Centre for Reformation and Renaissance Studies.
Translated from the Spanish manuscript, kept at the National Library of Madrid, written
between 1713 and 1716 by Madre María Rosa (Josefa de León y Ayala, 1660–1716) and
edited by Sister Josepha Victoria in 1722.
Includes bibliographical references and index.
Also available in electronic format.
ISBN 978-0-7727-2050-4

1. María Rosa, Madre, 1660–1716—Diaries. 2. María Rosa, Madre, 1660–1716—
Travel—Peru. 3. Nuns—Spain—Biography. 4. Abbesses, Christian—Peru—Biography.
5. Capuchins—Biography. 6. Women—Religious life—Spain—History—18th century.
7. Spain—History—Philip V, 1700–1746. 8. Peru—Description and travel. I. Owens, Sarah
E., 1969– II. Iter Inc III. Victoria University (Toronto, Ont.). Centre for Reformation and
Renaissance Studies  IV. Title. V. Series: Other voice in early modern Europe.  Toronto
series ; 1

BX4303.P47M3713 2010
271'.97302    C2009–906670–X

Cover illustration:
St. Claire with her Sister, Agnes and Nuns (oil on canvas), French School (17th century) /
Louvre, Paris, France / Lauros / Giraudon / The Bridgeman Art Library XIR232801.

Cover design:
Maureen Morin, Information Technology Services, University of Toronto Libraries.

Typesetting and production:
Iter Inc.

*For my dad*

*Raymond Owens*

# Contents

# *Acknowledgments*

This project began with a summer visit to the National Library in Madrid in 2003 when I first discovered María Rosa's original manuscript. As soon as I read it, I knew that this incredible story of travel and adventure had to be published. I am extremely grateful to the College of Charleston which has funded several return trips to the archives in Madrid and Seville. The College of Charleston also awarded me a sabbatical year during 2007. During that time I put the finishing touches on the translation and prepared the manuscript for publication. I consider myself fortunate to work at such a supportive institution.

I owe much gratitude to the many people who have helped me over the years, but I will only mention a few. The first steps of the translation were taken at a workshop (Mundo a Mundo) in Querétaro, Mexico, during the summer of 2005. I would like to thank the instructor of the course, Amanda Powell, and the other participants, for their helpful critiques and encouragement. Special thanks to my friend and colleague at the College of Charleston, Maricela Villalobos, who helped me revise countless versions of the translation. Heartfelt thanks to Jose Escobar and Nina Scott who reviewed specific sections of the translation. I need to acknowledge Patrick McCarty, the computer whiz from the College of Charleston, who crafted the two beautiful maps in this edition. I am particularly grateful to Lisa Vollendorf who read the completed manuscript and shared her astute insight with me. She is a true mentor. I would like to thank the editor of the series, Albert Rabil, for his careful editing and guiding me through the process of preparing the manuscript for publication. I want to acknowledge my parents, Miriam and Raymond Owens, for their unlimited positive support. Most of all I want to recognize my husband, Barry Hainer, who has been with me every step of the way.

# Introduction

## The Other Voice: Atlantic Nuns

In the early eighteenth century as fleets of European ships navigated the currents of the Atlantic, five Capuchin nuns boarded a Spanish vessel at the Port of Cadiz. They were about to embark on a remarkable journey that would literally take them across two continents and an ocean in between. This was a watershed moment for Europe: the Spanish War of Succession (1701–14) was still ongoing and the decaying Spanish Empire was fast yielding to more powerful nations such as Britain and Holland.[1] In these turbulent times, an amazing voice emerged from a woman who documented the compelling story of the foundation of a new convent in Lima, Peru.

María Rosa, the mother abbess of the future Capuchin convent in Peru, wrote a unique and fascinating manuscript, originally titled, "Account of the Journey of Five Capuchin Nuns." It was later polished and edited by another nun, Josepha Victoria, in 1722.[2] María Rosa held many things in common with other religious early modern European writers: she was brought up under the strict regulations of a Post-Tridentine doctrine and, until her journey, she had lived her life within the cloistered walls of a convent. What makes this document unique is that the sisters' lives were turned upside-down when they accepted the challenge of leaving Madrid and traveling to the New World to establish a convent in Peru. Their legacy is a riveting travel narrative of adventure on the high seas, pirates, violent storms, and the crossing of the Andes. María Rosa's account documents this experience and paints the sights and sounds of their travels through colorful brushstrokes. She enriches our perceptions of the Atlantic world by adding the depth and specificity of her personal experience. Hers is a remarkable text because it is one of the few travel accounts written by a woman for other women of this time period. It alters the traditional perspective that only men traveled and wrote eyewitness accounts of the Iberian Atlantic. Moreover, it attests to the direct

1. Holland, along with parts of Belgium and France, was originally known as Flanders.

2. The narrative is written primarily in the first person from the mother abbess's perspective, but there are several instances when Josepha Victoria interjects her own observations. These are usually short asides that mention whether or not a certain person had since passed away or had changed rank.

participation of early modern women in the expansion of the Atlantic world. Up until now María Rosa's voice has been relegated to the outermost margins of history. Thanks to this series, the English translation of her account is now accessible to scholars, students, and all those interested in women's history.

## Women's Role in the Atlantic World

The latest studies on gender and religion are providing a nuanced view of how early modern Spanish and colonial women negotiated the minefield of a patriarchal and misogynist society.[3] This body of scholarship suggests that women, including nuns, learned to work within the church-driven gender codes that governed their behavior. Those gender codes were put in place at the last session of the Council of Trent, December 3, 1563.[4] The Council mandated the strict enclosure of nuns within cloistered walls. An exception was made, however, for the founding of new convents.[5] The Capuchin nuns of Madrid

3. See Kathryn Burns, *Colonial Habits: Convents and the Spiritual Economy of Cuzco, Peru* (Durham, NC: Duke University Press, 1999); Stephanie L. Kirk, *Convent Life in Colonial Mexico: A Tale of Two Communities* (Gainesville: University Press of Florida, 2007); Jacqueline Holler, *Escogidas Plantas: Nuns and Beatas in Mexico City, 1531–1601* (http://www.gutenberg-e.org, 2002); Nora Jaffary, *False Mystics: Deviant Orthodoxy in Colonial Mexico* (Lincoln: University of Nebraska Press, 2004); Elizabeth A. Lehfeldt, *Religious Women in Golden Age Spain: The Permeable Cloister* (Burlington, VT: Ashgate, 2005); Joan Cameron Bristol, *Christians, Blasphemers, and Witches* (Albuquerque: University of New Mexico Press, 2007); Allyson Poska, *Women and Authority in Early Modern Spain: The Peasants of Galicia* (Oxford: Oxford University Press, 2005); Bianca Premo, *Children of the Father King: Youth, Authority & Legal Minority in Colonial Lima* (Chapel Hill: University of North Carolina Press, 2005); Kimberly Guaderman, *Women's Lives in Colonial Quito: Gender, Law and Economy in Spanish America* (Austin: University of Texas Press, 2003); Daniella Kostroun and Lisa Vollendorf, eds. *Women, Religion, and the Atlantic World* (University of Toronto Press, forthcoming).

4. *Canons and Decrees of the Council of Trent*, ed. Rev. H. J. Schroeder (London and St. Louis, MO: B. Herder Book Co., 1941, 1960), 220–21 [Twenty-fifth session, December 3–4, 1563, chapter 5].

5. Kostroun and Vollendorf affirm that the negative and isolating character of enclosure in cloistered convents has been overstated. They have written: "The mandate to enclosure for religious women cut some religious communities off from their livelihoods, yet opened up opportunities for engagement with education and reform, as seen in the influential case of Teresa of Avila's Discalced Carmelites." Introduction to *Women, Religion, and the Atlantic World*, 12. In reference to the Tridentine reforms Lehfeldt opines: "By examining the intertwined issues of monastic discipline, opportunities for religious expression, and secular patronage, it is apparent that Spanish religious women and their supporters negoti-

were following church mandates when they selected five sisters who were willing to undertake the transatlantic venture in order to create a monastery in the New World. María Rosa, one of the five selected, took it upon herself to chronicle the daily events of their travels so that their future sisters in Lima (and back in Spain) could trace the footsteps of their pilgrimage. The five original founders and their posts were: Madre María Rosa (abbess), Madre María Estefanía (vicaress), Madre María Gertrudis (turn keeper [*tornera*]), Madre María Bernarda (novice mistress) and the Madre Josepha Victoria (council member [*conciliaria*]).

"Account of the Journey" shows that the voyage and subsequent foundation of their new convent was also in accordance with the Spanish Crown's desire to imprint Spanish Catholicism onto Peruvian culture.[6] The use of missionaries to build empire had begun as early as the first voyages of Columbus and would continue until independence.[7] What makes this manuscript special is that it enables us to see, through María Rosa's narrative lens, that women played an active role in the colonial enterprise. She was among the first women to document her experiences as a woman of the church traveling from Spain to the New World.

---

ated a modified application of the reforms." *Religious Women in Golden Age Spain*, 11. Also see Ulrike Strasser for a discussion of nun's agency in Catholic Bavaria. She has written: "Nuns still were among the most powerful and influential women of the early modern state; because of the Counter Reformation's preoccupation with chastity and the Virgin Mary, some rose to greater prominence than they previously enjoyed." *State of Virginity: Gender, Religion, and Politics in an Early Modern Catholic State* (Ann Arbor: University of Michigan Press, 2004), 3.

6. For a general overview on missionaries in Peru see Juan Carlos Estenssoro Fuchs, *Del paganismo a la santidad: La incorporación de los indios del Perú al Catolicismo*, trans. Gabriela Ramos (Lima: Instituto Francés de Estudios Andinos, 2003), 36–46. See also Rubén Vargas Ugarte's *Historia de la iglesia en el Perú (1570–1640)* (Burgos: Imprenta de Aldecoa, 1959), II.225–68. See Holler for a similar discussion of the role of religious women in Mexico City. She considers them "as participants in and instruments of a conscious process of social transformation." *Escogidas Plantas*, 5.

7. According to Amy Turner Bushnell and Jack P. Greene, "The European encounter with the Americas inaugurated by the Columbian voyages provided the first step in the reconstructions of the Atlantic—and, more particularly, the American world. Over the next 350 years, Europeans, operating under the aegis or the blessing of the national politics taking shape on the northeastern fringe of the Atlantic Ocean, engaged in a plethora of efforts to bring the vast spaces and numerous people of the Americas under their hegemony." Introduction to *Negotiated Empire: Centers and Peripheries in the Americas, 1500–1820*, ed. Christine Daniels and Michael V. Kennedy (New York: Routledge, 2002), 1.

"Account of the Journey" was not a complete break from similar works produced by their male counterparts or from the constraints of patriarchal society. On the contrary, María Rosa (through later editing by Josepha Victoria) created a hybrid of several different genres accessible to her at the time. It took three years for this small group of nuns to navigate the Atlantic to their final destination of Peru. During the two years they were delayed on the Iberian Peninsula, they were very likely exposed to ideas and even books pertaining to the New World. Upon close examination, we can see a tapestry of influences in this manuscript, including the style of foundation narratives of new convents, travel writing by women (Saint Teresa of Avila), Post-Tridentine doctrine, and the traditional chronicles of the New World (especially that of José de Acosta).

María Rosa's writing style is lively and multilayered. She forces us to rethink many of our assumptions about early modern religious women, especially that of the nun isolated from the outside world. What's more, her text takes account of the politically complex landscape of the Atlantic world and is a salient example of women's roles in that world. For example, throughout her writing we see how these nuns were treated with reverence and high regard. Whenever they arrived in a large city, such as Santiago or Lima, the local population would come out in droves just to catch a glimpse of the nuns from Spain. The sophistication of her account is impressive, particularly since María Rosa, like other religious women of her time, had access only to informal mechanisms of education.

## María Rosa and the Capuchin Order

We know little about María Rosa, other than what is found in her "Account of the Journey." She was born in Madrid on January 14, 1660. Her parents were Joseph de León y Ayala (from Seville) and Estefanía Muñoz (from Villa de Herrera de Guadalupe). Her given name was Josefa de León y Ayala, but, as was customary, she changed it to María Rosa upon becoming a nun. She entered the Capuchin convent of Madrid at the age of seventeen in 1677. After she was appointed the first mother abbess of the new convent in Peru, she left Spain in 1712 with the four other founding mothers, none of whom was ever to return to her homeland. A month before her death on August 14, 1716, she stepped down from this position and her cofounder María Gertrudis was elected abbess. María Rosa died at the age of fifty-six.[8]

María Rosa and her companions came from a long line of Capuchin women who had taken to the road to found new convents. Moreover, their foremothers enrich our understanding of these brave women who crossed the Atlantic. A woman named María Lorenza Llonc founded the original order in the early sixteenth century in Naples, Italy. She was from Catalonia, Spain, but had traveled in 1506 with her husband to Italy with the court of Ferdinand "The Catholic." After his death she donned the garb of a third order Franciscan. She was forty-seven at the time. The convent she founded in 1535 in Naples (Monasterio de Jerusalén) was first part of the Order of Saint Clare but later became part of the Capuchins because the nuns yearned to follow a more austere lifestyle and wanted novices to be able to take their vows without a dowry.[9]

The first Capuchin convent outside Italy was the Monasterio de Jesús María in Granada, Spain, founded in 1597 by Lucía de Ureña. At the age of eighteen, she had dressed in the garb of a third order Franciscan and in 1587 traveled by foot all the way to Rome. She obtained an interview with the Franciscan Pope Sixtus V (1585–90), who granted permission for the new order in southern Spain. After the Capuchins established roots in Granada, they began to expand throughout Spain, France, and Portugal. The convent in Madrid, which later was to send the five nuns to Peru, was established in 1618.[10]

8. One of the few references to María Rosa is an entry on her by José Antonio Alvarez de Baena in *Hijos de Madrid, Ilustres en Santidad, Dignidades, Armas, Ciencias y Artes* (Madrid: Cano, 1791), IV.312–14. According to that source there was a *vida* (spiritual autobiography) written about María Rosa and it was sent to her sister Doña Teresa de Leon in Spain. I searched several archives in Spain and was unable to locate this document. See also Rubén Vargas Ugarte, *Relaciones de viajes (Siglo XVI, XVII y XVIII)* (Lima: Biblioteca Histórica Peruana, 1947), viii–xii. Vargas Ugarte cites María Rosa's parents' names as José de Ayala and Estefanía de Castro y Rivadeneyra. He mentions that María Gertrudis was the author of the vida of María Rosa; however, he does not mention the whereabouts of this document or the source of his information. The only other information about María Rosa and her founding sisters (two of whom became future abbesses at the convent in Lima) is in several letters housed in the Archive of the Indies in Seville. These letters were written after their trip and were addressed to the new Bourbon king of Spain, Philip V, beseeching him to grant their father confessor, Joseph Fausto Gallegos, an official post (with a pension) at their convent or within the bishopric of Lima. See Madre María Rosa, abadesa a Su Majestad, Cartas y expedientes: personas eclesiásticas (1704–15), Signatura, Lima, 536, Archive of the Indies.

9. For a summary of the origins of the Capuchin order, see Lázaro Iriarte, *Las capuchinas: Pasado y presente* (Seville: El Adalid Seráfico, 1996), 17–24.

10. Ibid., 49–57.

The impetus for the new convent in Peru came from the efforts of a group of religious lay women, who were living together in a *beaterio* (an informal spiritual community), to become Capuchin nuns.[11] This community in Lima was originally formed as a *beaterio* by an indigenous man, Nicolás de Ayllón[12] (later known as Nicolás de Dios) and his wife, María Jacinta—a *mestiza* woman—in the latter half of the seventeenth century. Together they began to take in orphaned girls from Lima, and they eventually converted their home into an informal house for third order Franciscans. After her husband's death, María Jacinta became the mother superior of the *beaterio*. The *beatas* dreamed of converting their house into a convent.[13] This was in their best interest because their situation as religious lay women was precarious at best. For the most part, *beatas* were viewed with suspicion by the Catholic Church since they lived just beyond the church's control.[14] In 1685 the pious laywomen, with the help of various Jesuit priests, began the lengthy process of establishing a convent. During these early years, they directed all of their correspondence to the ail-

11. In "Account of the Journey," María Rosa always refers to the future novices as *colegialas* (schoolgirls) and to the lay community as the *colegio* (school); she never uses the term *beaterio*. Other sources, however, use only the term *beaterio* to describe this community of laywomen. Vargas Ugarte's edition of the account includes another document that even has *beaterio* in its title: "The Account of the Origin and Foundation of the *Beaterio* Jesus, Mary and Joseph and the Life and Virtues of Madre María Jacinta de la Santísima Trinidad, the Founder." See *Relaciones de viajes (Siglo XVI, XVII y XVIII)*, 211–55; see also Manuel de Mendiburu's *Diccionario Histórico Biográfico del Perú Tomo I* (Lima: Solis, 1874), I.37.

12. Nicolás de Ayllón (1632–77) was viewed as a saint by the people of Lima. For biographical information and details on his canonization, see Estenssoro Fuchs, *Del paganismo a la santidad*, 468–92. See also Bernardo Sartolo, *Vida admirable y muerte prodigiosa de Nicolás de Ayllon y con renombre más glorioso Nicolás de Dios, Natural de Chiclayo en las Indias del Perú* (Madrid: García Infancon, 1684). According to Enrique Fernández García, *Perú Cristiano* (Lima: Pontifica Universidad Católica del Perú Fondo Editorial, 2000), 280 and n28, Nicolás de Ayllon also founded, with the help of the Jesuit José de Buendía, the Escuela de Cristo in the church San Diego.

13. For a general discussion of *beatas* and *beaterios*, see Francisca de los Apóstoles, *The Inquisition of Francisca: A Sixteenth-Century Visionary on Trial*, ed. and trans. Gillian Ahlgren. The Other Voice in Early Modern Europe (Chicago: University of Chicago Press, 2005), 1–11. For a discussion of *colegios*, see Josefina Muriel, *La sociedad novohispana y sus colegios de niñas: Fundaciones de los siglos XVII y XVIII* (Mexico City: UNAM, 2004), 25–32.

14. For an astute assessment of *beatas* in colonial Peru, see Stacey Schlau, "Angela Carranza: El género sexual, la comercialización religiosa y la subversión de la jerarquía eclesiástica en el Perú colonial," in *Nictimene...sacrílega: Estudios coloniales en homenaje a Georgina Sabat-Rivers*, ed. Mabel Moraña and Yolanda Martínez San-Miguel (Mexico: Universidad del Claustro de Sor Juana, 2003), 114–16.

ing king of Spain, Charles II. By 1699 the *beatas* received permission by royal decree (*cédula real*) to become a convent. The mother house of the Capuchin order in Madrid had been selected to send five nuns to found the new nunnery.[15]

Capuchin nuns were loosely affiliated with the friars of the same name (who, along with the Jesuits, often served as their confessors), but instead of mandates from the friars, their order was based directly on the Rule of Saint Clare of Assisi (1194–1253). The Italian saint had originally founded the order of the Poor Clares in Italy during the thirteenth century. Saint Clare was a contemporary of Saint Francis and was deeply inspired by his teachings. Her rule (the body of regulations that govern the conduct of its members) prescribed a lifestyle of austere poverty, strict enclosure, simplicity (no dowry or possessions), fasting, and an intense prayer schedule throughout the day and night. The nuns who followed the Rule of Saint Clare and other austere orders were known as discalced (barefoot) orders and were much stricter than the calced (shod) orders.

With the passage of time some of the convents founded by Saint Clare began to stray from the original teaching of poverty and austerity. By the early fifteenth century, several convents had relaxed their regulations to such an extent that they were considered calced orders. Young women who aspired to become nuns in a calced convent needed a dowry to be accepted and often brought great of wealth to a convent. They enjoyed relative freedom in that they could have their own cell (sometimes several rooms), a kitchen, and even servants and slaves. It was possible for a woman to enter a calced convent without a dowry, but she would have to profess as a white-veiled nun, could not hold office, and usually had to work as part of the servant class. In France, Saint Colette (1381–1447) became particularly disenchanted with the Poor Clares and set out to reform the order. During her lifetime, she founded seventeen convents called the Colettines (a branch of the Poor Clares). In addition to the original Rule of Saint Clare, she wrote a new set of constitutions (the fundamental laws and principles that govern each individual convent) that received official support from the church. The Capuchins adopted a version of the Colettine Constitutions as their own. In "Account of the Journey," the author, María Rosa, makes frequent reference to Saint Clare, but mentions Saint Colette only on one occasion. Obviously she views the

---

15. Several examples of this correspondence are in the Archive of the Indies, Signatura, Lima, 536.

former as the founding mother of her order. She is also quick to point out the lack of poverty and lax rule in certain Poor Clare convents, particularly those in Portugal.

Each Capuchin convent had the right to modify its own constitutions as long as it adhered to the basic tenets of poverty and austerity. For this reason, we can observe slightly different routines, hierarchy, and even dress, depending on the convent. Although the times could vary slightly, all Capuchins followed a very strict prayer schedule laid down in the Divine Office. The nuns would pray seven hours in a twenty-four hour day: a typical day would be marked by matins and lauds (considered as a single hour), prime, terce, sext, nones, vespers, and compline.[16] In the account, María Rosa specifically mentions vespers (the evening service, said around 6:00 p.m. or sunset), compline (usually before bedtime), and matins (usually said at midnight).

In addition to the prayer schedule, most Capuchin nuns followed a very strict routine of fasting. This does not mean that they gave up food altogether but that they limited their food to one main meal a day and one light meal called a collation. For the most part they avoided meat and poultry. Exceptions could be made for illness or other extenuating circumstances, like the long journey to the New World. Some Capuchins practiced bodily penance, such as self-flagellation or the use of hair shirts. Yet, this seems to be more of an exception rather than the rule, and María Rosa never mentions any of these practices in her narrative.[17]

Their dress was simple and austere. The nuns wore a brown or gray habit made of coarse wool. They had only one change of under tunic made of sackcloth (a very scratchy material conducive to penance). María Rosa makes reference to their dress several times throughout the document. She is proud of their poverty and the fact that they have only one habit for the entire three-year journey. The nuns also wore a wimple, which covered their head and neck, and a veil as well, when they were approached by the secular population. María Rosa complains that during the hot weather they felt suffocated by the heavy veil.

Every Capuchin convent had its own form of self-governance.

16. See *The Oxford Dictionary of the Christian Church*, ed. F. L. Cross, 3d ed. (Oxford: Oxford University Press, 1997), s.v. "hours, canonical."

17. See Asunción Lavrin, *Brides of Christ* (Stanford, CA: Stanford University Press, 2008), 188–200.

The abbess was a senior member of the community democratically elected by the other nuns. The vicaress was second in command to the abbess. Each convent elected eight "discreets" to serve as council to the abbess. Another duty of the discreets was to accompany nuns to the grille or turn (*el torno*)—a revolving window in a cloistered convent used to pass messages from the outside world into the convent. Their job was to make sure that there was no "inappropriate" communication. Among other offices every convent had a novice mistress to instruct the novices (for at least a year) and turn keepers who were in charge of supervising the turn. On average a community would come together once a week for chapter meetings. They would discuss a variety of spiritual, administrative, and financial issues. Every convent also had its own chaplain (confessor), an additional chaplain, and oftentimes two lay brothers, but for the most part they did not interfere in the abbess's control of her community.

Generally the young women who decided to become Capuchin nuns were from upper-class families or even nobility. This tradition carried over from the Middle Ages when convents in Spain were primarily for the daughters of the elite class. Despite the fact that the Capuchin order did not accept a dowry,[18] there was still only a limited number of nuns who could profess in any one convent (on average thirty-three) and this created competition. Aspiring nuns had to be legitimate daughters. Basic literacy was also most likely expected of novices. An elitist attitude toward class and race is quite evident in María Rosa's narrative. During their five weeks in Lisbon, the narrator describes the Portuguese nuns as beautiful but the servants as "dark skinned and ugly" (90v). She also mentions that the nuns were daughters of nobility. Many of these prerequisites carried over into the New World, and the convents became homes primarily for white women of Spanish ancestry (*criollas*).

Because of their austere lifestyle each Capuchin community was completely dependent on benefactors and alms. The nuns embraced poverty, but they had to be realistic and court donors. For example, María Rosa makes specific reference to each one of their patrons at the end of her account. Without their help a nunnery could not survive on its own.[19] Every convent would have a procurator out-

18. Although the Capuchins did not accept dowries, they did not turn down donations from nuns and their families. In María Rosa's account she tells how an aspirant nun of the new convent in Lima made a very sizable donation of 15,000 pesos to complete the church.

19. For an analysis of convent patronage see Lehfeldt's chapter, "Bound Together in Com-

side the convent to manage their funds and serve as an alms collector (*síndico*). Some convents would supplement their meager income by producing small items to sell to the outside world such as sweets, needlework, or silk flowers.[20]

## The Legacy of Women and Travel

The legacy of the Capuchin nuns' itinerant foremothers is deeply woven into the fabric of "Account of the Journey." Spanish nuns form part of a long heritage of European women travelers who have taken to the road and the seas since biblical times. Before the Counter Reformation and the strict mandates to enclose nuns in convents, religious women had much more freedom to leave their hometowns and travel to distant lands. In the early Middle Ages, the main impetus for travel was to make a pilgrimage to holy sites around Europe (Rome and Santiago de Compostela were very popular) and even further afield to such distant lands as Egypt, Constantinople, and Jerusalem. As early as 385, Egeria, a Spanish abbess probably from Galicia, wrote an account of her pilgrimage to the Holy Land in Latin. Her account of the journey is the oldest known travel document written by a woman. It provides a fascinating description of the geography and rituals of the sites she visited along the way.[21]

Egeria's travels differed from those of later Spanish nuns because she was not limited to the strict rules of a cloistered convent. She was much freer to embark on her pilgrimage to the Holy Land. Her fascinating description of the trip proves that religious women were interested in documenting their journeys. She set a precedent for many future pilgrims. Other religious women documented their travels in the early Middle Ages. Among the most famous were

---

munity," *Religious Women in Golden Age Spain*, 15–46. See also Alison Weber, "Saint Teresa's Problematic Patrons," *Journal of Medieval and Early Modern Studies* 29, no. 2 (Spring 1999): 357–79.

20. For more information on the Capuchin order, see *Saint Clare's Plan for Gospel Living: The Rule and Constitutions of the Capuchin Poor Clares* (Wilmington, DE: Poor Clares, 1989), 3–15; Jesús Mendoza Muñoz, *El convento de San José de Gracia de pobres monjas capuchinas de la Ciudad de Querétaro, un espacio para la pobreza y la contemplación femenina durante el virreinato* (Querétaro, Mexico: Cadereyta, 2005), 7–35; Luis Francisco Prieto del Río, *Crónica del monasterio de capuchinas* (Santiago, Chile: Imprenta de San José, 1911), ix–xii.

21. For further information on Egeria see Carolyn L. Connor, *Women of Byzantium* (New Haven, CT: Yale University Press, 2004), 35.

Leoba, an eighth-century Anglo-Saxon nun who traveled to Germany; Saint Birgitta (1303–73) of Sweden who established the Brigittines in Italy; and Margery Kempe who, after visiting all of holy sites in Europe and Jerusalem, wrote her well-known work *The Book of Margery Kempe*, considered by some the first autobiography written in the English language.[22]

Spanish nuns also have their own history of travel, much of which occurred during the climate of repression spurred by the Counter Reformation. As mentioned earlier, the Council of Trent had mandated the strict enclosure of nuns to the cloister. But this did not quench religious women's desire to leave their convents. Although nuns could no longer embark on a religious pilgrimage like their European foremothers, many became caught up in the missionary zeal that spread throughout this period. According to Ronnie Po-chia Hsia, "The spirit of missions that fired so many men in Catholic Europe burned with equal flame in many women."[23]

The world-renowned Saint Teresa of Avila (1515–82) shared in this missionary enthusiasm. At the tender age of seven, Teresa conceived a fervent desire, shared with many pious Catholics, to convert the heathen peoples of the world and to die a martyr. She and her brother Rodrigo even tried to run away from their hometown of Avila to convert the Moors. Her dream to die a martyr in a foreign land was never fulfilled, but she later focused her missionary fervor on reforming the Carmelite order. At the age of fifty-two she began numerous arduous travels around Spain on mules and in primitive oxcarts to establish and visit seventeen new convents.[24] She wrote countless letters documenting these foundations. Electa Arenal and Stacey Schlau have written: "Saint Teresa of Avila's impact on the lives and writing of Hispanic nuns can scarcely be overestimated."[25] Regardless of the fact

22. For information on Leoba, see Catherine Wybourne, "Seafarers and Stay-At-Homes: Anglo-Saxon Nuns and Mission," *The Downside Review* 114, no. 397 (1996): 247–48. For information on Saint Birgitta see *The Catholic Encyclopedia*. For further information on Margery Kempe, see Jane Robinson, *Wayward Women* (Oxford: Oxford University Press, 1990), 163.

23. Ronnie Po-chia Hsia, *The World of Catholic Renewal, 1540–1770* (Cambridge: Cambridge University Press, 2005), 150.

24. Saint Teresa was able to leave her convent even before her reformation of the Carmelite order and subsequent journeys. She had resided in a noblewoman's palace during the spring of 1562. See María de San José Salazar, *Book for the Hour of Recreation*, ed. Weber, 43, n24.

25. *Untold Sisters: Hispanic Nuns in Their Own Works*, ed. and introd. Electa Arenal and Stacey Schlau, trans. Amanda Powell (Albuquerque: University of New Mexico Press, 1989), 9.

that María Rosa mentions Saint Teresa only once, and in reference to her feast day, it seems highly likely that she would have been familiar with her life and works. During their long journey, the five pilgrims stayed with Carmelite nuns in several different convents, and María Rosa comments on their great admiration for that religious order.[26]

Not all nuns had the freedom to move around like Saint Teresa. The mandates of the Council of Trent meant that they were physically confined in their home convent. Yet several religious women from Spain, such as Sor María Agreda, learned to stretch these guidelines by embarking on spiritual journeys to the New World.[27] María Coronel y Arana was born in 1602 in the small town of Agreda in the north of Spain. Her parents were devout, and her father eventually transformed the family home into a Franciscan convent. María soon joined the order and, at a very young age, became the abbess of the community, a position she held for the rest of her life. She is known for her close friendship and correspondence with the king of Spain, Philip IV, but is best known for her work, *The Mystical City of God*, a biography of the Virgin Mary that she claimed to have written with the aid of revelations from the Virgin herself. According to Clarke Colahan, this shifted Mary's role from that of a passive and meek female to that of an active and powerful example for all women: "The biography, while a creation of the imagination, has offered thousands

---

See also Alison Weber, *Teresa of Avila and the Rhetoric of Femininity* (Princeton, NJ: Princeton University Press, 1990), 165; and Hsia, *The World of Catholic Renewal, 1540–1770*, 145.

26. Although she had no religious vocation, Catalina de Erauso (1592–1650), like Teresa of Avila, also garnered a lot of attention in her own day. Otherwise known as the *Monja Alférez* (Lieutenant Nun), Catalina escaped her convent in San Sebastian, Spain, as a novitiate at the age fifteen. She donned the garb of a man and traveled to the New World to fight in Spain's military battles against the fierce Indian tribe of the *Aracaunos* in Chile. She claims to have written an autobiography documenting her adventures, although there is controversy as to the authorship of that text.

27. Jane Tar has documented the widespread visionary journeys of religious women in Spain during the first third of the seventeenth century. She links this trend specifically to the Franciscans: "My research would seem to indicate that bilocations were particularly characteristic of visionary nuns of the Franciscan order." Tar examines the journeys of Madre Juana de la Cruz de Cubas (1484–1531), Madre Luisa de la Ascensión, Sor Juana Rodríguez de Burgos (1564–1650), Sor María de San José, Sor Beatriz de la Concepción (d. 1645), and Sor María de Agreda. "Flying Through the Empire: The Visionary Journeys of Early Modern Nuns," in *Women's Voices and the Politics of the Spanish Empire*, ed. Jennifer Eich and Jeanne Gillespie (New Orleans, LA: University Press of the South, 2008), 268. For more discussion on both spiritual and real journeys, see Elisa Sampson Vera Tudela, *Colonial Angels* (Austin: University of Texas Press, 2000), 1–13.

and thousands of readers a role model who is not passive, but active, powerful, even all knowing, and who was of fundamental importance in the history of the church and mankind in general."[28]

As an extension of her written works, knowledge spread across Spain of Madre Agreda's extraordinary bilocations to the New World.[29] Though she is said to have never left her home town of Agreda, she swore that Jesus, her guardian angel, and the Virgin Mary often carried her to the territories of northern New Spain. During these bilocations, Madre María claimed to have baptized and preached to the Pecos Indians, specifically to the Jumano of New Mexico, and she became known to them as the "Lady in Blue."[30]

Just as María Rosa never made any direct references to Saint Teresa, her account fails to mention Madre Agreda as well. Yet it is probable that she would have at least heard of her "traveling" foremother. The Spanish mystic from Agreda was a source of pride for the Franciscan order and was viewed by many as a role model. The obvious difference between Sor Madre Agreda and María Rosa is that the latter was able physically to embark on her transatlantic journey. Further, instead of wanting to baptize and convert the indigenous peoples of New Mexico, her goal was to bring young *criolla* women in Lima to the Capuchin order.[31]

28. Clarke Colahan, *The Visions of Sor María de Agreda* (Tucson: University of Arizona Press, 1994), 6.

29. The term *bilocation* comes directly from its Latin roots: *bis*, twice, and *locatio*, place; that is, the ability physically to be in two places at one time. For an excellent analysis of the acceptance of such phenomena in Golden Age Spain, see Stephen Haliczer, *Female Mystics in the Golden Age of Spain* (Oxford: Oxford University Press, 2002), 4.

30. See John L. Kessell, *Kiva, Cross, and Crown: The Pecos Indians and New Mexico, 1540–1840* (Washington, DC: National Park Service, 1979), 150–51. Supposedly Sor María Agreda appeared to the Jumano Indians wearing the "deep-blue sackcloth cloak symbolic of the Immaculate Conception." For further information on bilocation in the New World and the case of a Mexican *beata*, see Sarah Owens, "Journeys to Dark Lands: Francisca de los Angeles' Bilocations to Remote Provinces of New Spain," *Colonial Latin American Historical Review* 12, no. 2 (2003): 151–71. This short section on Sor María Agreda is taken from that article.

31. The young women who were to be nuns of the Convent of Jesus, Mary, and Joseph in Lima, were all *criollas*—the vast majority of convents were only for white Spanish women born in the New World. In some cases they also housed *peninsulares*—Spanish women born in Europe but who (like the founders) had made the long journey to live in the colonies. Descriptions from "Account of the Journey" lead us to believe that Joseph Fausto Gallegos was a *criollo* from a well-established Lima family. Despite the wealth his family might have attained in the New World, *criollos* were often viewed as second-class citizens by the crown,

## Nuns and Writing in the New World

Spiritual visions and/or extraordinary bilocations were obviously not the only way to travel to the New World. Several other Spanish religious women made the dangerous sea voyage. In 1530, at the request of the bishop of Mexico City, Juan de Zumárraga, six Franciscan *beatas* (religious laywomen) made the transatlantic crossing to teach young indigenous girls at a school in Texcoco, Mexico. During the next ten years at least twelve more *beatas* came from Spain to teach in ten schools for indigenous girls. However, these schools all were closed by 1540, and soon thereafter the Council of Trent enacted the strict enclosure of religious women.[32] In essence, the Catholic Church believed that these pious laywomen were too active and free, as they were not strictly supervised behind the walls of a cloister. After this initial experiment in Amerindian education led by the pre-Trent Spanish *beatas*, my research has led me to believe that only five Spanish communities sent nuns on the precarious transatlantic journey to set up new convents. The first three foundations came from the Capuchin order: Toledo to Mexico City (San Felipe in 1665), Madrid to Lima (1713), and Madrid to Antigua, Guatemala (1725).[33] A few years later, the aforementioned Brigittine nuns sent a small party of women from Vitoria, Spain, to Mexico City to establish a new convent in 1744.[34] The only other order that sent nuns to the New World was from the Companía de María: they were from Zaragoza, Spain, and established a new convent, Nuestra Señora del Pilar, in Mexico City in 1753.[35] These traveling groups of nuns were in the minority because

thus making it difficult for Gallegos to receive an official appointment. For detailed information on *criollos* and many of the obstacles they faced, see J. H. Elliot, *Empires of the Atlantic World* (New Haven, CT: Yale University Press, 2006), 234–45.

32. See Holler, *Escogidas Plantas*, Introduction, 1–2.

33. For detailed information on the San Felipe foundation, see Emilia Alba González, *Fundación del Convento de San Felipe de Jesús de Clarisas Capuchinas en Nueva España* (Mexico City: Ediciones Dabar, 2002). For information on the Guatemala foundation see Jorge Luján Muñoz, *Guía del convento de capuchinas de Antigua Guatemala* (Antigua, Guatemala: Editorial Jose de Pineda Ibarra, 1977).

34. See Josefina Muriel and Anne Sofie Sifvert, *Crónica del Convento de Nuestra Señora de las Nieves, Santa Brígida de México* (Mexico City: UNAM, 2001). See also Anne Sofie Sifvert, "Crónica de las monjas Brígidas de la Ciudad de México" (Ph.D. diss., University of Stockholm, 1992).

35. María Concepción Amerlinck de Corsi and Manuel Ramos Medina, *Conventos de monjas: Fundaciones en el México virreinal* (Mexico City: Grupo Condumex, 1995), 134–39.

*criolla* women already living in the colonies established the vast majority of convents and founded offshoots from these convents.

Only three convents were established in Lima during the 1500s. This was a relatively small number in comparison with Mexico City, which erected eleven between 1540 and 1601.[36] However, by the end of the sixteenth century Lima was already considered a religious center, boasting more than forty churches and chapels.[37] By the early 1700s convents were in abundance in the viceroyalty of Peru. In the heyday of this era more than 20 percent of Lima's women resided in a convent.[38] There was a wide variety of religious orders in Lima, among others, Franciscans, Dominicans, Augustinians, and Carmelites. However, there were no Capuchin convents in the viceroyalty of Peru during this time—a factor that likely aided these particular Spanish women from Madrid in receiving permission to establish their new convent in Lima.[39]

Travel, as we have seen above, was nothing new to nuns. The Capuchin order, for example, was renowned for its rapid growth throughout Europe and across the globe. If a novice were to take her solemn vows in one of the Spanish nunneries, she could easily learn about previous foundations and possibilities for travel. In Italy alone, for instance, after the establishment of the first Capuchin convent in Naples in 1535, growth was rapid and a grand total of forty-three religious communities was in existence by 1655.[40] From there the Capuchins traveled to Spain, France, Portugal, and the New World. The Madrid nuns continued their order's tradition of travel in the New

36. Nuestra Señora de la Concepción in Mexico City was the first convent established in the Americas in 1540. See Holler, *Escogidas Plantas*, Introduction, 2.

37. See Stacey Schlau, "Angela Carranza: El género sexual, la comercialización religiosa y la subversión de la jerarquía eclesiástica en el Perú colonial," in *Nictimene... sacrílega: Estudios coloniales en homenaje a Georgina Sabat-Rivers*, ed. Mabel Moraña and Yolanda Martínez San-Miguel (Mexico: Universidad del Claustro de Sor Juana, 2003), 112.

38. Mark A. Burkholder and Lyman L. Johnson, *Colonial Latin America* (New York: Oxford University Press, 2004), 105.

39. For a comprehensive study of the different female religious orders in colonial Latin America, including countries, cities, and dates of foundation, see Josefina Muriel's table at the end of her chapter "Cincuenta años escribiendo historia de las mujeres," in *El Monacato Femenino en el Imperio Español*, ed. Manuel Ramos Medina (Mexico: Condumex, 1995), 26–31. See also Amaya Fernández Fernández, *La mujer en la conquista y la evangelización en el Perú* (Lima: Fondo Editorial de la Pontificia Universidad Católica del Perú, 1997), 153–550.

40. Iriarte, *Las capuchinas: Pasado y presente*, 47.

World, because they used the three initial foundations (Mexico City; Antigua, Guatemala; and Lima, Peru) to establish many other nunneries in Latin America (and even as far beyond as the Philippines).[41]

The groups of nuns who made the transatlantic crossing documented their travels either through "foundation" narratives or letters. The narratives were written as official histories of the foundation of the new convent. They were often styled as a book manuscript complete with chapters. Scribes copied them so that at least one copy could be sent to the mother convent and another kept in the new foundation. The nuns left behind were anxious to hear about the details of the long voyage, and these texts were a way to provide the whole convent with a portrait of their travels. Not only were these narratives meant to document the official history of the convent, but they were also meant to be edifying for the new nuns and novices. The authors of these foundation narratives tell us of the hardships encountered during the journey, while they also expound on the devotion and perseverance of the founding nuns. The founding mothers are the true heroes of the narrative, but the reader receives only a polished, "official" version of the journey. This style of writing that presents an "idealized" version of events is reminiscent of the traditional hagiography—a term that refers to the writing of the lives of saints but can be applied to biographies of religious figures as well. The genre of hagiography was well known and embraced by all the orders. Kathleen Ann Myers has written: "By the sixteenth and seventeenth centuries in the Hispanic world, the hagiographic tradition had become intertwined with religious women's own spiritual writings and with clerical biographies of these women."[42] María Rosa was obviously very familiar with this genre and incorporated it into her narrative. This is most apparent in her description of Madre Estefanía's breast cancer and subsequent death. Early in the manuscript María Rosa tells her audience that their beloved María Estefanía stoically suffered from a very large breast tumor (*un zaratán*) which would later take her life upon their arrival in Buenos Aires. She is portrayed as an exemplary nun who takes joy in her own suffering. By glorifying the death of the nun, not only does María Rosa praise the Catholic religion, but she also elevates the status of the Capuchin order.

41. Ibid., 62.

42. See Kathleen Ann Myers, *Neither Saints Nor Sinners* (Oxford: Oxford University Press, 2003), vii.

## Stormy Waters: The Spanish War of Succession (1701–14)

When the nuns began their journey in 1710, the political climate in Spain and the rest of Europe was one of change and uncertainty. The Spanish War of Succession was ongoing and the nuns had been advised against traveling during dangerous times. Many ecclesiastical authorities feared for their safety. Nonetheless, the women believed that their trip was destined by God, and when they received permission, they did not hesitate to go ahead with their plans. Little did they realize that they would soon be captured by Dutch corsairs and become prisoners of their Protestant enemies.

The war stemmed from fighting among European nation states to decide who, after the death of Charles II, would be the new ruler of Spain. These thirteen years of fighting made for a murky time of political unrest not only for Spain but also for the rest of Europe. The nuns in the Capuchin convent in Madrid directly witnessed the bitter fighting that took place on Spanish soil. Initially they were present in Madrid for the arrival of the new French king Philip V. He ended the Hapsburg line of monarchs[43] and started the lineage of the Bourbon kings, still in Spain at the present day. Later, in 1706, the nuns witnessed the short siege of Madrid by another claimant to the Spanish throne, the archduke Charles of Hapsburg. The archduke entered Madrid again in 1710, but during this time the five nuns had already begun their journey and were themselves "prisoners" in a Portuguese convent in Lisbon.

This was an anxious time for the five pilgrims because they received several letters from their confessor (he was in Madrid securing new licenses) describing the siege of Madrid by Archduke Charles. According to María Rosa, the enemy troops did not respect the cloistered walls of their home convent. When their sisters in Madrid heard the soldiers banging on the doors, they had the novices shout for help from the convent's windows. The troops entered the convent looking for the count of Pinto, to whom they believed the nuns had given safe haven. According to the mother abbess in Madrid, this was just a pretext to rob the convent of all its precious possessions. Luckily the nuns had time to conceal most of the items in the roof of the convent, including trunks

---

43. For a concise overview of the end of the Hapsburg line of kings in Spain, see the editor's introduction to María de Guevara, *Warnings to the Kings and Advice on Restoring Spain*, ed. and trans. Nieves Romero-Díaz. The Other Voice in Early Modern Europe (Chicago: University of Chicago Press, 2007), 7–15.

of valuables sent by several of Madrid's wealthiest residents. The sisters in the capital suffered for three weeks under extreme conditions. They wrote that the only thing left to eat in the convent's dispensary was peas (*alverjas*). The narrator cuts her description short when documenting the atrocities committed by the enemy troops because, in her own words, "I do not want to stir up the bitterness in my heart" (131v).

Despite the unrest of this time, it is understandable that the nuns received permission to travel half way across the world. According to Henry Kamen, the consequences of the war were not as far reaching as originally thought. The majority of the soldiers were foreigners, and economically speaking there was only moderate damage to Spain.[44] Furthermore, the policies and government brought about by the new Bourbon monarchy were not put in place overnight. There were no drastic changes in the succession of the monarchy in 1700: "The decades before and after 1700 were a continuation of the unbroken course of Spanish history, merging into a middle ground of proximate solutions to permanent problems."[45] Furthermore, the Catholic Church still exercised great power in both Spain and the New World. During wartime the church and state were functioning well enough to provide the necessary licenses for the foundation of monasteries and convents in the New World—although the bureaucratic process was slowed down by the political unrest. According to John Lynch, the king did not have absolute control of Spain's government, but was rather part of a large bureaucracy with many controlling factors, including the church, the noble class, and the regional autonomies.[46]

These factors do not take away from the real dangers the pilgrims faced during the Spanish War of Succession. When the Dutch captured the Spanish fleet the women witnessed firsthand the wide cracks that had formed in the armor of the Spanish Empire. As we shall see in the next section, encounters with other European powers, such as the British navy, were no less daunting.

## The Atlantic World

By the time of the Spanish War of Succession, several European powers had long been navigating the waters of the Atlantic Ocean. Their

---

44. Henry Kamen, *Philip V of Spain: The King Who Reigned Twice* (New Haven, CT: Yale University Press, 2001), 99.

45. John Lynch, *Bourbon Spain, 1700–1808* (Oxford: Basil Blackwell, 1989), 1.

46. Ibid., 2.

ships sailed the same waters and inevitably came in contact at sea or on land. Furthermore, due to the unique experiences of conquest and colonization, countries such as Spain, Portugal, France, England, and Holland had shared some similar experiences. Nevertheless, the majority of historical analyses of the last century have focused on individual countries or cultures, thus implying that each country was insulated and acted independently of the others. Recent scholarship has begun to recognize that within the Atlantic world there were more similarities than differences. The experience of the Capuchin nuns confirms that judgment.

María Rosa's perception of Spain's position in the Atlantic world is well illustrated in a passage in which she describes her reaction to a massive British fleet entering the bay at Lisbon. She and the other nuns with her are awestruck by the pompous British navy and she expresses the humiliation she felt:

> That same day a British fleet entered the bay with an incredible pomp of bugle calls and many great ships. Their arrogance was revealed in the way they sailed into port. The English had made peace with Portugal and thought themselves to be the owners of the world. Only the Spanish were oppressed and humiliated (77v).

Without realizing it, María Rosa was describing perfectly the waxing of the British Empire and the waning of the Spanish at the outset of the eighteenth century. In the earlier years of its conquest, Spain's monopoly on free labor and precious metals from the New World was the key to the Atlantic economy. By the end of the seventeenth century, all this had changed; Spain's reliance on manufactured goods from the rest of Europe resulted in serious wounds to its whole economy, resulting in its weakening as a maritime power. When María Rosa penned this text, much of the gold from mines in Peru, Bolivia, and Mexico had flowed from Spain into the coffers of other, more productive European countries, thus interlinking all the major European powers.[47]

Yet this nexus between the major powers is not always so easy to define, and contemporary scholars hold differing opinions.[48] Bernard

47. See Bernard Bailyn, *Atlantic History: Concept and Contours* (Cambridge, MA: Harvard University Press, 2005), 87, 88.

48. For an overview of scholarship on the Atlantic world, see Donna Gabaccia, "A Long Atlantic in a Wider World," *Atlantic Studies* 1, no. 1 (2004): 1–27. In her view, research

Bailyn has written: "Atlantic history is the story of a world in motion. Its dominant characteristics shifted repeatedly." Conversely, he notes that we can trace some overarching patterns that connected the three continents of Europe, Africa, and America.[49] Some of these patterns date back to the initial period of conquest; for example, regardless of whether the conqueror was Spanish, French, British, or Dutch, the same brutal tendencies were evident in dealings with native peoples.

Many recent studies have focused on the similarities between Spain and Great Britain. J. H. Elliot has described the immigrant experience to the New World, citing the period 1500 to 1780 when more than 1.5 million Europeans made the transatlantic crossing.[50] The great majority were driven by the hope of riches. Although settlers came from distinct cultural backgrounds, all of them were moving from the known to the unknown, from the imperial metropolis to the peripheral colony. Furthermore, they shared the experience of comparing everything around them with their homeland. Elliot writes: "It was, in any event, only by reference to the familiar that they could make some sense of the unfamiliar that lay all around them."[51] This pervasive characteristic of comparing the New World to the home country is tangible in all the early Spanish "Chronicles of Indies," starting with the diary and letters of Christopher Columbus and continuing throughout the colonial enterprise. Nevertheless, Merry Wiesner-Hanks makes the point that these comparisons are almost always based on a man's point of view and experience. She speculates that if Columbus, for instance, had been a woman, his descriptions of the New World would have been different. She is also careful to contemplate that different does not necessarily mean better. When referring to female heroes of the past she writes: "When we turn to their *words*, however, we often find less to be thrilled at, for they are neither advocates for women's rights nor show any more understanding for other cultures than do their brothers."[52]

---

focusing on the major European powers during the period 1500–1800 has loomed large in the studies of Atlantic history. She calls for more studies that link this time period to the twentieth century. See also Lara Putman, "To Study the Fragments/Whole: Microhistory and the Atlantic World," *Journal of Social History* 39, no. 3 (Spring 2006): 615–30.

49. Bailyn, *Atlantic History*, 61.

50. Elliot, *Empires of the Atlantic World*, xiii.

51. Ibid., xiii.

52. Merry Wiesner-Hanks, "The Voyages of Christine Columbus," *World History Connected*, July 2006 <http://worldhistoryconnected.press.uiuc.edu/3.3/wiesner-hanks.html> (9 May 2008), 6.

This rings true with María Rosa's "Account of the Journey." On the one hand, this is a remarkably rich source written from a woman's perspective, but on the other, we must be careful not to idealize its contents. This applies especially to María Rosa's racist commentaries on the Amerindian population as discussed later in this introduction.

Jorge Cañizares-Esguerra has also described the influence of the Atlantic world in the colonization of the Americas, but from a different angle. In *Puritan Conquistadors: Iberianizing the Atlantic, 1550–1700*, he postulates that techniques used in the religious conquest by two seemingly different groups, Spanish Catholics and New England Puritans, were strikingly similar. He argues that both groups saw the New World as a harsh environment inhabited by Satan and his minions: "One way the Europeans saw colonization was as an ongoing battle against the devil."[53] Moreover, he argues, "The devil was the linchpin that in the early modern New World held all of these discourses together."[54] According to Cañizares-Esguerra, to counteract this constant battle, both Catholics and Protestants resorted to the trope of spiritual gardening. Europeans, for instance, saw Satan as controlling negative forces of nature such as natural disasters, earthquakes, violent storms, poisonous plants, or venomous snakes, but at the same time some pious Europeans viewed themselves as flowers in this garden of evil. They could grow and blossom and counteract Satan's negative influence. Nuns in particular were often described as flowers or were depicted in images or paintings with lilies, roses, or crowns of flowers.[55] Along the same lines, the five Capuchin nuns in all probability viewed themselves as Spanish flowers and gardeners sent to the New World to plant the seed of the Capuchin order in their new convent in Lima.[56] The trope of spiritual gardening is tangible also in the traditional chronicles of the Indies.

53. Jorge Cañizares-Esguerra, *Puritan Conquistadors: Iberianizing the Atlantic, 1550–1700* (Stanford, CA: Stanford University Press, 2006), 14.

54. Ibid., 30–31.

55. Ibid., 33. For numerous illustrations depicting nuns with flowers, see Alma Montero Alarcón, *Monjas Coronadas* (Mexico City: Círculo de Arte, 1999). See also Kirk, *Convent Life in Colonial Mexico*, 152. Kirk brings to light a poem written by a Portuguese nun in honor of Sor Juana. In this dedicatory poem that stemmed from a secret literary society (of which Sor Juana was also a member) she compares the Mexican nun's beautiful face with roses and lilies.

56. Holler explores the trope of spiritual gardening, explaining that the addition of a convent to a city in the New World meant prestige and prosperity: "The presence of holy women, then, was an honorable addition to a city; on a more prosaic note, it also demonstrated financial stability." *Escogidas Plantas*, 7.

## Chronicles of the Indies

There are striking similarities between the chronicles of the Indies and this document written by a nun. As mentioned earlier, the five Capuchin nuns traveled extensively throughout the Iberian Peninsula, staying not only in convents but also in many houses and palaces owned by the nobility. Although one can only conjecture as to the contents of convent libraries both in Europe and the New World (very few studies exist and the libraries varied greatly), we do know that nuns had some leisure time and access to books.[57] In their own convent or once outside the cloistered walls, it is quite possible that the five Capuchin nuns could have come into contact with accounts of the Indies. While María Rosa did not have a formal education, she obviously was an intelligent and literate woman who showed a natural curiosity for the New World and its wonders. The comparison of "Account of the Journey" with the chronicles dismantles assumptions that female religious were completely isolated from texts other than those containing purely church doctrine. It is difficult to ascertain whether María Rosa had read specific accounts, but her writing style appears to mirror certain motifs that permeated the early chronicles.

Many of the earlier accounts, such as Christopher Columbus's diaries, employed New World motifs. These included descriptions of flora and fauna, the noble savage, and legendary kingdoms filled with unimaginable riches. These Europeans constantly compared their new surroundings to those back home. Nonetheless, some tropes began to change over time as the Spaniards became more familiar with their new surroundings. Most notably, images of the noble savage, or that of an innocent and peaceful Indian population, later evolved into harsh criticisms or prejudices against those peoples. These depictions of the native peoples changed rapidly with the discovery that they held very different religious beliefs from the Spaniards. With graphic descriptions of human sacrifice and cannibalism, it became much easier for the crown to justify missionaries wielding the cross as sword.

57. Examples of common readings for women religious were biographies of saints, such as Saint Ignatius of Loyola and Saint Francis Borgia, mystical texts like the *Abecedario espiritual* (Spiritual Primer) by Francisco de Osuna, and Saint Teresa of Avila's *vida*. Individual convents also circulated unpublished manuscripts written by their own nuns. These included spiritual exercises, biographies, autobiographies, spiritual letters, histories of convents, poetry, and plays. See Asunción Lavrin, "Unlike Sor Juana? The Model Nun in the Religious Literature of Colonial Mexico," *Feminist Perspectives on Sor Juana Inés de la Cruz*, ed. Stephanie Merrim (Detroit, MI: Wayne State University Press, 1991), 61–85.

Page after page of these chronicles informed their European readers of barbaric practices. They recounted the native ways of life and, when possible, provided a summary of the Amerindian history before the arrival of the Spaniards.

María Rosa's derogatory remarks regarding the "ugly and heathen" Indians mimic the general negative perceptions of the native peoples by early modern Europeans.[58] Furthermore, she links them to the "Enemy"—her way of referring to the devil. She writes: "The Indians were so ugly looking (*feos*), that had we not been heavily guarded, we would have been absolutely terrified. Most were naked, giving them the appearance of devils (*unos enemigos*)" (160v). Likewise, her narrative breaks away from the early images of the Indies as the land of honey and gold. These are replaced with her nuanced critiques of the lack of wealth and poverty, especially in the remote outposts of Spain's global empire. For instance, María Rosa shows her evident distaste for the city of Mendoza, which she describes as bug and rat infested. Her perception of the decaying framework of the Spanish Empire influences her narrative, most notably in these subtle criticisms of the deserted Pampas of Argentina.

Despite these obvious differences in the writing styles between María Rosa's account and the early chronicles, we can still see some similarities, particularly in her description of the flora and fauna, in her tendency to compare the new environment to the homeland, and in her underlying belief that diabolical forces inhabited the new lands. All the same, several colonial and early modern scholars today dismiss the possibility of women reading the chronicles, let alone contemplating the chronicles' influence on the missionary machinery of Spanish nuns and convents in the New World.[59]

---

58. Her negative view of the Amerindian cultures could have been influenced by the works of other nuns. Saint Teresa, for example, almost always depicted the devil as dark, hideous, and repugnant. See Alison Weber, "Saint Teresa, Demonologist," in *Culture and Control in Counter-Reformation Spain*, ed. Anne J. Cruz and Mary Elizabeth Perry (Minneapolis: University of Minnesota Press, 1992), 175–76.

59. See Walter Mignolo's introduction to the recent English translation of Acosta's work. It eclipses the possibility of women's roles as active participants in the expansion of the Catholic Spanish Empire. He writes: "Soldiers, explorers, and missionaries produced an impressive amount of writing, codifying the information they learned about the people, places, plants, animals, atmospheric conditions, and 'elements' (as Acosta puts it, meaning air, water, earth, and fire) of the New World. The enormous impact this writing produced in the European mind (mainly men's minds and mainly Spanish and Portuguese) is not easy to imagine five centuries later." *Natural and Moral History of the Indies*, ed. Jane E. Mangan,

To the contrary, a close reading of "Account of the Journey" suggests strongly that the chronicles of the Indies impacted María Rosa. The early written accounts of the New World, along with those dealing with Peru, were in all likelihood on the shelves of the palaces, castles, and convents along María Rosa's route. Many of the chronicles followed the same formulaic descriptions of the New World and peoples. The authors liberally borrowed information from one another, sometimes lifting entire passages, so if María Rosa had the opportunity to read or even hear about any one of them she would have been exposed to a text influenced by several authors. It seems probable that the Capuchin nun had access to at least one of them on her three-year odyssey to Lima, most likely that of José de Acosta.

## The Influence of the Early Chronicles

The Spanish Crown was interested in documenting the riches of its newfound lands and welcomed recorded observations of its new discoveries. These accounts were intriguing for the monarchy and common folk alike. The early texts told amazing stories of cities filled with gold, monsters inhabiting the seas, and mythological half-beast and half-human land creatures. The first descriptions of the unknown continent came from navigational and military accounts by Christopher Columbus, Hernán Cortés, and Bernal Díaz de Castillo. These were soon followed by missionary accounts by Bartolomé de las Casas and Bernadino de Sahagún, which focused on the newly discovered islands of the Caribbean, Mexico, and Central America.

Early on the Spanish Crown began to sponsor official "Chroniclers of the Indies." One of the most famous was that of Gonzálo Fernández de Oviedo. He was appointed "General Chronicler" of the Indies in 1532. His five journeys to the new continent were the basis of his two extensive official histories: *Sumario de la natural historia de las Indias* (1526) and *Historia general y natural de la Indias* (1535–49).[60]

---

trans. Frances M. López Morillas (Durham, NC: Duke University Press, 2002), xx.

60. The genre of *Historia* (history) referred to large-scale works of history, oftentimes encompassing several volumes and incorporating moral and religious observations of the cultures under study. The other two important genres *Crónicas* (chronicles) and *Relaciones* (accounts) were usually shorter in length and, according to José Rabassa, "call for a weak plot that highlights the particularity of its contents and, above all, lacks the 'moralistic' resolutions that lend universal significations to history." *Inventing America: Spanish Historiography and the Formation of Eurocentrism* (Norman: University of Oklahoma Press, 1993), 5.

His work was the first of its kind to describe the natural world he saw, and his description served as an inspiration and model to many future historians of natural history such as José de Acosta.[61] Only the first volume of the *Historia general* was published in Oviedo's lifetime; however, many of the subsequent volumes circulated in manuscript form. In his analysis of Oviedo's impact on future chronicles, Antonello Gerbi writes: "The works of the chroniclers and scientists of the sixteenth and ensuing centuries contain innumerable quotations and obvious derivations from Oviedo...."[62] Even if María Rosa had never opened the cover to any of Oviedo's oeuvre, she would have seen the influence of his work in other chronicles.

As the Spaniards expanded their conquest from Mexico southward, the subject matter of the chronicles began to include South America. Soon after Francisco Pizarro's unprecedented defeat of the Incan empire in 1532, many new narrations of the Andean world were written. Following in Oviedo's footsteps, Pedro Cieza de León later wrote the first global history of the Andes, part one of which was published in Seville in 1553. Cieza de León died a year later in Seville and never saw the publication of subsequent volumes of his oeuvre, but part one was a bestseller with a total printing of 1,050 copies.[63] It also impacted the content of future chronicles. For instance, Gómez Suárez de Figueroa, who later changed his name to "El Inca" Garcilaso de la Vega—the famous *mestizo* chronicler—liberally plagiarized Cieza de León's work to write several sections on Andean history in his *Royal Commentaries of the Incas* (1609, 1616).

Garcilaso de la Vega was born in Peru in 1539. He was the illegitimate son of an Incan princess and a Spanish captain who had supported Francisco Pizarro. Garcilaso de la Vega left Peru for Spain at the age of twenty-one and never returned to his homeland. However, he later used his intimate knowledge of the Quechan language, culture, and dealings with the native informants to write his all encompassing

61. For a discussion on Oviedo's impact on chronicles in the New World, see Kathleen Ann Myers's introduction to *Ferndndez de Oviedo's Chronicle of America. A New History for a New World*, trans. Nina M. Scott (Austin: University of Texas Press, 2007), 3–6.

62. Antonello Gerbi, *Nature in the New World: From Christopher Columbus to Gonzalo Fernández de Oviedo*, trans. Jeremy Moyle (Pittsburgh, PA: University of Pittsburgh Press, 1986), 131.

63. See introduction to Pedro de Cieza de Léon, *The Discovery and Conquest of Peru: Chronicles of the New World Encounter*, introd. and trans. Alexandra Parma Cook and Noble David Cook (Durham, NC: Duke University Press, 1998), 17.

history of the Incan peoples. Both parts one and two of *Royal Commentaries of the Incas* were published in Lisbon in 1609 and 1616 respectively. According to Jean Franco, Garcilaso de la Vega was always viewed as an outsider since Spain placed a very high emphasis on pure blood (*limpieza de sangre*) and legitimacy. Nonetheless, in some ways his Incan ancestry served to his advantage.[64] It is difficult to ascertain whether the Capuchin nun had read or knew of this work, although she, like other Spaniards, might have considered his work a novelty and a way to understand a very foreign culture through the lens of an "insider." On the other hand, she might have viewed his work with guarded skepticism because he compared the Incan civilization to the great western civilizations such as Rome and because he postulated that the Incans were already on the verge of accepting Christianity before the arrival of the Spaniards. Overall, he painted the Incan civilization in a much more positive light than did his contemporaries.[65]

The Jesuit José de Acosta (1539–1616) was a contemporary of Garcilaso de la Vega. His writings, however, were much broader in scope than that of the Incan. In addition to Incan history, he included extensive information on the geography, flora, and fauna of the new continent. His extensive natural history titled *Natural and Moral History of the Indies* was published in 1590. Not only did his work enjoy widespread success in Spain, but it became a bestseller in the rest of Europe as well. It was translated during the colonial period into Italian, French, English, Dutch, and Latin. Acosta lived several years in Lima and Cuzco and traveled throughout the Andean region. He was a well-respected Jesuit priest who founded colleges in Arequipa, Pos-

---

64. Jean Franco writes: "At the same time these very characteristics made him uniquely suited to the task of relating Inca civilization to the great cultures of the West, a task he undertook in his *Comentarios Reales.*" See *An Introduction to Spanish-American Literature* (Cambridge: Cambridge University Press, 1994), 14.

65. I would be remiss not to mention the indigenous Peruvian Felipe Guaman Poma de Ayala's monumental work, *First New Chronicle and Good Government*, written between 1600 and 1615, but the manuscript was lost in the Royal Library of Denmark until 1908. Nonetheless, it goes without saying that this 1200–page manuscript, complete with illustrations, provides a fascinating and complex lens for viewing Andean history and the Spanish conquest. See Rolena Adorno and Ivan Boserup, *New Studies of the Autograph Manuscript of Felipe Guaman Poma de Ayala's Nueva corónica y buen gobierno* (Copenhagen: Museum Tusculanum Press, 2003); Rolena Adorno, *Guaman Poma: Writing and Resistance in Colonial Peru* (Austin: University of Texas Press, 2007); and Felipe Guaman Poma de Ayala, *The First New Chronicle and Good Government*, trans. and ed. David Frye (Indianapolis, IN: Hackett Publishing Company, 2006).

tosi, Chuquisaca, Panama, and La Paz. He spent his later years back in Europe. At the end of his life he was the rector of the University of Salamanca. A comparison of several excerpts from "Account of the Journey" with Acosta's *Natural and Moral History of the Indies* provides evidence that María Rosa was familiar with his work.

## María Rosa and José de Acosta

Acosta's *Natural and Moral History of the Indies* provides detailed descriptions of the flora and fauna of the new continent. Some scholars have interpreted Acosta's desire to understand nature as a way of knowing God the creator. With this knowledge, the Spaniards could better understand the environment of the indigenous peoples and convert them to Christianity.[66] Jorge Cañizares-Esguerra has analyzed Acosta's descriptions of the natural world from a different angle as a treatise on demonology. His study acknowledges that other scholars have explored the trope of demonology in Acosta's detailed descriptions of the Amerindian peoples but that it has been ignored as a factor in his natural history. Acosta does not make direct references to Satan, but after a close analysis we can see the trope of the devil embedded in his discourse. Snakes, for example, were widely held to be serpentine demons, controlled by Lucifer, and Acosta depicts them as inherently evil. Yet his portrayal of these "natural threats" stemmed from the worldview that pious Spaniards had the ability to counteract these evil manifestations. For instance, holding tight to a crucifix, along with other religious images or relics, was believed to ward off snake bites or even violent storms. Overall, Catholics saw God as winning the battle over Lucifer's control of nature.[67]

The interplay between evil and nature is also quite transparent in María Rosa's account. While crossing the barren plains of the Pampa, for instance, she tells a story of a poor man who was mortally bitten by a deadly serpent but who, after their arrival, made a miraculous recovery. Although she always gives credit to the Lord, she subtly relates how their presence was enough to counteract the deadly powers of Satan.

While in Spain and Portugal, María Rosa almost never writes about wildlife or nature (the only exceptions are her detailed descrip-

66. See Mignolo's introduction to *Natural and Moral History of the Indies*, xviii. See also Franco, *An Introduction to Spanish-American Literature*, 15.

67. Cañizares-Esguerra, *Puritan Conquistadors: Iberianizing the Atlantic, 1550–1700*, 120–41.

tions of the weather—she complains bitterly about the heat in Portugal). This does not mean that the countryside of Spain was bereft of evil—she describes their fear of bandits and thieves in the Sierra Madre. Her portrayal of the natural world, however, is mostly saved for the New World. First, she puts into relief the marine life of the Atlantic Ocean and later she uses vivid imagery to depict the barren lands of the Pampas and the jagged peaks of the Andes. Thus she follows in the footsteps of the male chroniclers who came before her. Like them, she sees the New World through Spanish eyes, often comparing wildlife to that of the Iberian Peninsula.[68]

The following quotes show how María Rosa's descriptions of nature and natural occurrences mimic several passages from Acosta's *Natural and Moral History of the Indies*. María Rosa saw the natural elements of the New World as controlled by evil forces and, like Acosta, she viewed herself and her sisters as cultivators of this new symbolic garden. They were winning the battle. In the first example we see how each of the authors depicted marine life.

> Acosta: Bk 3, Ch. 15: Of the Different Fish and Methods of Fishing of the Indians: I had good reason to marvel at sharks and their incredible voracity when I saw one that had been captured in the port I mentioned; they took out of its maw a large butcher's knife, a big iron hook, and a large portion of a cow's head with one horn intact—and I am not sure that there were not two horns. I once saw, as a pastime, a quarter of a horse hung high over a deep inlet formed by the sea and a group of sharks immediately attracted by the smell; to make the entertainment merrier, the horsemeat did not touch the water but hung a good many handbreadths above it. All around were these creatures I am describing, which leaped into the air and in one leap cut through flesh and bone with extraordinary speed. They lopped off the horse's leg as if it had been a stalk of lettuce, so sharp are the knives that they carry in their teeth. Little fish called *romeros*, pilgrims, or pilot fish, swim clinging to these savage sharks, and no matter how hard the sharks try they cannot dislodge them; these

---

68. See Mary Louise Pratt's seminal work *Imperial Eyes: Travel Writing and Transculturation* (London: Routledge, 1994), 1–11.

fish feed on what escapes from the sides of the shark's mouths.[69]

María Rosa: Ch. 8: Our Arrival in Buenos Aires and Other Things that Happened in that City: In between the worries and concerns one suffers on a ship, we did have some moments of pleasure. We had occasion to thank God for the variety of fish we spotted in different areas. Sometimes we would see whales, which was always a good sign because it meant that there was wind. To the contrary, on calm days the sharks would appear. The sailors loved fishing these animals that were about the same size as rams. Although they are not edible, they fished them just for fun. It was a pleasure to watch how easily the men would trick them. To give us a show they would rig up a cord on the gallery and then tie to it an iron hook, dangling a piece of meat from it. The sharks would bite the meat and get snared by the hook. The sailors would then hoist them out of the water. This was very entertaining, particularly to see their two rows of teeth and huge mouths that could fit a small child inside.

One day during the siesta hour a gigantic fish appeared. Although the sailors all had much experience with the different creatures of the sea, no one had any idea what this could be. It seemed to me to be a type of shark because of the shape of its head. I believed that it must have been quite old to have grown to that proportion. It calmly swam under the ship and did not cause us any problems or fear. It appeared to be about ten *varas*[70] long and six wide. The head was so large that two or three bodies could fit in its mouth. A whole school of small fish was playing on top of it. In conclusion, everyone who saw it was truly amazed; praised be He who creates such marvels.

These two texts are surprisingly similar. The description of the shark's mouth and teeth, the sharks attacking the dangling meat,

---

69. Acosta, *Natural and Moral History of the Indies*, 133.

70. A *vara* is a measurement of length of approximately thirty-three inches.

and the small fish that swim around the carnivorous creature, all resemble each other. Both narrators are awed by the shark's tremendous strength and ability to kill. So large and ominous is its mouth that María Rosa says a small child could fit inside. It appears obvious that Acosta and the Spanish nun both see the shark as inherently evil, but at the same time they point out that the Spaniards found a way to dominate this sea monster. They dangle the meat and torment the shark for the pleasure of the amazed spectators. Most notably, in the second paragraph, María Rosa ventures to identify the sea creature as a shark. Obviously she felt confident in her opinion and probably based it on her familiarity with descriptions of nature by previous Spanish chroniclers such as Acosta.

Another salient example of her probable familiarity with Acosta's work is rendered in a comparative account of their descriptions of the wildlife of Argentina's Pampas.

> Acosta: Ch. 35: Of Birds that Exist in Europe and how they came to the Indies: For there are also very large birds in the Indies resembling ostriches, which are found in Peru and even frighten the Peruvian pack animals when they are loaded…. Finally, in the Indies there are many species of animals and birds resembling those of Europe, which the Spaniards found there, such as the ones I have described and still more that I leave others to describe.[71]

> María Rosa: Ch. 14: The Departure from the *Chácara* and Everything that Happened on our Way to Mendoza and then on to the Mountain Range: There were many very large ostriches. Boys brought us their eggs so that we could see their size. I estimate that each one weighed somewhere between a pound and a half and two pounds. Also, they brought us partridge eggs. There is a great abundance of them all along the route from Buenos Aires. Many partridge eggs are so large that they look like hen's eggs, although there are also small ones, as in Spain.

---

71. Acosta, *Natural and Moral History of the Indies*, 234, 235.

Again, the parallels between these two descriptions of birds of the Americas are striking. María Rosa compares these birds to those of Spain, just as the chapter by Acosta does. Acosta invites future chroniclers to cite other birds found on both continents; and although it may be a coincidence, María Rosa answers his call by describing the partridge, a bird mentioned only in passing in Acosta's account. Was the Capuchin narrator actually filling in some of the blanks that Acosta left open for future chroniclers, such as in this section on native birds? Although María Rosa never makes any direct reference to Acosta (or to any other chronicler), at the very least she must have read or heard about parts of his natural history. It appears quite possible that she drew on several sections of Acosta's natural history, particularly those dealing with exotic fauna, to inform her own account. But we should not rule out the possibility that María Rosa was influenced by other chroniclers. As mentioned with Garcilaso de la Vega, it was common practice for these authors to "borrow" from one another's works; many of their depictions of wildlife are quite similar.

There are some critical differences, however, between Acosta's work and María Rosa's account. Her references to natural history are limited and make up only a small part of her overall narrative. She places much more emphasis, for instance, on painting a picture of other nuns and convents visited on their long pilgrimage. One of Acosta's main goals in writing his history was to create a document that would later help the Spaniards better understand the New World and with this deeper understanding be able to convert the indigenous peoples. The nun's narrative had little to do with the conversion of the indigenous peoples whom she viewed with skepticism and in some moments as ugly heathens. On the contrary, she wrote this unique chronicle for her sisters. The influences from the chronicles of the Indies are definitely tangible in this tale of Atlantic nuns, but it is only one of the many threads that run through this well-woven narrative.

## Content and Analysis of "Account of the Journey"

María Rosa is a master storyteller. Despite some repetition—she goes into great detail about the kindness and pious nature of all the nuns they meet along the route—for the most part, her narrative is lively and engaging. We can catch a glimpse of her unique voice as she weaves graphic descriptions of each new experience into her account, combining elements of humor, drama, and suspense. She takes the reader across the great plains of Spain, the coast of Portugal, the open waters of the Atlantic, and the towering peaks of the Andes. We are introduced to many well-known places, like the Giralda in Seville, that are considered major tourist destinations even today. Ultimately María Rosa treats her reader to the sights, sounds, and tastes of two continents. Yet, this is only one layer of this multitextured account. In addition to the route and fascinating journey, her text is complex because the author draws on several narrative techniques available to her at the time. In essence, it both espouses the windy rhetoric marshaled by the Catholic Church and is a staging ground for resistance.

María Rosa often crafts the account by using the third person, but there are certain instances in which she switches to the first person. Early in the document, for example, she does this when she is selected for the foundation; in all probability she felt empowered by her elevated status as a founder and the new mother abbess. It is clear that María Rosa's "Account of the Journey" is a highly edited version of the account, but these examples bring to light her use of oral textual strategies commonly found in a typical *vida* (spiritual autobiography). Along the same lines that hagiographies were spiritual biographies of saints or religious figures, the *vida* refers to the genre of spiritual and confessional autobiographies written by religious women. One colloquial phrase that María Rosa repeats several times is: "returning to my narration and what I was saying...." This type of conversational tone is reminiscent of Saint Teresa's natural speech in her *vida* and can be interpreted as a rhetorical strategy devised to circumvent the power of the church that viewed women's writings as suspect at best.[72] According to Arenal and Schlau, "An analysis of the act of writing, and especially linguistic usages, can illuminate questions of power and domination, submission and subservience, and can reveal some less obvious aspects of the society's hierarchical structure. Sixteenth- and seventeenth-century Hispanic nuns circumvented an ideology that promoted women's silence and learned to couch their thoughts in language acceptable to authority."[73] In this case, perhaps María Rosa incorporates the use of a more colloquial language to present herself in a position of submission, someone who does not have a formal education and does

---

72. For a comprehensive study on Teresa of Avila's oral language, see Weber, *Teresa of Avila and the Rhetoric of Femininity*, 5–16.

73. *Untold Sisters: Hispanic Nuns in Their Own Works*, 16.

not want her male contemporaries to think she is trying to surpass them in her literary prowess.

As discussed previously, María Rosa intended the final document to be an official historical account of the astounding journey and the establishment of their convent. Her Capuchin sisters constitute the audience that guides the overall content and style of her narrative. María Rosa specifically states as much: "My beloved daughters, mothers and sisters, I want to inform your esteemed reverences of the reasons why our Capuchin community decided to sponsor this new foundation…." (2). Thus she keeps both the journey and the retelling of their adventures within the sphere of a marginal world dominated by women. This differs from the traditional *vida*, however, because normally the female author would use some form of rhetoric of humility, declaring that holy obedience (*la santa obediencia*) to her confessor had obligated her to put quill to parchment. Distinct from those texts, María Rosa is direct about her intentions. She writes this account not because of a male ecclesiastical authority, but because she has received a request from her sisters: "I am writing this account of our journey because my beloved mothers and sisters of this house, Jesus, Mary, and Joseph, have asked me to do so…." (1).

From the very first pages of her account we see how María Rosa does not always conform to the rigid constraints of empire directed by men. According to several scholars, women in the colonial world "exist in a symbiotic relationship with the page, with official space, but provide a space for contestations and escape."[74] Through her retelling of the journey, the narrator provides her sisters with a feminine perspective of the Atlantic world. For instance, María Rosa always showed great respect for the male authorities, but when it came time for the selection of the five founders for the new convent, there were nuns who refused their charge. For whatever reason, they did not want to travel across the world; they voiced their objections, and their opinions were heard. María Rosa records this in her text. Furthermore, in another section the consolation of eternal salvation seems secondary to the passing of their beloved Madre Estefanía. She writes: "Our grief and that of our father confessor was beyond words since we had witnessed her leave the cloister only later to die in a foreign land" (20v, 21). She then goes on to say that it was all done for God's glory, but this seems more like an afterthought. It is one of

---

74. Lizabeth Paravisini-Gebert and Ivette Romero-Cesareo, *Women at Sea: Travel Writing and the Margins of Caribbean Discourse* (New York: Palgrove, 2001), 7.

the unique moments in the text when María Rosa expresses some resistance to the foundation.

The majority of the Capuchin nuns would never leave their convent in Lima, but they would always have the opportunity to "escape" to the exotic environs portrayed by María Rosa in her account. The history of their foundation had been written by one of their own. Furthermore, they are treated to a fascinating glimpse of life on the road in the early eighteenth century. María Rosa includes many details such as their daily prayer schedule, modes of transportation, sleeping accommodations, diet, the countryside, and the people they met along the route. The five nuns traveled in a carriage pulled by six mules, an extremely bumpy and uncomfortable mode of transportation. María Rosa tells us that her sisters were dizzy and sick especially at the beginning of the trip: "My sisters began to feel motion sick because all of the carriage curtains were tightly closed. One of my sisters really worried me: from the moment she stepped into the carriage she was extremely queasy" (28v). We learn also that the nuns were traveling in a small caravan. Among several other Spaniards heading to the New World to fulfill appointed positions, they were accompanied by Joseph Fausto Gallegos (their father confessor), by his brother Ignacio Gallegos (the future *oidor* of Chile), by Doctor Don Cipriano de Santa Cruz (the future precentor [*chantre*] of the Cathedral of Guamanga), by at least one male lay brother, and by the whole team of mule drivers.

When possible, the five nuns stayed in convents or houses of noble contacts, but there were times when they needed to spend the night in country inns (*posadas*). On some occasions, they were offered beds with luxurious sheets and mattresses, but the pilgrims always slept on the floor or on the hard wooden frame with just one blanket. The narrator often makes reference to the austere lifestyle of their Capuchin order. When an experience is particularly difficult, they enjoy offering their suffering up to God. Such humble rhetoric is part and parcel of María Rosa's narrative style. Furthermore, as part of their austere lifestyle, their order permitted them to wear only the habit on their backs and to have two undergarments. María Rosa mentions this fact several times along their journey, and it is difficult for the modern reader to fathom the condition of these garments even after a few weeks of travel, not to mention after three years on the road.

On some days the women's diet appears to be much more bountiful than their accustomed asceticism in their Capuchin convent. At the beginning of the journey, the bishop of Toledo made them promise that they would obey their confessor's wishes and not fast during the trip. Subsequently, whenever María describes a meal she reminds the reader that she and her companions were thoroughly distressed that they had to eat such items as sponge cakes (*bizcochos*), ring-shaped pastries (*rosquillas*), roasted chickens, and partridge. Seeing many tears and long faces she would encourage her companions to eat these delicious foods out of obedience: "I tried to encourage them so that our father confessor would not feel hurt. I reminded them that their obedience was also a type of sacrifice" (41v).

It is impossible to know the truth behind these self-sacrificing statements. Humble rhetoric was very common to nuns' writings during the period,[75] and although the five companions' opinions might have differed on issues, such as their diet during the journey, the narrator was unlikely to express these views in an account destined to be the official history of the convent. This was also going to be a public testimony, open to the male ecclesiastical community and, of course, members of the Inquisition. Thus it is not surprising that the narrator follows the traditional rhetoric expected of a woman of her status. Only in subtle instances, as in the introduction dedicated only to female readers, can we see a hint of María Rosa's unique voice.

Despite this humble rhetoric, María Rosa's narration offers valuable insights into Spain of the early 1700s, both to her sisters and to the modern reader. When entering Andalusia she was delighted by a bagpiper and his son who entertained the group. The rough mule drivers even danced to the music. They witnessed Andalusia at the peak of the olive harvest: "It was the olive harvest, the trail was full of olive trees, and many people were gathering them" (50v). Also, she makes a point of saying that they often had to close the curtains because many country folk were curious to see the traveling nuns. After visiting many small towns along the way, the group spent eighteen days in a convent in Seville (this later would be their place of residence for a year and a half after losing all of their official licenses to the Dutch corsairs). While in Seville the pilgrims had the opportunity to visit La Giralda, an obvious tourist destination even three hundred years ago. The women were very impressed by the tower:

---

75. For an excellent analysis of the rhetoric of humility, see Weber, *Teresa of Avila and the Rhetoric of Femininity*, 48–50; and Arenal and Schlau, *Untold Sisters: Hispanic Nuns in Their Own Works*, 15–17.

The distinguished canons honored us in many ways
and they delighted us by taking us to see the famous
Giralda. It is truly marvelous, because it is so high that
you do not need to climb any stairs to go up it—even a
sedan chair can easily go up. In order for us to hear the
tremendous force of the bells, they were rung outside
the ordinary prayer schedule. The bells were many
and large and even though we were ready, they nearly
scared us to death (60).

With such detailed observations, this narration at times falls
more into the category of female travel literature than a typical narrative about the foundation of a new convent. Her depictions of Andalusia are lively and upbeat. As mentioned earlier, María Rosa was re-cre-
ating the marvels of southern Spain for her sisters who stayed behind
and for those in the new convent in Lima. Most of them would never
leave the cloistered walls of their convent, but like armchair tourists
they were able to relive some of the sights and adventures of their sisters through the narrator. Not only has she and her four companions
undertaken this incredible transatlantic voyage, but she makes it possible for others, through her writing, to relive their experiences.

In the section on the capture by the Dutch corsairs, María
Rosa changes the tone of her narrative dramatically. She graphically
reproduces for her sisters the pitiful situation of the Spanish galleons
in comparison to the power of the Dutch (and later the British).[76] Furthermore, she exposes the nuns to a totally foreign culture, one that
she finds strange and repugnant. According to María Rosa, the Dutch
showed no mercy toward the majority of the prisoners. They looted
and sacked all the cabins, including that of the wife of the Chilean
presiding magistrate (*presidenta de Chile*). The nuns suffered when
they witnessed their cruelty to the other passengers:

The Dutch crew hauled down our king's flags and
raised their own with great pride and celebration. This
was very distressing to all the prisoners, whom they

---

76. As a former territory of Spain the Dutch had a long-standing tradition of animosity
towards the Spanish. Moreover, at times the Dutch government sponsored corsairs and jus-
tified their attacks on Spanish ships as part of their fight against Catholicism. For a detailed
study on piracy during this period, see Kris Lane, *Pillaging the Empire: Piracy in the Americas 1500–1750* (Armonk, NY: M. E. Sharpe, 1998).

began to treat with unspeakable tyranny, for they beat some of them with staves. Others, of higher status, although they were not treated like that, were taken to the enemy ships and given nothing better to eat than barley gruel; as they had taken all the provisions from our ships with them (71v, 72).

The only passengers who received some form of clemency were the five nuns. Apparently one of the Dutch captains treated them with the utmost respect. From the very beginning, the women were impressed by his genteel manners and courtesy. He ordered sentries to guard their cabin and offered them beer and butter (neither of which they accepted). María Rosa writes: "In this man I observed many good qualities: he was kind, well mannered, and not a tyrant like the rest" (83). The women took advantage of his kindness and hid ten or twelve passengers in their cabin. However, despite their kindness, the Dutch took all their possessions, including the five vestments they used to celebrate mass and all the other items they brought along for the new foundation.

After six days at sea "in the company of these barbarians" (76v), the Dutch commander finally decided to take the fleet to the Port of Lisbon. On April 2, 1710, when they reached the port, their situation was grave. Except for their habits, the nuns had lost all their possessions and most importantly the official licenses for the new foundation in Peru. Their benefactor, Joseph Gallegos, had been stripped of his entire fortune. Ninety Jesuit missionaries made it to shore with just the clothes on their backs. The future archbishop and viceroy of Lima, Pedro Levanto,[77] never left the ship; instead he was taken as prisoner to Holland where he would have to wait a year and a half before the Spanish Crown would trade prisoners for his release. María Rosa was horrified at the way the Dutch treated this very important figure of the Catholic Church. According to her account, not only did they mistreat him physically by practically starving him

---

77. Pedro Francisco Levanto Vivaldo (Seville 1662–1729). After his release, Levanto traveled back to Spain from Holland via land. He made two memorable stops on the way home. First he was greeted in France by Louis XIV and later in Madrid he kissed the hand of the new Spanish king, Philip V. Subsequently Levanto renounced his position as viceroy and archbishop of Lima and accepted another post as the bishop of Badajoz, Spain. This was an apparent step down, but in light of his lengthy ordeal Levanto obviously wanted to remain in his home country. See Justino Matute y Gaviria, *Hijos de Sevilla señalados en Santidad, Letras, Armas, Artes o Dignidad* (Seville: Oficina de El Orden, 1887), II.121–23.

but they ridiculed his Catholic faith: "They mocked the religious prints right in front of him, they smeared the image of the Señor Saint Joseph with bacon, and they used the holy oils that he had brought as a dressing for their food" (75v).

The Capuchin nuns did receive a surprise when they made their final preparations to leave the ship. During their farewells, María Rosa tells us that the captain took her hand and tried to kiss it. She pulled back and did not let him do so, but she used the occasion to ask him to return some prints that had been left on the altar (soon thereafter he sent them to her). The nuns were later told that he was secretly a Catholic.

The Dutch captain could have been Catholic; after all, the Low Countries had been a part of Spain until the late 1500s. Moreover, there still was an underground Catholic presence in the Netherlands at this time.[78] Whether it is true or not, it certainly adds to the suspense of this narrative. María Rosa plants a seed of hope even at the lowest point of their journey. According to her myopic vision, only truly good people must be Catholic. It would not have been possible that they could have been treated so well by Protestants. In her introduction to *Crossing Boundaries: Attending to Early Modern Women*, Anne Lake Prescott writes that "religion may have provided women with opportunities for transnational contact and for escaping restrictive spaces within nations, but religion may also have challenged notions of ethnic or cultural differences."[79] In this case, the five women are exposed to a man from a totally different culture; however, his kindness and later confession that he is secretly a Catholic challenges their prejudices against the Dutch. This captain in particular is not seen as a "barbarian." By documenting this in her account, María Rosa is exposing her readers to a new way of looking at a different culture.

Much later in their journey, in Valparaiso, Chile, the nuns were to meet three French captains who offered them passage on their ships to Lima. In stark contrast to her dislike of the Dutch (with the exception of the captain), María Rosa was very impressed with these men. She makes a point of stating that they were observant Catholics. She did not seem at all concerned that they were Frenchmen, an

---

78. See Christine Kooi, "Popish Impudence: The Perseverance of the Roman Catholic Faithful in Calvinist Holland, 1572–1620," *Sixteenth Century Journal* 26, no. 1 (1995): 75–85.

79. Anne Lake Prescott, introduction to *Crossing Boundaries: Attending to Early Modern Women*, ed. Jane Donawerth and Adele Seeff (Newark: University of Delaware Press, 2000), 20.

attitude that coincided with the mindset of the Spaniards during that time period: their new king was French, and they saw the French as their main allies during the Spanish War of Succession. Furthermore, Catholicism was a much more uniting factor than nationality.

The nuns had the same positive reaction toward the Portuguese. It did not matter that Spain was at war with Portugal at the time. When the nuns entered Lisbon's harbor, they felt a sense of relief to be in Catholic waters. This is the point where María Rosa incorporates some humorous moments into her narrative. Not only does the narrator seem interested in edifying her new community, but she has an eye for drama, spicing up certain parts of the journey. After being captured by Dutch corsairs, for instance, the five pilgrims were required to spend six weeks as "prisoners" in two Lisbon convents while they waited for safe passage back to Spain. This part of the chronicle is quite humorous because María Rosa lets us glimpse her annoyance at the opulence and lack of religious piety in the Portuguese convents— evidently the nuns were from the upper echelons of Lisbon society. She pokes fun even at their status as "prisoners" because they were treated like royalty. Clearly the Portuguese nuns were thrilled to have the Spanish pilgrims as their guests. They lavished the Castilian women with gifts and would not let them have a moment of peace.

In contrast to the Portuguese, the indigenous culture of the Southern Cone was totally foreign to the Spanish pilgrims. Before crossing the Pampas to the Andes, the women spent several weeks on a *chácara* (the narrator informs the reader that this is the term used in the Indies for hacienda). They spent fifteen days on the rustic ranch owned by a gentleman from Buenos Aires, Don Joseph Arregui. This was the nuns' first experience with the native population. According to María Rosa, there were about a hundred "barbarian" Indians living at the hacienda (almost all of them women and children since the men of their tribes had been killed in war by the Spaniards). With the help of a Franciscan friar, Don Joseph took it upon himself to indoctrinate the indigenous population in the Christian faith, and the nuns admired him for his dedication to those people.

María Rosa dedicates only a small section of her narrative to her portrayal of the ranch and the native peoples. Her worldview is obviously colored by the Spaniards' overall impression of the Amerindians as an inferior race. She takes pity on their status as heathens, while she praises Don Joseph's efforts to indoctrinate them. She writes:

> When we arrived at the aforementioned *chácara* there
> were close to one hundred Indians living there. The
> majority were very young. There were also a few old
> women who were completely unable to grasp anything
> pertaining to our holy faith. It was pitiful to see them in
> this state. That fine gentleman had the utmost concern
> that both the old women and the children be taught
> and instructed in Christian doctrine (152v).

These are her brief observations. It is very difficult to ascertain the real treatment of these native peoples from her narrative. However, we know that the situation was not as idyllic as she describes it.[80] In her editing of the account, Josepha Victoria interjects: "I have since heard that the Indians got smallpox (*viruela*) and more than eighty have died…." (153). Her words were a dark premonition: by the end of the nineteenth century virtually all the Southern Cone's indigenous population would be completely decimated by war and disease.

   These nuanced discrepancies in María Rosa's observations remind us that we must be careful not to take her descriptions at face value. Since her account was soon to become a public document, she had to be wary of its content. The men of the Arregui family were powerful players in the colonial enterprise of Argentina and Peru. They were also potential donors to the new convent, so it makes sense that María Rosa would praise them.

   Criticisms of Spaniards living in the New World are absent from the document, but María Rosa is not inhibited in passing judgment on certain places, such as the frontier town of Mendoza. The

---

80. At least one source specifically calls into question the benevolence of the Arregui family towards the indigenous populations: The *Diccionario Biográfico Nacional* from Buenos Aires has an entry on Juan de Armasa y Arregui, one of the Arregui brothers who visited the nuns on the hacienda. According to the entry he was originally from Buenos Aires and the brother of Gabriel Arregui, the bishop of Cuzco. At the end of his life Juan Arregui would also become the bishop of Buenos Aires. He first held the position of the *corregidor* of Cuzco and later became the governor of Tucumán in 1732. According to this biographical entry, he was inept at his job, cruel, and vengeful: "Dando margen con su inacción a una de las más cruentos y formidables invasiones de los naturales que recuerdan los anales de la historia local de aquel territorio" (His lack of action made way for one of the most bloody and formidable invasions by the natives that has ever been recorded in the local annals of that territory). The viceroy dismissed him from his post in 1735. He died a year later on December 19, 1736. See Carlos Molina Arrotea, et al, "Juan de Armasa y Arregui," *Diccionario Biográfico Nacional* (Buenos Aires: Rivadavia, 1877), I.336.

small party stayed approximately eighteen days in Mendoza while their confessor sent for mules and saddles to cross the Andes. María Rosa was far from impressed with this small town on the edge of Spanish civilization. Although she thanked the governor's wife and also the vicar for their generosity, she made a point of discussing the plague of giant bedbugs (*chinches*) that attacked them in the late evening hours: "The adobe walls were infested with creatures quite similar to bedbugs, but they are much larger; each bug is four to six times the size of the ones in Spain. You don't see them at all during the day, but every morning we would awake covered in bumps" (162). These graphic descriptions of life on the pampas probably were quite accurate. The sisters had all taken a vow of poverty, but they were accustomed to a more civilized lifestyle in the capital of Spain.

In this section of the account, María Rosa has no qualms about expressing her obvious dislike for the uncivilized areas of the peripheries.[81] Her description speaks to the whole social milieu that made up colonial society. It is my impression that her portrayal of Mendoza would be very similar to that of any other Spaniard (male or female) who had just arrived in the New World.[82] Furthermore, at the end of the narrative, María Rosa sharply juxtaposes this dusty town of the Pampas to the opulence of Lima.

In spite of María Rosa's criticisms, for the most part her narration leans toward awe and wonder. In addition, she intersperses elements of humor that provide surprising moments of comic relief. One such example comes from the most difficult part of the journey: the crossing of the Andes. In this section, the nuns would abandon the relative comfort of their oxcarts for the backs of mules. They were to traverse one of the most treacherous mountain ranges in the world. María Rosa had never ridden on the back on any type of animal, nor had she ever seen a woman undertake such a feat. She describes herself and Bernarda as horrible riders. They fell on at least two separate occasions. Also, María Rosa feels sorry for the mules because she is quite large: "We were both poor riders [referring to Bernarda] and I had the additional problem of being quite fat, causing the mules to

81. See Turner Bushnell and Green for their discussion of the division within the colonies. They posit that the colonies were divided into core areas (the cities) and the peripheries (areas dominated by indigenous populations). "Introduction," *Negotiated Empire*, 2.

82. Unlike their experience in Mendoza, the four women really enjoyed their stay in Santiago. The narrator declared this city to be the closest to Spain they had seen so far, especially because the people and the climate were both very similar.

tire easily...." (164v). María Rosa's playful voice shines through in this vivid illustration. She does not mind poking fun at her rotund figure, while she provides the reader some comic relief.

It would take another five months until the founders would finally enter the doors of their new convent. May 14, 1713, was chosen as the official day of their foundation. The last chapter of the manuscript is dedicated to the last days before this official date. By this time the four women had been living in Lima in another convent for several months and had visited with all of Lima's dignitaries and met most of the nuns living in the other twelve convents. In political terms the pilgrims from Spain had paid their respects to the upper crust of Lima's noble society, and they had secured the necessary funds to finish the construction of the cloister and the church, which was completed in 1721.

On May 14, 1713, the four sisters left by coach the Convent of the Madres Trinitarias. After being dropped off at the cathedral, they walked in procession the five blocks to their new convent. According to María Rosa, the streets were packed with people; everyone wanted to see the nuns who had made such an incredible journey from the other side of the world: "Everyone in Lima, both healthy and infirm, came out to see us; the route was so filled with people that they could not all fit in the streets" (200v). Whether or not throngs of people really came out to greet the nuns, it seems clear that María Rosa shapes her narrative to emphasize the sister's spiritual role in the New World. Ultimately she positions herself and companion nuns from Spain as cultivators of a new spiritual garden in Lima.

The end of the manuscript follows the traditional format of foundation narratives.[83] First, María Rosa records all the names of the *colegialas* who then took vows as new Capuchin nuns. She then thanks their confessor, Joseph Fausto Gallegos, who funded the entire trip and continued to function as their spiritual advisor. Next, she documents the building of the new convent and the church, making references to specific monetary donations. In particular, the new abbess carefully includes all the names of the men and women who had made the foundation possible. She views the new foundation as a collective endeavor, one that was ultimately guided by God, whom she thanks at the very end for making all of this possible: "May His Divine Majesty be eternally praised for His works and especially this one that

---

83. For a concise overview on the typical contents of a foundation narrative, see Josefina Muriel's introduction to *Crónica del Convento de Nuestra Señora de las Nieves*, 13, 14.

has required innumerable trials and tribulations...." (207v). She hopes that "His Divine Majesty" will be praised by all that they have endured. To a certain extent she also puts the authorship of this official history in God's hands. Inasmuch as this is a public document—open to both her sisters and any male ecclesiastical authority (with the potential of being scrutinized by the Inquisition)—she closes it in a protective layer of humble rhetoric.[84]

## Significance and Afterlife of María Rosa's Account

"Account of the Journey of Five Capuchin Nuns" provides testimony that Spanish women actively participated in the widening of the Spanish Empire. These nuns were a part of the microcosm of the complex Atlantic world. During their long pilgrimage, they came into contact with people from all the major European powers: Dutch, English, Portuguese, Genoese, and French, and, to a lesser extent, the disappearing indigenous population of the Southern Cone. They traversed two continents and an ocean between to reach their final destination. Through the lens of María Rosa, we witness firsthand the consequences of the Spanish War of Succession and its far-reaching effects even on the fringe of the Spanish empire. At one point, when referring to the British navy, the narrator even comments on waning Spanish power.

The manuscript is rich and diverse. To create this unique account, María Rosa draws on a multitude of sources readily at hand, creating a patchwork quilt with many colorful pieces. The "Account of the Journey" sews together elements of the early chronicles of the New World, particularly José de Acosta's descriptions of the natural world. María Rosa's narrative style also includes elements of traditional rhetoric from hagiographies and *vidas*. It is influenced by Saint Teresa and other religious foremothers. Foremost, María Rosa crafts her account for her Capuchin sisters. She is writing the official foundation narrative for the new convent and they are her audience. This manuscript joins the ranks of travel literature written by women and for women. María Rosa (along with the editing skills of Josepha Victoria), acknowledges the help she received from her male counterparts, especially that of her father confessor, but ultimately this document attests to the power of women in a time when misogynistic doctrine and thought dominated Spanish society. Despite a publication of the ac-

---

84. Neither María Rosa nor her writings were ever investigated by the Holy Office.

count in Spanish in 1947,[85] the amazing pilgrimage of these Capuchin nuns has remained virtually unknown to scholars (in both Spanish and English). Nonetheless, the account provides a testament to the history of nuns in the Atlantic region. It is my hope that this introduction and subsequent translation have paid sufficient homage to these remarkable women and that María Rosa's account will change the way we view the role of Atlantic nuns in the history of the New World.

## Note on the Translation

This translation is based on the 414-folio manuscript that I found in the National Library of Madrid. It was surprising to me to discover that this document had never been translated and was not mentioned in any scholarly works in English about the Spanish colonial enterprise.[86] I soon discovered that there already existed a published tran-

85. See Rubén Vargas Ugarte, *Relaciones de viajes (Siglo XVI, XVII y XVIII)*, 259–381.

86. Scholarship on the writings of female religious from early modern Spain and colonial Latin America has grown considerably in the past twenty years. In spite of this boom in scholarly attention, few English translations of women's works from the Hispanic world exist. Electa Arenal and Stacy Schlau's seminal work, *Untold Sisters* (1989) still remains groundbreaking for its bilingual edition of Spanish and Latin American religious writings. The translation and new edition of one of Saint Teresa of Avila's works was most recently completed by Henry L. Carrigan: Teresa de Jesús, *The Way of Perfection*, (Brewster, MA: Paraclete Press, 2000). Nina Scott, Kathleen Myers, Amanda Powell, and Grady Wray have also translated works by Sor Juana Inés de la Cruz, María de San José Salazar, and Madre María de San José, among other colonial religious women. See *Madres del Verbo. Mothers of the Word: Early Spanish American Women Writers, A Bilingual Anthology*, ed. and trans. Nina M. Scott (Albuquerque: University of New Mexico Press, 1999); Sor Juana Inés de la Cruz, *The Answer/La Respuesta Including a Selection of Poems*, ed. and trans. Electa Arenal and Amanda Powell (New York: Feminist Press at City University of New York, 1994); and *The Devotional Exercises/Los Ejercicios Devotos of Sor Juana Inés de la Cruz, Mexico's Prodigious Nun (1648/51–1695)*, ed. and trans. Grady C. Wray (Lewiston, NY: The Edwin Mellen Press, 2005); María de San José Salazar, *Book for the Hour of Recreation;* Madre María de San José, *A Wild Country Out in the Garden: The Spiritual Journals of a Colonial Mexican Nun*, ed. and trans. Kathleen A. Myers and Amanda Powell (Bloomington, IN: Indiana University Press, 1999). The Modern Language Association has acknowledged the growing importance of the field of early modern Hispanic gender studies by including two new volumes (on Saint Teresa and Sor Juana) in its Approaches to Teaching Series. Except for an edition on the "Lieutenant Nun" and the secular writings of Sor Juana, the vast majority of translations focus on spiritual or autobiographical works. There are no English translations of foundation narratives (with the possible exception of the edition on Madre San José), let alone a travel diary such as the one translated here. Few studies to date have focused on nuns' travels and their role in the Iberian colonial enterprise.

scription of the Spanish text from 1947 by Rubén Vargas Ugarte, a Jesuit Priest in Lima, Peru. Vargas Ugarte's transcription is based on another copy of the document housed in the convent of Jesus María and Joseph in Lima.[87] Almost certainly the nuns of both convents (in Lima and Madrid) were interested in having a copy of this major accomplishment. It is difficult to ascertain whether one version was the original and the other a copy. They were probably both copied by a scribe because they were already fashioned in book form with seventeen well-organized chapters (including titles) and paragraphs. Moreover, the handwriting of the Madrid manuscript is very precise and clear and appears to have been that of a professional. There are only minor discrepancies between the two versions, and where appropriate I have used footnotes to point out small differences between the two documents; but for the most part they are very similar.[88]

I have had two goals in crafting this translation: to make it accessible and readable to a modern-day audience of English language readers and to maintain the unique voice of the nuns. The organization of the original manuscript with its chapter titles has all been left intact. The translation incorporates modern spelling and punctuation. When I refer to the translation in the introduction I use the pagination from the original Madrid manuscript. Throughout the translation, where necessary, I have used brackets for textual clarification or I have left the original Spanish word to suggest the flavor of this early eighteenth-century document. For example the word *madre*, when used as a title, has been left in the Spanish version instead of being translated as "mother." As opposed to the title "sor" (derived from the Latin *soror*, meaning sister), mother is a designation generally reserved for the elevated position of a nun who has been elected abbess of a convent. Madre María Rosa, except for the first paragraph when she writes "madre sor," uses the term *madre* for her traveling companions. This seems appropriate since two of them were to become future abbesses of the convent in Lima. However, she also uses the term for Madre Estefanía, who died of breast cancer before making it to their

87. Vargas Ugarte's edition, however, only includes a brief introduction to the text and very few notes. See his introduction, *Relaciones de viajes (Siglo XVI, XVII y XVIII)*, viii–xi. Fidel de Lejarza also has an overview of the foundation of the new convent; see "Expansión de las clarisas en América y extremo oriente," *Archivo Ibero-americano* 55 (July–Sept, 1954): 296–310. Other than these sources, this document has never been studied at length.

88. Since I have not had the opportunity to see the original Peruvian manuscript, I have had to rely on Vargas Ugarte's transcription for a comparison.

final destination. Most likely she opted for *madre* instead of *sor* due to their elevated status as founders of the new convent. Furthermore, when referring to the four nuns in general, María Rosa calls them "mis madres compañeras." In this case, instead of using the direct translation of "mothers," which sounds awkward in English I have opted for "my sisters" (at times during their travels she does refer to other nuns as sisters and she refers to the *colegialas*—the future nuns of the Lima convent—as sisters).

Several dictionaries were essential to this translation. Sebastián de Covarrubias Orozco's invaluable work of 1611, *Tesoro de la Lengua Castellana o Española* (Madrid: Editorial Castalia, 1995) has provided me with a lens to the time period and language that informed this account. I frequently turned to multiple editions of the *Diccionario de la Real Academia*, especially the early versions of *Autoridades* (1726–70).

We must keep in mind that in the original Spanish text, María Rosa was not aiming her account at the erudite elite, but at her Capuchin sisters and potentially male church officials. This is not to say that her writing is overly simplistic. She had a gift for the Spanish language and often incorporates creative metaphors into her writing style, some of which were thorny (to say the very least) to translate into English. I have tried my best to maintain her lively and readable style. A glossary of key Spanish words has been added at the end for further clarification.

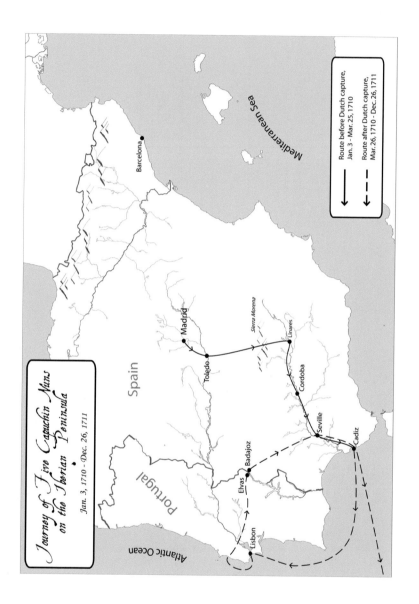

Journey of Five Capuchin Nuns
on the Iberian Peninsula

Jan. 3, 1710 - Dec. 26, 1711

Atlantic Ocean

Mediterranean Sea

Portugal

Spain

Lisbon

Elvas

Badajoz

Seville

Cadiz

Cordoba

Linares

Toledo

Madrid

Barcelona

Sierra Morena

Route before Dutch capture,
Jan. 3 - Mar. 25, 1710

Route after Dutch capture,
Mar. 26, 1710 - Dec. 26, 1711

Spain to Buenos Aires
Dec. 27 - Apr. 12, 1712

Andes

Amazon River

Lima

Andes

Atlantic Ocean

Mendoza

Buenos Aires

Santiago

Pacific Ocean

Andes

Journey Across South America
(Buenos Aires to Lima)
Apr. 13, 1712 - Feb. 4, 1713

## Account of the Journey of Five Capuchin Nuns Who Travelled from Their Convent in Madrid to Found the Convent of Jesus, Mary, and Joseph in Lima [1722]

### How the Foundation Was Established

Here begins the account of the journey of five Capuchin nuns who traveled from their convent in Madrid to found the Convent of Jesus, Mary, and Joseph in this city of Lima.[1] This account also contains other details regarding the foundation of the convent. All this is based on the notes left by Madre Sor María Rosa, one of the five founders who came to Lima as the mother abbess. Later, Madre Sor Josepha Victoria, one of the cofounders, organized and put the notes in order and added some other materials about things that happened afterwards. The year 1722.

In the Name of the Holy Trinity. Amen.

At the request of my beloved mothers and sisters of this house of Jesus, Mary, and Joseph, I am writing about our journey from Madrid to this city of Lima, our time as prisoners, other hardships, the appointment of the five founders, the obstacles posed by the prelates to grant the foundation license, our departure from the court, and about how the foundation took place. The five founding nuns were selected by the Illustrious Bishop of Sión Don Benito Madueño de Ramos, member of His Majesty's Supreme Council, Canon [*Canónigo*] of the Cathedral of Toledo, and General Superintendent of Monasteries and Houses of Prayer of that archbishopric. He issued this appointment after receiving an order given by the venerable dean[2] and city council of the aforementioned cathedral since the seat of the [bishop of Madrid] was vacant at that time. May all this be for God's glory.

---

1. The Madrid manuscript includes a short paragraph before the subtitle "How the Foundation Was Established." I have chosen to omit this section because it is very similar to the first sentence of the account, "Here begins the account…."

2. Throughout the document, María Rosa uses the title of dean to refer to the position of the person in a cathedral who served as the head of the chapter of canons. This title ranked after that of a bishop. See below, note 18.

# Chapter I
## Some of the Things that Preceded the Acquisition of the Foundation License,
### How It Was Obtained and the Nuns Appointed

My beloved daughters, mothers, and sisters, I would like to inform your reverences of our community's motives to accept this foundation. For years, many prayers had been offered for this to happen. On several occasions, the Lord had shown his pleasure at this prospect; nonetheless, He never revealed in what part of the world the new convent would be established. It was only known that it would be in a far off land and that to reach the foundation a sea voyage and crossing of many rough roads would have to be endured. The nuns who were to make the journey and all those who would accompany them could be seen [in a revelation]. In later revelations they learned that a church was being secretly built without a license from the king. Upon asking about the church and the convent, they were told that it was for Capuchin nuns.[3]

On another occasion as the nuns were praying after compline,[4] one of these good souls sensed that she had gotten distracted from her prayers when she saw five nuns prostrate [*postradas*].[5] For this reason she could not see their faces, but their number remained imprinted on her brain. When the time came for the appointment of the nuns and there was some discussion about allowing six, she replied: "I am certain that God only wants five. I know this because I have not been wrong with the other events I have foreseen, least of all in this one, since I paid careful attention to it. I also noticed that one of them was dressed in white. At first this made me believe that she was a sister of the third order [*hermana lega*], but I later realized that she was not part of the group of five because she still had to become a novice and everything else that this entails." She also saw that a nativity scene

3. The Spanish version of this paragraph is also very vague. María Rosa never directly says who received the revelations, but it appears that she is referring to one or more nuns from the Madrid convent (perhaps even herself).

4. Compline is the last of the canonical hours, usually said just before bedtime. It is part of a series of prayers said at fixed hours throughout the day, otherwise known as the Divine Office. See introduction. See *The Oxford Dictionary of the Christian Church*, ed. F. L. Cross, 3d ed. (Oxford: Oxford University Press, 1997).

5. In English, the word *prostrate* implies lying face down, as in submission or prayer, but in addition to this definition, according to the *Real Diccionario de la Academia*, the word *postrar* can also mean to kneel down.

must have been set up because [the nuns] were prostrated in front of it. Everything happened to the letter of the word.

On yet another occasion, the same nun, as she was praying in her cell to the images of Jesus, Mary, and Joseph, saw the Lord holding the foundation in His hands in the form of a globe of light with two people kneeled before Him. The nun recognized the one woman, but she did not know the man. She could only sense that he was a very special person and that His [Divine] Majesty had destined him to protect his work. The Lord made this even clearer when He said: "For her (pointing to the woman) I do this work and he (pointing to the man) will play a large role in it."

We have seen the results of both those two souls. First, Madre María Jacinta[6] (may she rest in God's presence) was the one who attempted, with her great spirit, to obtain what seemed to be the impossible. With her pious zeal she launched the founding mothers from Spain [to Lima] to establish this house for the most austere religious order of God. Although she did not have long to live in this world, the Lord granted her prayers for help by providing her with the Illustrious Señor Don Juan González de Santiago who at that time was a fiscal minister of the high court and later—at the time of his death—the bishop of Cuzco.

This gentleman so enthusiastically took up the cause of promoting this poor house, that through his position he was able to obtain the license from His Majesty[7] [the king]. With his own money and everything he was able to collect, he paid for the construction and materials until his death. The brevity of this account does not provide space to specify all his admirable qualities and virtues, but let it suffice to say that God had granted him great attributes. I[8] can also say the same of Madre Jacinta, leaving for another time a description of all the things that the Lord instilled in her soul and in this house and many details about her life. I will now continue narrating the rest of

---

6. Madre María Jacinta and her husband Nicolás de Dios were founders of the original house for orphaned young girls (also referred to at times as a *beaterio* and *colegio*—see introduction), and she later sought to have the house to become a convent.

7. Carlos II granted the royal decree for the *beaterio* to become a Capuchin convent in 1699. This letter granting the license from the king and several others concerning the foundation are housed in the Archive of the Indies. See Cartas y expedientes: personas eclesiásticas (1704–15), Signatura, Lima, 536, Archive of the Indies.

8. This is an important moment in the account, because it is the first time María Rosa uses the first person.

the story, all of which has already been manifested to the world.

The Illustrious Señor Don Juan González and Madre María Jacinta wrote to our convent in Madrid asking for founding mothers for this house of Jesus, Mary, and Joseph. They said that the afore-mentioned Madre María Jacinta and her companions were fervently prepared to follow a religious lifestyle. As has already been stated, our community was well aware of God's wishes for this foundation, and therefore their request was accepted. After everything had been re-ceived—all the letters with the licenses from this city, a report from the viceroy and all the other necessary documents that were to be proc-essed by the council—our prelate spoke to the señor cardinal of the request. He said that if His Eminence did not object, then our convent in Madrid was already prepared to execute the request from Lima.

After his Eminence saw that all the required documents were in order and the nuns—whose obedience was clear—were eagerly prepared to embark on the journey, he gave both his authorization and blessing for everything to proceed as necessary. The king and the councils, once they had been informed of our request, also gave their approval without any further ado.

All the necessary steps were being carried out with such joy that it seemed miraculous. Never in their previous foundations (there had been five that had stemmed from our [Madrid] convent) had eve-rything gone so smoothly.[9] Everything was moving along so quickly that they thought they were going to be able to take the first available ship. However, great works are never achieved without the counter-balance of difficulties. These calm seas soon erupted into such a fierce storm of contradictions that everything that had been achieved now seemed to be lost. His Eminence, who at first had been so supportive, all of a sudden changed his mind, saying that it would be impossible for nuns to travel to such distant places. Although he was given sev-eral examples, like our foundations in Mexico[10] and Sardinia, and sev-eral people went to speak to him on our behalf, he would hear noth-ing of it. When the Viceroy Castell dos Rius[11] said that the founding

9. These five foundations were: Toledo (1632), Plasencia (1636), Cordoba (1655), Sassari, Sardinia (1673), Coruña (1683), and then later Lima (1713) and Guatemala (1725). Many of these foundations went on to found even more convents. See Iriarte, *Las capuchinas: Pasado y presente*, 47.

10. The convent in Mexico was founded by nuns from Toledo. See preceding note.

11. Manuel de Oms y Santa Pau de Semanat, Marqués de Castell dos Rius (1651–1710, Barcelona—Lima). He served as viceroy of Peru, 1707–10.

mothers could accompany him, this seemed like a sure thing. Despite the fact that he liked this proposal, it turned out that this was not the right time for him, and he posed many obstacles to the responsibility of chaperoning the nuns. The viceroy's reluctance gave His Eminence more grounds to deny his permission for the nuns to travel until there was a peace treaty.[12] He said that he felt a great love for our convent, but if he signed the license for them to travel, and then they were taken prisoners, he would never forgive himself because we were the apple of his eye. Although he really wanted the new foundation, he would not permit it as long as he was still alive.

Despite His Eminence's resistance, the señor bishop of Cuzco still sent him letters informing him of the situation, but nothing could convince him. On various occasions many gentlemen, both ecclesiastical and secular, all with authorization from Madre Jacinta, approached the cardinal, telling him about their great wish to chaperone the nuns, but all these requests fell on deaf ears.

After some time had passed, they returned [to the cardinal] to remind him that the servants of God [in Lima] anxiously wanted to become nuns. He was also told about the building that was to be constructed. He responded by telling them to return another day. They left, happily believing that the cardinal was prepared to grant them their wish. The nuns conducted extraordinary exercises and prayers in the community, and they returned to the bishop to see if he had had a change of heart. He granted them an audience, called all his servants to come into the room and then said: the reason that I have gathered together all my people is so that they can serve as witnesses to the fact that I deny the license for the Capuchin nuns to travel to Lima during wartime.

The community was devastated by his decision. Nonetheless, they venerated the esteemed judgments of the Almighty and knew that His power could also achieve the impossible when it was His will. Prayers kept pouring out to the Lord, imploring Him to shorten the wait, and seven months after the meeting, the Señor Joseph Fausto Gallegos arrived from Lima. He delivered letters from Madre Jacinta with new appeals. Actually we hardly had the heart to listen to the grievances expressed by this servant of God and all her daughters. They explained in the letter that the bearer of the letter was a person of true virtue and that he very much wanted to accompany the founding mothers to Lima because he felt great

12. She is referring to the Spanish War of Succession (1701–14).

esteem for this house and he was their current confessor. He spoke to the mother abbess who brought him up to date on all the details surrounding the foundation. She told him that, barring a miracle from God, they had lost hope. When Joseph Fausto Gallegos heard these words he laughed and said: "My daughters have faith, keep me in your prayers and I will take care of the rest."

He did everything possible to make this happen, exerting great effort to sway the cardinal in our favor. His Eminence was very gracious to him, but gave him the same response he had used with everyone else. Furthermore, he said that many people had come to him, speaking of their zeal for the foundation, but that they had only used this as an excuse to achieve their own ends. Joseph Fausto Gallegos politely and humbly answered him and he never stopped visiting His Eminence while he was still alive. He also visited several members of his inner circle who were of very high rank (and also very adamantly against the foundation); he left no stone unturned in an attempt to change their minds.

As he had no authority over these people, the Lord led him on a new path by taking away three subjects who had the greatest influence on His Eminence. It was clear that this was not a punishment because they had good intentions and were guided by prudent decisions, but the Lord, who was ready to console that community and make its members' wishes come true, began to cut a path through impassable terrain that had detained this foundation for so many years.

The cardinal was struck by an illness that worried everyone at court, especially us. We had always been very fond of him (we knew that his unwillingness to grant us the license stemmed from his love for us, just as a vigilant Shepherd keeps his flock out of danger). His illness took a turn for the worse and the time came for the Lord to take him out of this world, which broke our hearts.

Our father Don Joseph Fausto Gallegos[13] was the first to offer his condolences to us. After he had paid the customary words of courtesy in that matter, he changed the subject and said: "My daughters, now our happiness will begin. I will soon depart for Toledo where I will present our case to the gentlemen of the city council. I have confidence that the Divine goodness will arrange everything for me. Your reverences should not stop asking Him to grant us this because it will all be for His honor and glory. We increased our petitions and prayers and he left for Toledo. He had to be very persistent in his business

---

13. The Peru transcription calls him José Justo Gallegos.

because he was confronted with countless obstacles; before [the death of the cardinal] the foundation only hinged on one voter, and now the whole council was against it. Yet his great virtue and patience helped him bear these mortifications that seemed never-ending. He took refuge and solace by visiting Our Lady of the Tabernacle [*Nuestra Señora del Sagrario*]. He entreated her [the Virgin] to intercede on behalf of his request—I mean to say his goal[14]—and asked her to let those gentlemen see the light and that she grant him the right words to sway the hearts of those who had been so against the proposal.

The Señor Bishop of Sión Don Benito Madueño de Ramos, who was then the governor of the archbishopric, was also strongly against the foundation (as he later acknowledged). On the occasions that he would travel to Madrid, we spoke to him about our endeavor, but he would try to hide his true feelings because he was a very discreet person. Nonetheless, he could not help but become angry at what he considered a very misguided proposal. Our father confessor[15] went to talk to this prince of a man. He spoke to him in great detail of his plans, updating him on the status of the licenses from the king and council that had all been granted. He told him of the *colegialas*'[16] yearning desire to become nuns which was increasing by the day. He also said that there was an opportunity to embark on a very decent and safe ship. Don Andrés Martínez de Murguía's ships would be sailing to Buenos Aires with a document of safe conduct granted by Queen Anne.[17] Moreover, the passengers were all very respectable and if we

14. The author corrects herself here. She does this several times during the account. This use of colloquial language could also be a writing strategy—perhaps she even purposely corrects herself to appear less erudite to a male reader. See the section on "Content and Analysis" in the introduction.

15. María Rosa refers to Don Joseph Gallegos as their father or father confessor throughout the account. In most instances I have chosen to use "father confessor" instead of just "father" to avoid confusion with other priests.

16. These were the young women in the *colegio* (informal school) in Lima who were yearning to become nuns. The narrator refers to the young students in the *colegio* as *colegialas*. These girls are to be the convent's future novices. Throughout the document she uses the terms *colegio* and *casa* (house) interchangeably. This seems appropriate since the informal *colegio* (also referred to as a *beaterio*—see introduction) was housed in the home of the original founder, Madre Jacinta.

17. Queen Anne of Great Britain (1665–1714) ruled the British Crown during the Spanish War of Succession (1701–14). Although England supported the Archduke Charles II of Hapsburg to succeed to the Spanish throne, by 1710 England was ready to seek peace. It was most likely for this reason the queen had granted the passage of safe conduct for this Spanish fleet.

lost this chance we would not have another one for many years. Our father confessor gave His Illustriousness full control of this endeavor and told him that since he was a great supporter of God's glory he should use all his influence to set the wheels in motion for this blessed purpose. All these arguments made an impact on his expert judgment and he completely changed his mind. He offered to present our case to the distinguished canons, and he also enlightened our father confessor on the best channels through which he could achieve his goal in the shortest period of time.

His Divine Majesty saw to it that the reports presented by His Illustriousness started to soften the hearts of the city council. When the city council met on October 9, 1709, some of the gentlemen were ready to give their approval and others still said no. The señor bishop spoke to them with great fervor and eloquence. He told them of the importance of this foundation and how he believed it would be for God's glory and the salvation of souls.

Finally the time had come that had already been determined by the Almighty. The Holy Spirit spoke through the bishop, moving everyone's heart and every single one of the council members voted for the foundation. They later acknowledged that they did not know what had come over them, as they had all changed their minds. Praise be the Lord who does not need to depend on any of His creatures when He wants something.

## Chapter II
### The Appointment of the Nuns and the Señor Bishop's Visit for that Purpose

The members of the city council came out of their meeting and called our father confessor, who all the while had been fervently praying for this important endeavor. He went to the distinguished prebendaries[18] who notified him that since the license had already been granted, it was necessary for him (if he wanted the nuns to travel in the manner appropriate to their position) to sign a deed binding himself and his property to the endeavor. Only then would they entrust the nuns to him. Our confessor met all their requirements, but this was not enough for him; he also swore his complete allegiance up until the day he brought the founders [the nuns] to the city of Lima and handed them over to its dean and city council. He followed everything to the letter of the law, completing every task with such great charity, humbleness, and patience that not only were we thankful to him, but we also learned a lot from him.

After this meeting had taken place, our father confessor hurriedly sent a messenger to our convent to give us the good news of all that he had achieved and to let us know that the señor bishop would accompany him to the court to appoint the nuns who were going to found the new convent.

On the eleventh day of October, [1709] we received his letter and we immediately went to the choir [coro][19] to sing *Te Deum Laudamus*.[20] That same day at dusk, the señor bishop and our father confessor arrived in Madrid. His Illustriousness sent word that he would come to us the next morning to say Mass. However, when it came time for him to put on his vestments, he realized that he had

---

18. María Rosa uses the term *prebendados* to refer to the cathedral canons. This ecclesiastical title refers to the secular clergy belonging to a cathedral. The canons along with the dean of a cathedral formed the "General Chapter" that would vote on certain issues pertaining to their diocese. The term *prebend* or *prebendary* also exists in English but is not as common as canon and was used in the early Middle Ages. This is the only time she uses *prebendados*, throughout the rest of the document she calls them *canónigos*—a synonym for *prebendados*. See *The Oxford Dictionary of the Christian Church*, ed. Cross, s.v. "canon" and "prebend."

19. A separate room with stalls on one side of the church for use by the cloistered nuns. The choir was separated from the church by a grille. The nuns could see the altar, but they were hidden from the parishioners seated in the congregation.

20. *Te Deum Laudamus* is an early Christian hymn of praise, still used in the Roman Catholic Church today.

only his street clothes with him; as it turned out his vestments had fallen out of the coach. It was a feast day, so a vestment was brought to his house, and he then sent for other ones from Toledo. This was all a lot of work, expense and concern for our father confessor who also had to say Mass at one o'clock, but he was just happy to see how quickly everything was progressing.

The next day His Illustriousness [the bishop] came to say Mass for us. He was staying at our father confessor's house very close by. He spoke to the community and commanded us to ask God to help guide us in the choice of the individuals who were to be appointed for the trip. Each one of us was to seek guidance from God as if we were to be the one selected and given the responsibility of such an important work; we were also to consider the very long and unavoidable risks of a ship journey. He added that every nun who was appointed should speak freely: if she felt ready to embrace the task she should say so, and if she did not want to go she should give her reasons. No one was bound by holy obedience to go; all were free to voice their concerns or to accept the proposal. Each nun made her own individual prayer; all thought themselves completely unworthy of this endeavor, but they resigned themselves to Divine Will.

The next day His Illustriousness returned and gave another speech to the community. He warned us that for this selection the procedure would be different from previous ones. Regarding the appointment, normally the prelate, the confessor and the abbess would appoint the founders, but in this case, he instructed the vicaress and the convent's eight discreets [*discretas*]²¹ also to take part. Each one was to write on a piece of paper the names of five nuns whom their conscience deemed the most apt for this task. They should then fold the paper and give it to the abbess who would then hand it to His Illustriousness. He also stated the conditions pertaining to the age of those who were eligible for appointment: the oldest should not be over fifty, the rest should be younger, and the last should be under thirty. It would not matter if the youngest had only taken her vows five years earlier as long as she was capable; seniority would not be needed in the company of the other nuns. This foundation could not use elderly nuns because there would be a question about their ability to perform the difficult work ahead of them. After this, Doctor Don

---

21. The discreets were elected advisors to a mother abbess and vicaress—most of the Franciscan orders, including the Capuchins, would elect eight discreets. The discreets were also used as chaperones, accompanying their charges to speak to visitors at the grille.

Martín Soriano, a very learned and virtuous person, went to speak privately to our father confessor by whom he was briefly updated on the positive attributes of each of the nuns.

The next day on October 14, [1709] His Illustriousness, accompanied by father Don Joseph Fausto Gallego, a notary and several witnesses, came to the choir grille to name the founders. The whole community gathered together, all of us wearing our veils and then the grille was opened. The bishop explained how he truly hoped that the right nuns had been chosen. He then told the notary to read the names aloud and they were: Madre María Rafaela, Madre María Rosa, Madre María Coleta, Madre María Bernarda, and Madre Josepha Victoria.

After he had finished reading the list, the señor bishop instructed each nun to respond whether she accepted or not, but all of them remained silent. Madre Rafaela was named first, but since she was younger than Madre Rosa[22] she did not dare speak. The mother abbess then said: "Señor, would your Illustrious Lordship require Madre Rosa to speak since she is the senior nun." I obeyed the order by saying I accept, although I did not have any confidence in my own strength, which was nothing. Nonetheless, if Divine Will and the intercession of the Holy Mother wanted to use such a useless instrument in their glorious work, then I resigned myself to their wishes. I would even give my life for the cause. Next in line came Madre Rafaela whose response surprised everyone. Up until that point she had been a great supporter of the foundation, always expressing her wish to be a part of it; so much so that every hour lost seemed like a century to her. Yet, the minute she heard herself nominated she forgot all this and felt such an unbearable weight on her heart that she answered that she was incapable of accepting the charge.

The prudent señor bishop listed all the difficulties that she [Madre Rafaela] was most likely to encounter, telling her that she should trust in the Lord, and since He had chosen her He would provide what she lacked according to His knowledge (none of this took away from the fact that she was a very good and ideal nun, but that the Lord had other tasks in mind for her and this was not one of them). She listened to all the bishop's arguments, to which she responded: "I will only go if you order me to do so by holy obedience, otherwise I will not change my mind." He responded by saying that under no circumstances would he command her to do so and that she would

---

22. There are places in the document where the author refers to herself as Rosa instead of María Rosa.

only go by agreeing like the others. When she heard this she said: "In that case, señor, I do not accept." The bishop turned to the notary and instructed him to put Madre María Gertrudis in the place of Madre Rafaela. The next to respond was Madre María Coleta who said she needed to speak to him in private. He received the same response from *madres* Gertrudis and Bernarda.

When it came time for Madre Josepha Victoria to respond, she was very flustered. She said that she was not the right choice because it had only been seven years since she had taken her vows and that she had not learned everything she needed to know in order to teach others. The señor bishop told her that he was well aware of her status and that she should consent to it despite this shortcoming. When Madre Josepha Victoria heard this, she surrendered herself to God's Will, offering up all the hardships she was to suffer to His love. His Illustriousness came inside so that all the nuns who had asked to speak to him in private could do so. Madre María Coleta went to him and told him all the precise reasons why she could not accept. Foremost she suffered from very poor health. In sum, the bishop was satisfied and enlightened by the many reasons that she had listed for him. She was followed by Madre Gertrudis who tried to excuse herself, claiming her humility. This was not accepted as an excuse because God specially had chosen her even against the father confessor's wishes. He had tried to prevent her from joining us in order to console one of the nun's [biological] sisters. Other people also tried to influence His Illustriousness on behalf of other nuns, but this was to no avail. When Madre Rafaela was excused from the list, the prelate realized that the one [Madre María Gertrudis] he had excluded out of consideration for her own flesh and blood was the one whom God had chosen for the foundation. Madre María Bernarda also tried to persuade the bishop that she was unworthy for the foundation, but he told her that she should resign herself to the task and there was no way out of it.

We were now four founders and His Illustriousness was told to appoint Madre María Estefanía as the fifth. By this time she had absentmindedly left the meeting to go to the refectory where she was preparing a light meal for her sisters. God had granted her good health, and she was so humble that she was always greatly inclined to serve and make lighter the work of her sisters. When she was told that the señor bishop had summoned her she responded: "They want me? I'm just a little worthless nothing and among so many better choices

I am very happy with my fate." She said these words even though she really wanted to be part of the foundation. Her desire came after four years of prayers and [spiritual] exercises (previously she had been very much against it and would get very angry at any mention of it). She suddenly changed her mind after the death of a very exemplary nun from our community, who had vehemently supported the foundation. Without any inhibitions, Madre Estefanía told everyone that Our Lord had passed Madre Augustina's vocation on to her. At the time of writing this she is also deceased. God had only taken her out of the cloister because she had shown the way as a great model nun to the community: she was so penitent that she fasted only on bread and water for more than fifteen years; she never ate any treats because she believed herself unworthy of any earthly pleasures; she never missed choir; she was unflagging in her work; and she can be equally praised in all her other virtues, the same as He can be praised for generously endowing her with all these qualities. She was very devoted to the Blessed Sacrament. Every day that she took communion, tears would well up in her eyes. Her innocent soul was like that of a four-year-old child and her humility and silence were extreme. In sum, she shone as one of our community's most virtuous nuns, and for this reason and her good health she was nominated for the foundation.

Nevertheless, as God knows what is right for all of us, when she left for the foundation she became ill with a cancerous breast tumor [*zaratán en un pecho*].[23] Yet with great mortification and suffering she was determined to hide this. She did so to such an extent that she would not even apply a small compress, and she only did so later under duress of holy obedience. The whole journey was very difficult for her, due to the pain she suffered. It wasn't until we arrived in Buenos Aires, where she was much sicker than during the ship voyage, that she finally received some treatment, but really there was nothing that could be done for her comfort. Her condition kept worsening so that she was given no hope of recovery. When the dean received this news he visited the patient [Madre María Estefanía] and asked her if she would like to be buried in the bishops' plot of that city. In her accustomed humble and lowly manner, she responded that she

---

23. According to Covarrubias this is the Arabic word for cancer. See Sebastián de Covarrubias Orozco, *Tesoro de la lengua castellana o española*. Breast cancer was nothing new to nuns. It was even referred to by some in Europe at the time as the "nuns' disease." Modern science tells us that childless women are more susceptible to this malady. See James S. Olson, *Bathsheba's Breast: Women, Cancer & History* (Baltimore, MD: Johns Hopkins University Press, 2002), 21, 22.

appreciated the honor, but as a daughter of obedience, her will was that of her abbess. It was her wish (although she did not believe that she deserved a better burial than in a rubbish heap), to ask for a tiny corner in the Convent of our Father Saint Francis. The dean left with a feeling of bewilderment since he had never met anyone who spoke so calmly about her own burial. She was accompanied to Our Lord [to the convent of Saint Francis] in a public procession by hordes of the city's people. She was so at ease that it was hard to believe she was on death's doorstep. She felt so much at peace that she did not remember the convent or anything else, except that she was going to enjoy the Glory of God, something she had desired for a very long time. She took this to such an extreme that she was ordered not to ask His [Divine] Majesty to take her away.

When she was close to the very end, our father confessor asked her how she felt. She replied: "My body is filled with pain, but my soul feels an intense peace. It's longing to fly to its Creator, like a little bird that one holds in the hand, only waiting to have its feet released to be free." She was given the Extreme Unction[24] and we stayed by her side along with our father confessor, but she was still so lucid that she knew it was our bedtime and insisted that we leave her to go rest. To make her feel better we lay down a bit, but since we were so worried about her we really could not rest. She assured us that we should not worry, that she would let us know when the time had come. She spent the night in acts of love for God and in resignation, and when dawn was approaching our father confessor asked her if she would like to take communion. She said: "I can't because I can't hold down the cordial[25] that I have been sipping." Our father said Mass, and just as he began the confession the patient informed us: "It's time. I'm about to die," and without another word or movement, except to bow her head, she passed away. The Mass was offered for her blessed soul.

Our grief and that of our father confessor was beyond words since we had witnessed her leave the cloister only later to die in a foreign land. Nevertheless, we did have the comfort of knowing the merciful prize she would enjoy for all her work and suffering and that she never wavered in her wish to follow Divine Will. She knew from the very beginning (later we learned this from our father confessor) that she would never make it to the city of Lima. She also

---

24. This term, also referred to as the Anointing of the Sick, is a rite given to patients on their deathbeds.

25. She was taking an alcoholic medicinal tonic.

knew that we would never get the chance to meet Madre Jacinta. When we first arrived in Buenos Aires, and we received word that Madre Jacinta had passed away, Madre Estefanía said: "Now that I see that this prediction has come true, I also feel in my heart that I will die in this city." Blessed be the Lord who let us feel this suffering so that we could offer it up to Him.

Madre María Estefanía was buried in the Convent of Our Father Saint Francis with all solemnity. In attendance were the presiding magistrate[26] and all the religious orders. Each community said Masses for her as if she had been a nun from their order. After she had passed away, Fray Juan de Arregui, Custodian [of the Franciscan convent], sent the majority of his friars to keep vigil for her and to say Masses for her in their chapel. He also had the kindness to preside over her funeral service, but he was so emotional that during the last prayer he broke into tears, and the deacon had to finish for him. Her body was laid to rest by the main altar. I am leaving out details relating to her worldly and religious virtues as well as concerning her funeral rites. All I have mentioned is but a shadow of what I could have said, but although I will write about this later on, I thought it necessary to write a brief summary about her so those who read this will learn a little about this servant of God.

Returning to my account, Madre María Estefanía went before the bishop, and he asked her whether she wanted to participate in the foundation. She beamed with delight and at the same time was obedient and resigned to Divine Will. However, because of her humble nature, she felt unworthy of this task, and she said that she would only accept it under the condition that she be given no other task than to serve the nuns. The señor bishop heard her request and said: "My daughter, the most important thing is to become one of the founders. Do not worry about having a task or not; this is not a pretext to excuse yourself." By eight o'clock in the evening, the appointment of the founders was completed.

The next day on the Feast of Saint Teresa [of Avila, October 15, 1709] His Illustriousness returned to the convent. He ordered the whole community to vote for the five founders and the positions for each one. Although I was the least deserving of all, I was elected the abbess according to the precepts of our convent; Madre Estefanía was

---

26. That is, the presiding magistrate (*el presidente*) of the high court (*audiencia*), oftentimes the viceroy himself.

the vicaress, Madre Gertrudis the turn keeper [*la tornera*],[27] Madre María Bernarda the novice mistress, and Madre Josepha Victoria the councilor [*conciliaria*].[28] The señor bishop approved the election and then asked us if we wanted Señor Doctor Don Joseph Fausto Gallegos as our confessor. We gladly responded that we would if he accepted this charge with everything that it entailed, as he would be the most important part of this foundation.

His Illustriousness bid his farewells and left for Toledo to wait for news about the fleet's departure. In the interim he gave permission for Don Joseph Fausto Gallegos to hear confession from the five of us. We began to prepare for the journey, but we did not relinquish our duties to our blessed community. Since all my sisters were young and capable, they did not remain idle. We loved all the nuns [in our community] dearly and they were extremely upset at seeing our departure so near. Our sorrow was no less than theirs, having to say goodbye to such a caring group.

Three months after our appointment we received a letter from Cadiz telling us to depart immediately. Our blessed community would not allow it until after the Christmas season. The bishop was informed of our departure so that he could come and take us out of the cloister as he had offered to do. He arrived at the court [of Madrid] on the Eve of the Feast of the Circumcision of Our Lord [January 1, 1710]. As soon as the people of Madrid heard of his arrival, everyone became very excited because they knew of his intentions. Since they wanted to accompany us out of the city, they wanted to know the exact date, but it was kept hidden to avoid a loud gathering. The señor bishop told us to be prepared to leave on the third of January, but that he was going to tell the city another departure date because there would be many attempts to take us to various places.

On the day I have just mentioned, as we were waiting for His Illustriousness, our mother abbess told us to go drink a crock of hot chocolate.[29] She wanted to give us this gift before the ceremony that

27. The turn keeper was the woman in charge of the turn [*el torno*], a revolving window in a cloistered convent that was used to pass messages—verbal or written—from the outside world into the convent. See introduction.

28. Advisor to the mother abbess—often there was more than one in a convent and, if so, they would make up a general council. In this case, Madre Josepha Victoria was most likely to become head of the future council of their convent in Lima.

29. Chocolate, a pre-Columbian delicacy in Mexico, later became a very popular drink in Europe. Due to its popularity and exotic origins, some religious orders banned chocolate,

awaited us, but this kind gesture turned into a bitter farewell. The turn keepers [*torneras*] burst into tears and so did we when we realized that this would be the last thing that we would receive from that blessed community and that we would never see them again. Our father confessor arrived while this was happening and tried his best to console them. He reminded them of what an honor it was for their community to provide God with so many fruitful new foundations, especially because this was the sixth one. As was typical of his generosity, he then gave them a donation; despite the major expenses of the new foundation, he always helped that convent in Madrid. We then left the turn and while we waited for the señor bishop we went to the antechoir to say goodbye to the [figurine] of the Christ Child on the nativity scene whom I loved dearly since I had been his keeper for many years. I said to Him: "God, my little child, you stay here, nicely bundled up in your bed as we go out into the world. We will spend many a cold night for your love and we will even die for you; all with the hope of harvesting many souls that will serve and praise you."[30]

---

claiming that it broke prescribed fasting. Despite the controversy, many women religious did drink chocolate (like these Capuchin nuns) and did not believe that it interfered with their fasts. To learn more about the importance of chocolate in convents both in Spain and the New World, see Electa Arenal, "Monjas chocolateras: contextualizaciones agridulces," in *Nictimene...sacrílega: Estudios coloniales en homenaje a Georgina Sabat-Rivers*, ed. Mabel Moraña and Yolanda Martínez San-Miguel (Mexico: Universidad del Claustro de Sor Juana, 2003), 135–55.

30. Dolls and figurines of the Christ Child were quite common in convents both in Europe and the New World. See Christiane Klapisch-Zuber's chapter "Holy Dolls," in *Women, Family and Ritual in Renaissance Italy*, trans. Lydia Cochrane (Chicago: University of Chicago Press, 1985), 310–29.

## Chapter III
### How We Left the Cloister and the Manner in which the Señor Bishop Handed Us Over to Our Father Don Joseph Fausto Gallegos

At this point everything had been set in place by Divine Wisdom, and the foundation would be completed at the appointed time. It had been sought after with many prayers and tears, in our convent [in Madrid], as well as [here in Lima] in this house of Jesus, Mary, and Joseph.

The community was advised that the señor bishop was waiting at the door for the five founders. In front of all the other nuns we prostrated ourselves to receive the blessing of our mother abbess; like everyone else, she was a river of tears. After we received her blessing and kissed her hand, we said goodbyes to our sisters with inexplicable sorrow. Madre Josepha Victoria took the Christ [statue] and we processed out through the main doorway where His Illustriousness awaited us with our father confessor and with many other gentlemen. Although the date had been kept secret, many people came out to see us because they were greatly devoted to our blessed [Capuchin] order.

His Illustriousness spoke to the mother abbess and to everyone else, telling them that they should be very thankful to God for having guided them to that sanctuary, whence many servants of His [Divine] Majesty had already taken the standard[31] of the holy cross to very diverse parts of the world so that many souls could be saved. From this foundation [in Lima], he also awaited very fruitful results because he himself had witnessed visible miracles. Next he had the notary read aloud His Majesty's royal decree and the license that had been granted by Toledo's honorable dean and by its city council. The license explained how we had been entrusted to the care and guardianship of our father confessor, Señor Doctor Don Joseph Fausto Gallegos, until he handed us over to the prelates of Lima's cathedral.

Afterward His Illustriousness called me to him and took me by the hand. My sisters were also taken by the hand by other high-ranking officials, and we were thus escorted to the area of the presbytery[32] of our church where we prostrated ourselves to receive the blessing of the Blessed Sacrament. It broke our hearts to hear the muffled sobs of the women inside. We left the church with great difficulty because the masses of people would not let us get through. A

31. Type of flag or banner.

32. Part of the chancel of a church beyond the choir.

carriage from the queen was waiting for us in the portico. We only used it to travel two leagues [*leguas*][33] because our father had rented a carriage for our journey; he was so generous that he did not spare any expense on our account.

After we had entered the carriage my sisters humbly pledged their obedience to me. Although it had been almost three months since our appointment, we had really done nothing about it. I felt very embarrassed as their prelate, but at the same time I felt comforted to know that such blessed subjects would kindly tolerate my defects.

We left Madrid on the third day of January in the year 1710. I looked around at my homeland and I thanked God for letting me leave it for such a holy purpose, because I was feeling a great tenderness for it. I asked His Divine Majesty to shower the land with blessings so that many blessed souls would spring forth. I also asked Him to bless our kings and prince with good health and peace. After we had traveled some distance the people who accompanied us said their goodbyes. My sisters began to feel motion sickness because all the carriage curtains were tightly closed. One of my sisters really worried me: from the moment she stepped in the carriage she was extremely queasy. The señor bishop came to our rescue by telling the drivers to open the curtains, letting in a breeze so we could get a breath of fresh air.

We arrived at Illescas where there is a convent of nuns of our Mother Saint Clare. We spent the night with them and they treated us with a love that cannot be described. They gave us dinner right away when they heard that we had had nothing to eat the whole day except for the small refreshment that I have already mentioned when we drank the hot chocolate in the turn room of our convent. When the señor bishop heard this he felt really guilty because he thought we had eaten something before we left, but we had thought nothing of it since we had wanted to continue our observance of professed fasting.

Those pious nuns made a big fuss over us. They brought us to the choir to see the nativity scene. They sang several hymns to Him [the Christ Child], and as faithful daughters of our Father Saint Francis they solemnly celebrated the mystery [of His birth]. They are good nuns, and since they were the first we met, they hold a special place in our hearts. I pray to Our Lord to let them remain as faithfully observant as we found them. They took us to retire for the night and they had prepared comfortable beds for us. But we implored them to take them down because we only wanted to sleep on the wooden frame with one

33. A league is a measure of distance of approximately three miles.

blanket, according to the discipline we use. The next morning after we took communion and heard Mass, they gave us a small bite to eat so that we would be able to continue with our fasting. The time had come to leave this convent, and they all wept as if we had lived together for a long time. The mother abbess gathered her community together and we processed out of the choir together singing the *Miserere*[34]—just as when we entered we had sung *Te Deum Laudamus.*

We continued on our day's journey to Toledo and fasted that whole day as we had the previous one. When we arrived in that city many people came out to greet us. We were given lodging in the convent of our Capuchin mothers. Like true sisters they gave us a joyous welcome, singing *Te Deum Laudamus* as they accompanied us to the choir. The señor bishop, along with our father confessor and the Señor Inquisitor Don Juan de Ovalle, entered the cloister. His Illustriousness then sang a prayer. After they visited the convent they departed, leaving us alone with the nuns, who greatly entertained us. We went to a room where they kept the nativity scene; it was very well cared for. It was a great joy for us to have met those servants of God, and to see that their observances were the same as those in our community. Despite the fact that they had left our community many years earlier to establish this foundation, they had not changed any detail of our religious devotions. God had instilled in us a great love for one another in such a short period of time that none of us wanted to leave.

The convent is housed in a small fortress [*alcázar*], originally founded by Señor Cardinal Don Pascual de Aragón. Here one can see a richness, which does not compromise the strictness of the Capuchin order. His Eminence had his own tomb carved in the nuns' vault of the convent. After his death his body was transported to this place, but in accordance with his mandate, his heart was to be left with the Capuchin nuns in Madrid whom he had cared for deeply. On a daily basis he had given alms for the sick nuns and for the ecclesiastical benefices[35] of the community. He was very pious and gave everything he had to one or the other of the two Capuchin convents. Prayers from both communities have compensated him very well.

The next day the señor bishop and the distinguished canons arranged to take us to see the blessed church [the cathedral] and the

---

34. A piece of religious music derived from Psalm 50/51—the Latin version begins "Miserere mei, Deus."

35. Ecclesiastical offices that were awarded revenues (to provide a living).

Chapel of Our Lady of the Tabernacle. The indescribable relics and precious items located there are beyond words. It was a great joy to be granted such an unexpected treat. His Illustriousness told us to meet him at noon to try to avoid the masses of people. I do not know how they found out, but so many people gathered at the main gate that in order to trick them, he said that he was going to leave for lunch and that no time had been set for our departure. He returned around two o'clock in the afternoon, trying his best to do this secretly, but his precautions were not enough to free us from the throngs of humanity. At one point, so many people had gathered that we felt suffocated when we left the convent.

We arrived at the cathedral and went to see and touch the same stone the Holy Virgin Mary had touched with her feet when she appeared in the tabernacle and gave the chasuble [*casalla*][36] to Saint Ildefonsus.[37] We continued on to Señor Cardinal Portocarrero's tomb where we said a prayer for his soul. We shed many a tear as we asked God to help his soul; and if he were still in purgatory we asked God to take him to his resting place. He was a very pious prince of a man. We were then led to the sacristy, which is a slice of heaven on earth. The distinguished canons treated us very well, especially Señor Don Juan de Pimentel, son of Their Excellencies, the Señores Marquis of Tobar. At the time he was archdeacon and archbishop-elect of Zaragoza, but he renounced that position because he did not want to leave the holy Cathedral [of Toledo]. He was such a dedicated and ardent admirer of our Capuchin order that he outdid himself by accompanying us the whole afternoon, dressed in his surplice [*sobrepelliz*].[38] He also carried a small candleholder so that he could light up the way for us to see the grandeurs of that sanctuary.

They showed us the splendid garments of a statue of Our Lady. One dress in particular was embroidered with such large pearls that it would be impossible to find any bigger ones. The crown was gold and adorned with many precious stones. The bracelets were made of the same material and they kind of wrapped around her

36. A long sleeveless vestment worn by a priest when celebrating Mass.

37. The author is referring to the alleged miraculous apparition of the Virgin Mary to Saint Ildefonsus in the early seventh century. Supposedly the Virgin appeared to Ildefonsus in the Cathedral of Toledo and gave him the priest's robes. Pilgrims still visit the cathedral today to see the spot on which the Virgin touched her feet. Saint Ildefonsus is the patron saint of Toledo.

38. A white liturgical vestment.

wrists. We saw a large jewel chest that held so many diamonds I couldn't count them, and other precious gems, many of which were set on unique and exquisite rings. We saw a sash with two strands of diamonds given by our King Carlos II, may he rest in peace. Among all these jewels, we also saw a very large jet ring. This was a gift from Queen Doña Urraca, and they keep it because it was so old. There were many miters[39] decorated with diamonds and other precious gems. In sum, all this was great cause for admiration of the craftsmanship, as well as the grandeur—the sumptuousness, as well as the riches. The monstrance [*la custodia*] was a wonder. For all that I would like to say about it I lack the words to describe even the smallest detail. Since it was getting late we returned a second time to the Tabernacle of Our Lady. We said our goodbyes to her, leaving our hearts at her feet. We implored Her Majesty [the Virgin] to be our guide during our long and dangerous pilgrimage.

When we returned to the convent it seemed impossible to get to the gatehouse because of the crowd of people gathered there. We found the nuns very upset that we had spent the afternoon away from them, especially because our departure was set for the following day—the day after Three Kings Day[40] [January 6, 1710]. Since it was the eve of Epiphany, Doctor Don Antonio de los Cobos, may he rest in peace, had sent a large meal for the whole community. He was a canon of that holy cathedral and also confessor to the nuns. He treated us very well. After the meal—and we gave thanks for it— we went to a room that had a nativity scene. My sisters as well as the nuns from that community entertained us so much that the time passed quickly and we stayed until eleven in the evening. We wanted to go to matins,[41] but the señor bishop had said he would only permit it on the condition that we made it to bed early. The mother abbess was not to let us go if we did not meet this requirement. By the time we hugged and said our goodnights it was already midnight so she accompanied us to our dormitory and then went with her sisters to matins. I knelt down to pray matins on my own and then I wrote a letter to our blessed convent of Madrid, telling them all the things that had occurred up until that point.

39. A ceremonial headdress worn by a bishop.

40. Three Kings Day [*El Día de los Reyes*] is celebrated in the Catholic Church on January 6. This day is also called the Feast of Epiphany.

41. Matins (prayer usually said at midnight) is part of a series of prayers said at fixed hours throughout the day, otherwise known as the Divine Office. See introduction.

At five o'clock in the morning the mother abbess came for us. She ordered a fire to be brought to us because it was very cold. Afterward we went to the choir to take communion, to hear Mass, and then to pray the hours[42] with the whole community. During our prayers someone kept ringing the turn bell and when the turn keepers answered the door, they discovered that the Señor Inquisitor Don Juan de Ovalle had sent us an *arroba*[43] of chocolate so that we could drink it together with the whole community—he had obtained permission for all of us. We highly appreciated this gift, and I asked the mother abbess to consider it as a good deed. This was a novelty in the convent since this treat was normally prohibited there. Afterwards, His Illustriousness called us to the convent parlor [*locutorio*] and I told him how readily [his permission to drink] had been obeyed. He got a kick out of this and then asked the mother abbess to give us an early meal because he would come for us at ten in the morning. That blessed señora went to tell the cooks to hurry up because she wanted all of us to eat together in the refectory. At the same moment that they rang the bell to eat, someone was ringing the turn bell with such vigor that it crashed to the ground. The turn keepers responded and discovered that the señor bishop, who was accompanied by the señor inquisitor, by our father Don Joseph Fausto Gallegos, and by other people of authority, had come to take us out of the cloister.

This was very distressing news, and all the rejoicing turned into a flood of tears. The nuns asked the bishop to let us stay and eat, but His Illustriousness said that we needed to come with him because several important persons accompanied him, and he did not want to make them wait. I did not come down right away, and in order to buy a little more time the nuns told the bishop that I had had a little accident. When he heard this he became very alarmed and wanted to enter the cloister. I hurriedly came down and he told me breathlessly: "Mother abbess, what happened to you?" I responded: "Señor, with all the confusion I couldn't find my veil." He then said: "Thanks be to God that it was only a small thing." The truth is that the Lord gave us this blessed father, I mean to say, this saintly prince, for our father and protector of this endeavor. He treated us with such affection and care that we will never be able to thank him for all his acts of kindness, and we will always remember our obligation to him

42. In reference to the hours of the Divine Office.

43. Approximately twelve kilos.

as his perpetual wards [*capellanas*]. We had a very touching farewell with the nuns [from Toledo]. We thanked them for their warm hospitality and left their loving company feeling very enlightened by their strict religious observances and saintliness.

## Chapter IV
### Our Departure from Toledo, Our Farewell to the Bishop and All the Things that Happened before Our Arrival in Andujar

We left the convent accompanied by many persons. The blessed nuns were greatly mortified by the fact that we left without eating. They packed up the meal, with all the trimmings allowed by the austere Capuchin order, so that we could eat it on the road. We really appreciated this, but since we were traveling with such important persons, we gave it all to the carriage drivers who thoroughly enjoyed it. What we received was a note from the mother abbess telling us about all the problems she had dealing with the cook—she had fallen apart when she heard that we were not going to try the food she had prepared with such dedication and love. We continued on our way, and after a while a lay brother named Pedro de la Soledad, whom we had brought with us from our Madrid convent, came to say his goodbyes. He is a humble servant of God and very faithful to our convent. For many years he had attended to each of us like a father, and if it hadn't been for the fact that the Madrid community still needed him, without a doubt we would have brought him to our convent in Lima. Here [years later] we remembered again our mothers, and this was an occasion to ratify the sacrifice we made to Our Lord.

After this, the señor bishop, and the rest of the gentlemen accompanying him, got out of the carriage. He said that the time had come for him to return [to Toledo]. In the same manner since we had left Madrid, His Illustriousness helped each of us get down from the carriage, and then he helped each of us into the carriage we were to use for the journey. He would never let anyone else help us. After he made sure we were all settled in, he shed so many tears as he said his goodbyes that he practically washed the coach's running board. He spoke to us with so many kind and feverish words—his passionate speech was with such spirit and eloquence—that it was as if he could foresee all the trials that we would later endure. He said he was very sorry that he was not able to accompany us on the entire trip and that although he was not inclined towards bishoprics in the Indies, he would accept one just to have the opportunity to help us. Between our great love for him, due to the excellent qualities that God had given him, and the sadness of separating ourselves from his presence, it seemed as if we were going to die from the pain of it. It

is impossible to express what took place at that moment. His Illustriousness then mandated that we obey our father Don Joseph Fausto
Gallegos to whom he gave all his authority. The bishop ordered our
confessor not to allow us to fast on the journey because we did not
know exactly how long the trip was going to last and we needed to
keep up our strength and energy in order to carry out God's plan. We
told him how we wanted to continue following our austere lifestyle.
He responded that our obedience would make up for everything that
our father confessor put in front of us, and we should accept it all
like poor religious souls who have nothing. He also told us to keep
him up to date during our whole journey; he would be very happy to
hear from us. Whenever possible we would write to him during the
journey, and we do so even now that we are finally established in this
blessed house. God has now given us thirty-two religious women,
twenty-six of whom have already professed. We also owe much piety
to the Señor Viceroy Don Diego Ladrón de Guevara,[44] who was also
the Bishop of Quito, because he helped construct the running water
as a great convenience to our community. All of this must have given
him [the bishop of Toledo] great pleasure for the great love God has
instilled in him for his poor little daughters.

   After we said goodbye to our blessed prelate [the bishop of
Toledo] and continued along the route, tears kept streaming down our
faces, realizing that we were leaving our homeland and familiar faces
and that we were about to travel all by ourselves as poor nuns to a
strange land. The only person we knew was our father confessor, on
whom after God, we relied to protect and console us. At that time,
however, we had just gotten to know him and we didn't feel at ease
around him. All this lasted just a short while since he is such a friendly
and warm person. He was extremely reliable and he kept all his promises; only God can repay him all the many things he did for us. I will
only say that his humble and modest nature served as such a perfect
example for us that we felt embarrassed by it. When he saw how we
were suffering after our goodbyes to our prelate, he prudently gave us
some time to grieve and to heal our aching hearts. After a long time he
came and asked us how we were doing and whether we needed anything. He also said we were very close to our resting place for the night.

   We arrived at a country inn [*posada*]. As the dinner was being prepared we were given a very fine refreshment of sponge cakes

44. Doctor Diego Ladrón de Guevara Orozco Calderón (1641–1718) was the viceroy of
Peru (1710–16); earlier he had been the bishop of Quito (1703–10).

and ring-shaped pastries, since that whole day we had had only the crock of hot chocolate to drink. Our father confessor left and shut the door so we could go about our business, returning later in the evening to set the table with his own two hands. We thought we were going to have fish for dinner, as we were inspired to fast the whole journey, but the exact opposite occurred. When they brought us hens for dinner, at first we thought it was cabbage because they looked so white. But when my sisters realized it was chicken, they felt awful. Without saying a word they looked at one another, and none of them wanted to eat. As I witnessed this depressing situation, I remembered that His Illustriousness had mandated us to obey our father confessor and not to harbor illusions of keeping up our fasting on such a long journey. I served a plate for each of them and they shed many tears as they ate it. I tried to cheer them up so as not to embarrass our father confessor. I told them that there was a lot of merit in their obedience. Afterwards we prayed matins and then turned in for the night. We got up early the next morning and processed to the local church; this was our practice wherever we went. Our father confessor heard our confession, gave us communion and then said Mass for us. Doctor Don Cipriano de Santa Cruz, who was also traveling with us, then said another Mass for us. He was to be the future cantor of the Cathedral of Guamanga [Peru]. He was a virtuous and upright gentleman, and seeing him so resigned helped us greatly to accept all the difficulties of our endeavor. After the two Masses we returned to the *posada* where we ate some breakfast before we continued our journey. Since this was the first day, our father confessor personally arranged everything as he saw proper; he gave us some toasted bread with chocolate. We were happy thinking this small bite was meant to help us continue our fasting.

We traveled to Consuegra. A member from our party had gone ahead (as was always done) to arrange our stay for the night. Later when we went into the *posada* we only asked for a drink of water, and although our father confessor wanted to give us more refreshments, we would not accept them so as to keep up with our fasting. His Grace [our confessor] just smiled and let us be, but at that moment I suspected what would happen later. He shut the door, as was the routine, and left. At the dinner hour he opened the door and set the table by himself; he did not trust anyone else with this task. He had us sit down, and when the food was brought to the door he and his companion Don Cipriano took it to us. He did not let anyone else enter our room. First they served us two roasted pullets [young hens], and afterwards, as if that wasn't enough, two well dressed partridges. If the previous evening there had been tears, now it was even beyond that; my sisters cried that they shouldn't eat meat because the Rule forbids it, and after all we were not ill, so why should we be treated like this? I felt terrible seeing the suffering of my blessed sisters and I tried to console them, telling them it was very important to obey and to eat everything we were given, especially because our mortification would be even greater than the times we were required to eat codfish in our blessed convent [of Madrid]. I felt really sorry for our father confessor, who on that day felt badly about the situation. Yet, from that point onward his spirits lifted, and he did what his prudence dictated. We all yielded to his wants and wishes, offering up to God our desire to follow a more austere lifestyle.

That day we arrived in Membrilla in the afternoon. We stayed in a convent of nuns from the Order of the Conception whose servants of the Lord welcomed us with great love and charity. After dinner all of them came to visit with us, although there were very few of them. They live an exceptionally difficult life because they are extremely poor and their house is very uncomfortable. Their convent is in ruins and they do not even have any dormitories or cells; when they go to the choir in wintertime they get wet and in the summer they roast. We felt very sorry for them and even more so because there was nothing we could do to help them. The majority are quite elderly and to console them God brought them a wealthy and lovely señorita. She had just taken her vows and all by herself she wanted to take on all the convent's offices. She was afraid that the convent might be closed if she did not do this. We spent the night in the señorita's cell where they had beds prepared for us. Nonetheless, we slept on the floor with our blankets, since we never accepted anything else. The next morning, after we had said confession and taken communion, we said a teary goodbye to those nuns. God had instilled in them such love that it was as if we had been living with them for many years.

That day we traveled without stopping until the afternoon when we arrived at a place called La Torre de Juan Abad. We were put up for the night in the house of a noble señora who had recently been widowed. She treated us very well and we tried to return the favor by comforting her as best we knew how. The next morning before sunrise we went to a small chapel [*ermita*]. There was such rain and wind that the going was extremely tough, but in order not to delay the day's journey we had to get up early so that we did not miss Mass and communion. After we had breakfast and said our goodbyes to the señora, we continued on our way.

As I have already mentioned above, our father confessor had arranged for a member of the party to go ahead and arrange our lodging for each evening. After we entered the room in the place that was set aside for us, we all prayed the Divine Office [*Oficio Divino*] as a community (whenever possible we tried to adjust our prayer obligations to our travel schedule). We were quite a large group since we had many people accompanying us. Our father confessor treated the coachmen with kindness and generosity so that they would take very good care of us. He had them warn us whenever they had other passengers so we could shut the curtains. The coachmen took their job so seriously that we praised the Lord for it, and it pleased us to see how dedicated they were to this task. The first days on the route they swore and cursed, uttering blasphemies whenever they found themselves in a difficult stretch or even for the littlest thing. This caused us great sadness and we told them to control themselves, not only because of God's displeasure, but because in our company we did not want to hear anything else but praises to the Lord. They promised to make amends and they did this very well. The oldest coachman had the worst habits, but he held his tongue out of respect for what we had said to him. On those occasions when he exercised control and to show us how much he had improved, he would say to us: "*Madres*, I am already a saint. On my life, since I have been around you, I pray a lot and I do not swear at all."

We had entrusted this good man with watching over us, and on one occasion he took his job so seriously that he raced past many people, I mean señoras.[45] As we were nearing a small town the mayor's wife and other noble women were waiting for us on the route, but once the coachmen saw them they told us to close the curtains, whipping the mules with such gusto that we flew by them. All the señoras and other women were running and shouting for them to stop, but the coachmen completely ignored them. After the señoras were left far behind, the drivers were very proud of themselves, saying: "What is it about the madres that those curious women want to look at? No way, they'll never see 'em."[46] Since our father was traveling behind us in

---

45. The author corrects herself.

46. María Rosa is imitating the colloquial language of the coachmen. The original Spanish reads: ";Qué querrían las curiosas ver a las madres? No lo conseguirán eso no más faltaba" (45v).

another calash [*calesa*],[47] he had no idea what had just happened. He felt really bad when he heard the complaints from the señoras. I also felt bad, but at the same time I endured that mad rush because I did not want the coachmen to stop taking care of us on future occasions.

We arrived at La Mancha. We had passed through Santo Cristo del Valle, a place where Christ had miraculously appeared a few years earlier. At that time many people worked in this valley, but because it was very isolated they were not able to hear Mass on feast days. It happened that one day two pilgrims came to this place and asked the inhabitants to let them rest in a granary[48] nearby. When the inhabitants went to look for the two pilgrims they didn't find anyone, only a very large charcoal painting of the Blessed Christ on the wall. It's a beautiful composition and the hands that painted it are well known. That place now has its own church and very fine chapel. There have been many miracles in that land and now the inconvenience of not having Mass has been solved. To get there we lost a half-day's journey, but we were very pleased to see that sanctuary.

We arrived that night in the foothills of the Sierra Morena [Mountains] at a place called Alcuvillas. We were completely soaked because the carriage's curtains were not enough to protect us from the fierce rain and windstorm. We went to the house of the priest who was a very good person and has the best house in the town, but it caused us a lot of trouble. In the large doorway [to the patio] he had a fireplace with a roaring fire; since we were very wet and did not have any change of habit, we dried out little by little in front of it (as children of my Father Saint Francis, we do not have more than two tunics and one habit). Afterward, we prayed the Divine Office and then the priest took us to his room which we were going to use. He had to take out the bed so that we could get in; otherwise there was no way all of us could fit. Not only was it very small, but it also had an earthen floor and walls. The window was actually a hole and a two-handled basket was used to cover it. The decoration of that room consisted of two or three very old chairs. Benches were found so that we could all sit down at the table. Finally we had dinner and when we asked for a pitcher of water—actually, we originally had wanted to travel further that day, but the fierce storm had held us back, and for that reason our cargo, which contained all our necessary supplies, was not there—we

---

47. A type of light carriage.

48. *Una trox* (also spelled *troj*) is a granary. The Peru transcription says "casa" instead of "trox."

were brought a large jug that seemed more like a drinking trough for chickens or pigeons. Don Cipriano de Santa Cruz was the one who had brought it in and with his usual good humor he said: "*Madres*, here I have brought you this elegant flowered pitcher." No matter how we tried to hide it we couldn't help but laugh because it amused us to see such a ridiculous thing. When it was time to turn in for the night we just didn't have the heart to put our blankets on top of so much dirt. It then took a long time to find an old mat. When I asked if the door had a lock and key, I was told no. I took a closer look at it and realized that there was an open space, about the size of a hand, both under and above the door. We were very frightened at being so exposed, and when I asked our father confessor to stay by the door—otherwise we would never have any peace of mind—he replied, "Don't worry. I don't have any other place to sleep except at this doorway." We felt much more at ease, even though it upset us to see that servant of God on the ground. Before five in the morning the señor priest accompanied us to the church; after our father confessor said Mass, he then said another one for us.

We continued that day's journey through the Sierra Morena. We were concerned about attacks from bandits that happen in this area; nonetheless, we were also confident that Divine Providence would take care of its wives. It's a very beautiful mountain range covered with trees and flowers that give cause to praise the Lord. It takes two and a half days to cross the mountains. The first place where we spent the night was the Venta de San Andrés (in this area there are no towns, only *ventas*).[49] The second night we stayed in the Venta de Carpio. All the men who were accompanying us stayed up the whole night to guard us. In front of the venta there is a large encina tree[50] about which we were told a story. We learned that in that place a Capuchin friar had confronted an important man who lived a scandalous lifestyle. The friar had tried to get this man to amend his appalling ways, but this certain señor was so filled with rage that he hung the friar from the encina. From that day onward all the acorns that grow from the tree have been marked with the sign of the Capuchin order. This was the way that God had decided to honor his servant.

We then traveled to a place they call "la barranca" [the precipice]. This is the most dangerous part of that deserted area. All the men from our party readied their firearms, but His Divine Majesty did not

49. Like a *posada*, but even more rustic.

50. A type of live oak tree.

deem that necessary and we passed on through without any problems.

At nine o'clock at night we arrived very tired at Linares, but very thankful to God Almighty for letting us safely cross the deserted area. After saying our prayers and eating our dinner we entered the room where we were going to sleep. It was very small and completely taken up by two beds. Since we do not use beds, we had them taken out, but when our father confessor saw that the floor was quite humid he had straw mattresses placed on the ground. We tried to get settled, but it was extremely difficult because the five of us really did not fit. The room was so small that the mattresses could not be separated and we had to climb over one another. The vicaress [Madre María Estefanía], (may she rest in peace), laid down on one end of the mattress and I on the opposite end. I ended up with my face stuck up against a mouse's nest. I had a horrible night: on top of the foul odor of the mice and my fear of them, I was also very uncomfortable, spending the whole night without a blanket; the same thing happened to the mother vicaress.  Although we slept dressed in our habits, it was so cold that we certainly had something to offer up to the Lord. My other three sisters were in the middle and fared somewhat better than us. The vicaress and I, however, slept without a blanket because the others kept pulling it off. May the Lord be well served by all this.

The next morning we went to church (as on other occasions). We left very early and continued our journey through some really difficult stretches, including a very steep ascent, with one league up hill. God miraculously saved us that day from falling off a cliff. On that occasion, Madre Josepha Victoria, who was sitting on the outside carriage step, felt tired, but not knowing why, decided to change to the other side. This then caused the mules to lean so far over to the right that the twelve carriage wheels on that side came off the edge of the trail and were airborne. Those who saw this episode from a distance thought we were doomed.

We arrived at an open plain where the coachmen stopped the carriages and got out to wait for the rest of the group to catch up. While there, a bagpiper and his son appeared and when they saw us they began to play and sing. We took pleasure from their joyfulness, while at the same time we were shocked at seeing such a horrendous thing—the bagpiper looked like the Enemy [the Devil] himself, he was so ugly. The coachmen began to dance, and if our father confessor had not arrived, they would have continued with their party. The coachmen were extremely happy to have been saved from that tragedy. We laughed for a long time as we remembered their dancing and that horrible sight.

We had now entered Andalusia: it was olive season and the whole trail was filled with olive trees and people who were harvesting them. For this reason we had to be careful to keep the curtains shut, and although many people asked to see us, the coachmen, in their amiable way, kept a careful watch. Thus, we avoided many courtesy visits and conversations; they were, however, all very devout and wanted to talk to us.

## Chapter V
### How We Arrived in the City of Andujar
### and Our Stay in the Convent of the Capuchin Nuns

We arrived in the beautiful city of Andujar, its friendly inhabitants devout followers of the daughters of our Mother Saint Clare. We were taken to the Capuchin convent, a foundation which had originally come from Cordoba. Those servants of the Lord gave us a very warm and loving welcome. The vicar, who was a very upstanding gentleman, accompanied us with many people—he is the nuns' confessor and they all hold him in high esteem. It was the hour of compline and thus only the mother abbess and the portresses came out to greet us so that the rest of the nuns would not miss the choir. When they finished, we went into the choir to receive the blessing of the Blessed Sacrament. Afterward we all went together to enjoy the nativity scene; since they knew we were coming they had left it up and they gave thanks to the Christ Child. Afterwards they took us to see their house, which was very small and very damp. All the lower cells were inhabitable, and to open each door felt like opening a crypt. A better convent was being built, but since the founder's death the construction had been halted. God's Will had it that the church and the upper and lower choir were built first (by no means the least important) so there was a somewhat comfortable place to pray the Divine Office. They are very lovely nuns; two of the founding mothers are still alive, but one of them has been ill for a long time.

We were very pleased to meet them and to see how well they had established that foundation [in Andujar]. We felt particularly attached to them because two of the founding mothers had come from our convent in Madrid to found one in Corboba.[51] One of the nuns was called Madre María Josepha and the other was Madre María Isabel.

The latter was a nun of noteworthy virtue. For the glory of God, I will tell a very unique story that took place at the time she left [the Madrid convent]. When all the preparations were being made for the Cordoba foundation, she could always be heard saying that she was going to go. It was very strange to hear her say this because she was a very quiet nun who spent a lot of time in seclusion and she was also sickly. The mother abbess would humiliate her by asking how such a thing could come out of her mouth when she was so worthless. As is customary, she would prostrate herself on the ground in front

51. They went on to found the convent in Andujar.

84

of the abbess to hear the reprimand, but then she would get up smiling and would repeat again that she was going to go. When the time came to select the founders, no one thought of mentioning this nun [María Isabel] for that task. Yet, she never wavered in her hope, so much so that it encouraged everyone else to poke fun at her naiveté. The habits were made for the new founders and she asked permission to do the same for herself. The day was set for the departure and the Dukes of Useda (who were the patrons of the new convent) came to publicly take the sisters out of the cloister. All of Spain's dignitaries had been invited for this occasion. It just so happened that the day before the departure one of the founding sisters had such a high fever that it appeared to be a *sincopal*.[52] The mother abbess was extremely worried about this; everything was ready and the trip could not be suspended. The prelate came (he was given the news that one of the founders would not be able to go due to her grave illness) and he was also told about Madre María Isabel's wish to participate; despite the fact she was a very virtuous nun, they did not think at first that she was the right candidate for the foundation. Nevertheless, from the onset of the preparations, she had assured them that she would be one of the founders and that now it seemed that God, by hindering the other one's departure, wanted her to go. The prelate called her to him and she gladly said: "Señor, here I am, ready to go. I am even holding my prayer book under my arm." The prelate and the whole community were amazed to see how readily something they had deemed so senseless, was carried out to the letter of the word. Her father confessor told everyone that much earlier she had told him that this would take place and that is exactly what happened.

Madre María Josepha and four other nuns were the first founders of this community in Andujar. However, she and three others who came from Cordoba died in the new convent because of the dampness of the place. Only one of the founders was left with a novice and she asked permission to return to her community in Cordoba. Her request was denied since the community would die out completely. The señor bishop decided to send new founders, among whom the most important was the aforementioned Madre María Isabel. Not only had the Lord destined her for the first foundation in Cordoba, but also for the second in Andujar.

---

52. In English, a *syncope*, refers to a blackout. The *Diccionario de la lengua española* also refers to it as a type of fever.

Returning to my narration and what I was saying about how we were so well treated by this community, all the nuns wanted us to spend at least one day with them. Yet this was not possible because the convent was under construction and we were under a lot of pressure to make the departure date.

We said a very tender goodbye to them and continued on to the city of Cordoba. It is one of the most important cities of Andalusia. The Capuchin nuns of Cordoba (as I have already mentioned) are daughters of our convent in Madrid. They were very excited about our arrival and so they notified all the gentlemen, relatives and benefactors of their convent so that they could come out to greet us. They all greatly honored us. We entered the church (which is quite small) and after a prayer was said to the Blessed Sacrament we processed to the convent's gatehouse. The whole community was waiting for us and we were lined up in a procession and rang bells as they sang *Te Deum Laudamus*; the mother abbess then sang a prayer. They didn't have enough time with us because many members of the leading families of Cordoba came to visit us. This greatly angered the Capuchin nuns, and all the other convents had the same complaint. They said that these noble persons took up the precious time that we were to be in their city. After we were left in the convent, the nuns entertained us by singing several hymns. They had lovely voices. We were very happy with those saintly nuns because it seemed as if we were in our own convent: there is no difference whatsoever between our two communities, even in the smallest of ceremonies.

The following day, as we prepared for our departure, a very amusing thing happened. The young girls in the convent, who were very creative (they had written several *romances*[53] before our arrival), formed a line of two choruses with us in the middle, and they sang for us like little angels. As we were enjoying their performance, we were notified that our father confessor, along with all the noblemen of that city, were waiting for us at the main door of the convent so that we could depart. This news greatly deflated my little singers and they started to cry. We were so rushed that it reminded us of our departure from Toledo.

They took us to the cathedral where they showed us all the exquisite things housed there, honoring us in all possible ways. The person who made the greatest effort (because he is a very saintly gentleman) was the señor viscount of Puebla, a great benefactor of

---

53. A type of verse narrative.

the Capuchin nuns. He and his mother, my Señora Doña Urraca, treated us very well. Doña Urraca and one of her maiden daughters accompanied us as we left the holy cathedral. Both of them got into the carriage with us and, since they wanted to ride with us, they didn't mind the inconvenience of sitting on the running board. They thought this was only going to be for a short distance, but it turned out to be quite the opposite.

We journeyed that day to the city of Ecija where Doña Urraca had a married daughter. She was very upset with her daughter, and despite many attempts and efforts to get them back together, she still did not want to speak to her. Nevertheless, Our Lord, who is the keeper of hearts, changed her mind to such an extent that she was not free to return to Cordoba, as was everyone else who accompanied us. Before she was to return, she told her son, the viscount, that she wanted to go to Ecija with us. He and everyone else were amazed to hear this, since she had always been against making that journey. It was even more surprising considering her uncomfortable mode of transport, as I have already described. We felt a great comfort by all this; it was a very good thing for the mother and daughter and also for the three families. We were so occupied the whole day that by five o'clock in the afternoon the saintly señora still hadn't eaten breakfast. She looked so pale that I asked her if she was ill. She said no, but that she had left her house in such a hurry, wanting to accompany us that she had forgotten to eat anything. We felt very sorry to think that in order to favor us she would have endured such discomfort. We gave her some sponge cakes [*bizcochos*] to tide her over until we arrived at a venta where our father confessor and the señor viscount had arranged a meal for us.

We continued on the route and arrived very late in the city of Ecija (it is ten leagues away from Cordoba). The daughter of the viscountess, accompanied by other señoras, who were relatives of her husband, came out to welcome us. We stayed in her house which is one of the best in the city. Although there were convents in Ecija, it was God's Will that we make these friendships, and thus He arranged that we would arrive so late in the evening that it did not seem fitting to bother any of the religious communities. This made those señoras very happy; they were especially pious women and felt very fortunate to have us stay in their house.

We spent a good part of the night conversing with them. We did not have the heart to go to bed since they appeared to be greatly comforted by spending time with us. We became friends with the daughter, the son-in-law, and the mother-in-law, and from that day onward they were very attached to us. Those señores showered us with a thousand favors, and the next morning they accompanied us for a long stretch of the route. We will always be thankful for their kindness. On occasion I have written to them as a reminder that we have not forgotten them.

## Chapter VI
## All that Took Place until We Arrived in Cadiz

After we said our goodbyes (as I have already mentioned) we traveled to Carmona. This is a long day's journey, and the climb to the town was very difficult. It was probably around ten o'clock in the evening when we arrived. We did not know that the señor archbishop of Seville had arranged our lodging. Apparently we were to have spent the night in a convent of Augustinian nuns. They were supposed to have come out and welcomed us with the ringing of their church bells, but none of this came to fruition. We had arrived so late and we were so tired that it did not seem appropriate to disturb anyone, so we went to a *posada*. Very early the next morning we went to the church; it was extremely cold outside. Since none of our companions knew which door opened to the church, they spent a long time knocking, but nobody seemed to hear us. After a while they looked around another side of the church where we found an open door. When the sacristan saw us he was beside himself with guilt; he was quite worried saying, "What am I going to tell the vicar? He had given me instructions to let him know when Your Reverences had arrived." We comforted him, assuring him that we would speak for him. After we heard Mass and took communion we left immediately.

We left for Seville. We made an early stop at a farm run by Jesuit priests, resting there for a while. At the farm we met several gentlemen who came trickling in from the city [Seville] and also from Lima, who happened to be traveling there at the time. The señor archbishop sent his confessor and other persons to accompany us to our sisters of the Capuchin convent in Seville. The mother abbess (who is the Señora Palafox)[54] and all her holy community were waiting for us. They followed the same routine as in other convents. Once the formal ceremonies were completed, the saintly abbess and all her daughters entertained us. We loved this convent dearly as if it were a piece of our own heart. Not only was it a place of comfort on this part of the

---

54. Sor Josepha Manuela de Palafox y Cardona (1649–1724: Zaragoza—Seville), founder and first abbess of the Capuchin convent in Seville, Monasterio de Santa Rosalía. Her uncle, Don Jaime de Palafox, archbishop of Seville had built the convent. She was author of several texts including: *Una muy instructiva memoria en obsequio de su instituto, con el título de testamento suyo el año de 1702*, printed in 1724 in Seville; and *La carta de edificación*, published after her death by the new abbess, Sor Clara Gertrudis Perez Navarro in 1730. Félix de Latassa y Ortiz, *Biblioteca Nueva de los Escritores Aragoneses* (Pamplona: Domingo, 1800), 4.399, 400.

journey, but we also had the privilege of staying with their gracious company for a year and a half after our time as prisoners.[55] During both visits we felt loved and spiritually uplifted by them.

Later the señor archbishop sent us alms and Señor Don Pedro Levanto (who was not there) had left more alms before leaving. The latter, who was the archbishop elect of Lima, was particularly fond of us and always showed his very generous nature to us as he is a father to all poor people. Later he came to visit us. We were all very happy that we were to travel together, although not on the same ship, because His Illustriousness needed a whole cabin to himself. We were going to share our cabin with the *presidenta* [wife of the presiding magistrate] of Chile and for this reason we would not all be able to fit on one ship. We felt very sorry about this because from the day we met him we felt a great love for him.

We spent eighteen days in that convent, treated very well by those saintly nuns. At the end of this time we prepared to leave for Cadiz. For this reason the Señor Don Pedro Levanto came and first took us to the cathedral where we were shown everything that there is to see (although it pales in comparison with the Cathedral of Toledo). The distinguished canons honored us in many ways and they delighted us by taking us to see the famous Giralda.[56] It is truly marvelous, because even though it is so high you do not need to climb any stairs to go up it—even a sedan chair[57] can easily go up. In order for us to hear the tremendous force of the bells, they were rung outside the ordinary prayer schedule. The bells were many and large, and even though we were ready, they nearly scared us to death.

We did not leave the church until very late. Señor Levanto made arrangements to take us to his house, which is like a palace. He did not permit us to return to the convent because we would be departing within the next day and a half. Later when we were in his home he demonstrated his great devotion to us—he kept wanting to

---

55. The author is referring to their capture by the Dutch and their subsequent time as prisoners in the Portuguese convents. After their stint in Portugal, the five nuns returned to this same convent in Seville where they waited over a year and a half for their father confessor to obtain the necessary licenses that had been lost to the Dutch.

56. The famous bell tower of the Cathedral of Seville. The tower is what was left of the ancient minaret (the first two thirds) of the Almohad mosque and at one time was the tallest building in the world. The oldest part of the tower dates back to the twelfth century.

57. A sedan chair [*silla de manos*] is a portable chair for one person, having poles on both sides and carried by two people.

give us more. He treated us with such veneration that it embarrassed us; for example, he insisted on serving us at his own table where we ate with his saintly mother who is a very elderly lady and is particularly virtuous. Her advanced age did not inhibit her from following the religious lifestyle of the Carmelites which was very uplifting to us. She has served as a wonderful example for her sons because all of them have turned out to be very well educated and virtuous. It was very comforting to get to know all these señores, especially His Illustriousness. He told us that Saint Francis Borgia[58] had been put up in the very same room where we were staying. We felt very fortunate to have this privilege. The day we spent with him he took us to the Benedictine Convent of San Pedro de las Dueñas where two of his sisters were nuns, and they treated us very well, which befit their upbringing.

The next day we left Seville. His Illustriousness, [Señor Levanto] along with many other gentlemen, accompanied us, and after they had traveled a long way with us we all said goodbye. As he blessed us, we felt very happy to think that we would be seeing each other again within a few short days in Cadiz.

We arrived in Utrera (which is a fortified town). Don Juan de Alva had been the sergeant major there and was the father of my sister, Madre Gertrudis. It had been two years since his death, and we didn't know how this happened but it was obviously God's Will (from what I can understand) because we ended up staying at a *posada* next to the church where this gentleman was buried. This was despite the fact that there was a convent in that town, but since we arrived very early no one thought of taking us there. The next morning we went to the church to take communion. We dedicated a suffrage [*sufragio*],[59] along with the Masses, to his soul. All of us, along with our father confessor and Don Cipriano, said a prayer for his soul. I don't think any nun has ever personally visited her father's grave after twenty years behind closed walls.

From there we traveled to the Venta de Vizcaína where some amusing things happened, although they didn't seem so at the time. It was very cold and rainy, and we really wanted to find a place to have a light meal. We found a very rustic shelter, not much better than an open field; the room was so wet that we could not sit down and the rain fell right down on us. This was very upsetting to our father

---

58. St. Francis Borgia (1510–72) was a Spanish Jesuit who held the title of father general in charge of the entire order. He was canonized in 1671.

59. I.e., a short intercessory prayer.

confessor, and since he is such a generous soul, he tried to fix up the place as best he could so that we could spend the night there. The next morning Our Lord consoled us by having a chapel quite close by. Although we still got a bit wet, we enjoyed offering this up to the Lord. We returned to the shelter—which was a good place to suffer—where His Divine Majesty had us spend that day and night; the weather was so stormy that we could not leave that day. The next day we woke up to the same bad weather. We resigned ourselves to God's Will, since it seemed as if He wanted us to be so uncomfortable that even getting something to eat would be a major accomplishment. The innkeeper was paid very well, but she kept complaining and we had to listen to everything. She was staying so close to us because she was sick, but she could not keep her mouth shut the whole day. We entreated God to calm her down. One of the members of the party got so angry that he threatened her by saying that we were carrying a royal decree from the king so that no one should deny us anything, and that if she did not help us then she would face grave consequences. After this she seemed to realize her mistake, and we spent a pleasant time speaking to her because she had a witty tongue.

In the afternoon the sky started to clear and we left for Jerez. Before entering the town there is a very long narrow street. It was so flooded from water on either side that it looked more like a sea. In order for the coachmen to avoid that quagmire they turned off the royal road [*camino real*], yet after a short while they found themselves in an even worse situation. Seeing that there was no alternative and that turning back was not an option, they suddenly lunged forward, the six mules and the carriage, all falling over an embankment. We invoked Our Lady of Carmen to save us as we were falling down. The carriage jerked violently but it did not turn over or split into pieces. My sisters and I fell on top of one another, and I was so frightened that I got sick.

When we entered Jerez we were really fortunate because we were immediately provided with braziers[60] so that we could dry out. Since we had not brought any more clothes than our one habit, we did not have anything to change into; this fact brought solace to our hearts. The next morning we went to the Convent of Our Father Saint Francis. While we were listening to Mass, the sacristan of the discalced nuns who resided in that town spotted us. He quickly went to tell the nuns, who then told the señor vicar, who felt very bad that he had not known about our arrival. He had been instructed by the señor archbishop to

---

60. Metal container for fire, a type of primitive heating device for a room.

take us to the convent no matter what our arrival time. He apologized profusely to us and obligated us to stay with the discalced nuns. He said that there was no reason for us to be out in the streets, since we had a place to stay with the nuns. Since we had just arrived in the manner I have described, we couldn't think of anything better than getting out of the carriage that was soaked with water. We thanked the señor vicar for his goodwill and for all that was done for us by those saintly nuns who welcomed us with great hospitality and respect. Those discalced daughters are very observant of our Mother Saint Clare. They enthusiastically celebrated our arrival, within the limits of their order, and we were very pleased to spend time with them. Despite this, we were anxious to continue on to Cadiz, but the heavy rains would not allow it. We asked them to pray to God to let it stop raining. They humorously replied that they had already prayed to God to let it rain for many days so that we would not be able to leave them.

We spent two days with them and after that we left for the Port of Santa María. While there we stayed with the nuns of the Convent of the Immaculate Conception who treated us with exceptional kindness. We felt very sorry for them because their convent was in a practical state of ruin. This all occurred when the British had entered the port and destroyed their sanctuary. They had profaned the Virgin Mary and all the sacred images. Now, after the attack, the nuns only had a very small room that served as the church. I do not have the words to describe how uncomfortably they lived; we understood this because after our time as prisoners we spent forty-five days in that convent. Going to the choir was very inconvenient because we would get just as wet as if we were out on the street, but on the occasion that I am describing now, we only spent one night. We left the next morning, accompanied by all the city gentlemen—who made many efforts to favor us—to board the ferry. That day we felt a great comfort when we saw the sea, although that pleasure was soon to be cut short because my sisters got very seasick.

We arrived at the docks of Cadiz where we were awaited by a cathedral dignitary,[61] by Andrés de Murguia and many other high-ranking officials. They had brought with them the governor's carriage to transport us. It was very elegant and when I saw all the mud I felt very bad that we were going to soil it with our wet feet. I said this in such a soft voice to my sisters that I thought no one could have heard us. Yet this was not the case. A poor soul quickly took off his cape

61. A cathedral dignitary (*maestrescuela*) who teaches divinity.

and put it on the ground so that we could step on it. I was so embarrassed that I wanted to throw myself down and kiss his feet. Later, the
cathedral dignitary imitated this good man when we got out of the
carriage at the main entrance of the Convent of the Discalced Nuns of
the Conception. Those pious nuns affectionately received us as guests
as the bells rang *Te Deum Laudamus*. As soon as they saw that we had
fasted that day and were still queasy from the ferry crossing,[62] they
gave us breakfast and then took us to lie down. This treatment helped
us feel much better after our bout of seasickness from our first ferry
ride. They had prepared a cell for each of us. This, along with the very
affable reception from those servants of God, made us feel as if we
were in our own community.

---

62. They most likely had taken a ferry from the Port of Santa María to Cadiz.

## Chapter VII
### Concerning All the Things that Happened
### before We Were Taken Prisoners and Brought to Portugal

I have already mentioned the great kindness we received in this convent. Although we thought our delay would be only a few days, our departure was held up for forty-six days, since setting sail involves many unforeseen circumstances. We were well cared for by the holy company at the convent, and it seemed we were all one in love and sincerity. Although their order differs from ours in many ways, especially in the established schedule, we share much in common and we attended as many of their community activities as possible. We took comfort in this and also from [the nuns] who were genuinely pleased with the time we spent with them. There will always be a special place in our hearts for this convent, which is one of the most perfect we encountered during our entire pilgrimage.

From the convent we saw the arrival of the fleet with many ships; although they were to detain us even longer, we had a great time watching them from here. This very beautiful convent had wonderful views of the sea, thus allowing us to see the fleet's arrival and praise God for it. A few days later our prelate, Señor Levanto, arrived. Señor Levanto then extended us the favor of a visit, which was his custom. We were also visited by the señor bishop of that city [Cadiz], and by the bishop of Buenos Aires who was to set sail with us. During one of his visits, the bishop of Buenos Aires was inspired by divine grace and said: "My sisters, I am very pleased to travel with you, but I fear greatly that the restless Enemy [the Devil] of this undertaking might try to set a snare for us."

Our departure was arranged for the Feast of Our Father Saint Joseph [March 19, 1710] to the dismay of the holy sisters of the convent who told us they could scarcely resign themselves to our going. Although we felt bad, the wish to go on with our purpose held greater sway over us. Near midday we were summoned to the turn to meet with a captain of one of the ships on important business. I was quite alarmed, and seeing me in this state, the captain told me to calm myself, because even though he did not bring good news, there was nothing to fear. He told me that it was still not time for our departure because His Majesty had sent an order to delay the ships until the arrival of a judge, whom he was sending to Buenos Aires. We had to offer up to God the postponement of the day of our much anticipated departure.

My heart was in my mouth from the moment the fleet arrived because I was told that the sea would be filled with our enemies as soon as they learned of the assembled fleet. With this new delay, I feared that by the time we set sail they would know all about us. I did not tell a soul about this, but afterwards we found out that the very day we were supposed to have set out was when the Dutch left their ports to capture us. The aforementioned city judge arrived at last and our departure was set for the Feast of the Incarnation[63] [March 25, 1710]. On the appointed day Señor Levanto came to take us out of the cloister. The señor bishop of Cadiz excused himself due to illness; but instead he sent us his confessor, his attendants and his own carriage so that they could accompany us. Countless people filled the church and its portico. The Señor Bishop of Buenos Aires Don Fray Pedro Fajardo[64] and many other important people gathered to be with us.

Everyone was waiting for our father confessor, who surprised us by not being the first to arrive. He was late, and we feared the worst because of his delay. He was searched for everywhere and after about an hour he arrived, looking extremely pale, and spoke in private to the señor archbishop and the bishop of Buenos Aires. He told them he had been delayed because he had received a very troubling message that two corsair ships were lurking just outside the harbor. In order to confirm this, he had sought out the governor who told him that a fishing vessel had also seen these ships. Our father confessor then called on Don Andrés de Murguía, the owner of our ships, telling him that under no circumstances would he depart until he found out whether this message were true. He convinced our father confessor that all had been a misunderstanding and assured him that there was nothing to fear, especially since he had the greatest [financial] interest in the voyage and for his own assurance had procured a safe-conduct from Queen Anne. Seeing our father confessor's alarm, Andrés de Murguía spoke all the more encouragingly, but he later admitted when we saw him again that he had been sick with fear.

What is clear is that Our Lord allowed them all to make mistakes and in doing so gave us a chance to become more deserving. When the señores who were waiting had heard this, they said that there was no cause for alarm. If we met with the English, we had Queen Anne's safe-conduct and if the corsairs were Moors they would

63. More commonly known as the Feast of the Annunciation.

64. Pedro Fajardo (1664–1729) was appointed bishop on May 22, 1713, but was not ordained in Buenos Aires until January 19, 1716.

never dare to attack such large ships. We placed ourselves in God's hands and, with this fear and our sorrow at seeing the teary-eyed nuns, we made a very sad departure. We reached the bay where our well prepared vessel awaited us. The Señor Archbishop Levanto and the bishop of Buenos Aires accompanied us to our cabin where they blessed us, telling us that they would come the next day to say Mass. Things occurred quite differently because we would not see them until more than a year later, after all involved endured indescribable trials, especially His Illustriousness [Señor Levanto].

We set sail that day with great joy. When we had lost sight of Cadiz we saw a brightly colored small boat, which alarmed us since it was too far out to sea to be a fishing vessel. At nightfall we lost sight of it and gave thanks to the Lord for setting us on our path to this city of Lima.

Very early the next morning, even though we were seasick, we said our devotions—the Divine Office—and had Mass and communion. Then just at daybreak two large ships sailed into view, heading towards us under a very favorable wind. I cannot express the sorrow in my heart and the fear of death I felt thinking they were Moors.

Everyone on board took up arms; the drums sounded; and in a very short time the ships came so close to us that we could speak to them from the stern. They hoisted their flags to identify themselves, and they were thought to be English. Everyone breathed a sigh of relief thinking that the safe-conduct would save us, but this was not the case because they said that they were from the Dutch States, that our letter of safe conduct meant nothing to them, and that we were their prey.

They boarded our ship and carefully searched it to see if there were any Frenchmen aboard. Our Captain, Don Joaquín de Triviño, came into our cabin with the Dutch captain, which startled us greatly. The Dutch captain, upon seeing us, merely bowed and then left. Our captain explained as best he could who we were, and since he was then to be taken to the Dutch ships and could no longer take care of us, he asked the Dutch captain to look after us. At this very moment God saved us by a miracle; with all the fear and commotion no one was steering the ships, and they collided with a terrible crash. Thanks be to the Lord for saving us from a possible disaster.

After our captain asked the Dutch captain to take care of us, he put a sentry by the door of our cabin to watch over us. Something quite different happened to the wife of the presiding magistrate of Chile. This woman was staying in a middle cabin and the Dutch crew broke into her cabin and looted it, taking away everything she and her maids possessed.

All this occurred on the twenty-sixth day of March in the year 1710. It was six in the morning when we were taken prisoners. The Dutch crew hauled down our king's flags and raised their own with great pride and celebration. This was very distressing to all the prisoners, whom they began to treat with unspeakable tyranny, for they beat some of them with staves; others, of higher status, although they were not treated like that, were taken to the enemy ships and given nothing better to eat than barley gruel. They took all the provisions from our ships with them.

It took all day to transfer all the captured passengers to their vessels. The Dutch crew did nothing but come and go in the launch, filling it with whomever they could get their hands on. It was pitiful to see how some of the passengers tried to hide. Eleven or twelve of the passengers (as many as could fit) sought refuge in our cabin. Our Lord saw to it that the food given to us nuns was enough for all of us. The food was brought to us by a lay brother who had come along to assist us and to whom the Dutch crew showed respect for being part of our order.

We experienced great favors from our God, for the roughest of men cared for us with such great courtesy that we never wanted for anything. The captain and the rest of his officers sent messages to us, saying that if we would allow it they would like to come and serve at our table. We appreciated their politeness, but we told them through the interpreter (who was a Jesuit priest) that our order did not allow men to see us. Also, the Dutch crew learned about our way of life and was very amazed to learn of our professed vows of poverty. When we went to pray the Divine Office from the balcony above our cabin they came to listen.

They showed great respect for our father confessor, offering him items that they use a lot of, such as beer and butter, with the intent that he would give them to us. We never accepted anything directly from the Dutch. We did not think any of these offers was appropriate, and our hearts pounded to see everyone controlled by the enemies of our faith with their evil dispositions. We knew that they loathed people devoted to God. We continuously beseeched our Divine Majesty to free us from their power and from such tribulation. We spent many a sleepless night listening to the gibberish of their language without knowing their plans. At times they said they wanted to take us to Holland, and at other times to Cape Verde. It was all so very frightening. The Lord who governs all did not give them favorable winds for any of these options and they only had enough wind to go to Lisbon, as I shall later relate.

Our father confessor's sorrow was immeasurable with so many worries that just kept growing. He saw his first attempt to praise God with this new foundation as lost, along with all his fortune. Yet, since he was such a saint, he resigned himself to God's Will and encouraged us to do the same. We really needed his example and comfort in order to compensate for our distress. Even our health was compromised what with seasickness and grief. Our anguish was not only for ourselves but also for very important people who had lost their assets. All of them had brought jewels and precious gems for their wives and families, and at that point in time they did not own anything more than the clothes on their backs. However, if their clothes were of high quality, then even those were not safe from the Dutch who coveted everything.

The Dutch were evil in other ways. They would act very pleasant and then ask for the keys, saying that they would keep them safe. There were those who believed them; others, who saw that if they did not show them everything the Dutch would get even more upset, were forced to give them everything. They took all our possessions, in particular five vestments used to say Mass, and a very ornate lamé cape that our father confessor's brother,[65] the future judge [*oidor*] of the high court of Chile, intended for the statue of Our Lady of Loreto. He had given us the cape in the hope of seeing it spared, but there was no place safe from their hands. Even though the Dutch promised that all our belongings would be returned to us, not even their superficial kindness toward us seemed to make a difference. They did not keep their word, and we were in anguish a long time before we saw our robes and blankets again.

One day the Dutch, through an interpreter, told us that if we had saved any precious items for the foundation we should hand them

---

65. In my archival research I could not find any information on Joseph Fausto Gallegos, but I did learn more about his brother, Ignacio Gallegos—most likely because he was the *oidor* of Chile, although he only held this position from May 14 until November 13, 1713. According to the *Diccionario Biográfico Colonial de Chile*, he had problems with the *Corregidor* Pedro de Raso due to his trade with the French. He was transferred to a prison on the Island of Maule, escaped, and then sought refuge in a Dominican convent in 1723. See José Toribio Medina, *Diccionario Biográfico Colonial de Chile* (Santiago: Elzeviriana, 1906), 99–101.

over with the promise that they would return them to us. I told the father—who was one of the missionaries to Chile and since he was Flemish understood their language—that he should tell them the following: we were very poor and did not own anything more that a few raggedy bags of things, and for this reason we lived much happier than with all the treasures of the world. The interpreter repeated again that if we had hidden any items from other passengers among our things that we would certainly lose everything. I did not pay any attention to that, but he urgently called our father confessor and as I have already said, he asked for the keys, and the sainted man gave them to him. They also made him hand over the small chest that contained all the necessary items to say Mass, which, amid all our suffering, we had the pleasure of hearing every day. Later we were denied Mass, even on Easter Sunday. The ship's chaplain and the Jesuits also missed Mass, as they also lost everything they had brought for their mission.

One day the señor bishop of Buenos Aires came to our cabin with great secrecy and shared communion with us, shedding so many tears that it renewed our sorrow. Since he still hadn't been ordained[66] (what I mean to say is, he was still only wearing the frock of a Trinitarian friar), he requested that those of us who knew him not treat him as a bishop but as a poor friar. This served him well because otherwise the Dutch would have done the same to him that they did with the Señor Archbishop Levanto whom they took as a hostage to Holland until the king of Spain ransomed him by freeing some of their prisoners in Spain.

They subjected this saintly archbishop to a thousand wrongdoings and treated him with great tyranny, so that one day when he was so tired due to lack of food, he ate a piece of bread and cheese given to him by a cabin boy. They profaned religious images right in front of him, they smeared the image of the Señor Saint Joseph with bacon, and they used the holy oils he had brought as a dressing for their food. Many other similar types of things happened on the other ship that we did not see but that saddened us greatly. We were thankful that it was the holy season of Lent so that we could accompany our sweet Jesus in his sorrows, seeing ourselves prisoners for His love. All these events were reason to have His Divine Majesty present and to make us pray for everyone. The seas were very calm and there was no wind to take us where they wanted; the Dutch crew was heard saying

---

66. He was not yet wearing his bishop's robes since he was going to be ordained in Buenos Aires. See above, note 64.

that if there was enough wind for Lisbon then they would go that way. All the passengers rejoiced when the Dutch informed us of their plans [to head to Lisbon]; we gave thanks to God for His mercy.

As we were about to take communion and fervently praying to go to Lisbon, I took out a cross from a servant of God[67] and some authentic rosary beads from Saint Juana.[68] I tossed them into the sea, and just at that moment we began to have favorable weather to take us to Portugal so that everyone took this event as a miracle. This was the last day of March, six days after we had been captured by these barbarians. We continued in the comfort of knowing that we were heading towards a Catholic country; and even though Portugal was at war with Spain at that time, we were hopeful that they would treat us kindly.

I do not want to hesitate to tell about some incidents that occurred amid our suffering, causing us laughter, such as the times that the commander came to visit us, and even though he asked our permission to enter, he and his other men acted with great modesty and courtesy, never sitting or wearing a hat and always trying to please us. One of my sisters, Madre Bernarda, got such a fright from seeing them that she turned white as a ghost. She was so nervous that she could not find her veil to cover herself. She then hid among the others and did not get over her embarrassment for a long time. Very little happened to the gentlemen who took refuge in our father confessor's cabin that was right next to our cabin. Whenever they heard the Dutchmen coming to visit us, they would run and hide with great fear because they did not feel safe anywhere, and since this area was so small they had to hide under the bunks, one on top of the other. We felt great pity for them.

With these hardships we continued to sail until the second day of April. Since I am a great believer in Saint Francis of Paola,[69] I put [a statue] of him out on the gallery [*corredor*].[70] begging our holy God to bring us to the port of our salvation. We dropped anchor in the Port of Lisbon, but with great maliciousness the Dutch stationed the ships very far away from shore so as to torment us even more. That same day a British fleet entered the bay with an incredible pomp of

---

67. In Spanish she says *una sierva de Dios*. Since she is using the feminine version of servant it appears that she is also referring to Saint Juana.

68. There are several Saint Juanas so I am not sure of the one to whom she is referring.

69. Saint Francis of Paola (1416–1507), born in Italy, was founder of the Roman Catholic Order of the Minims.

70. A platform or balcony at the stern of a sailing ship.

bugle calls and many great ships. Their arrogance was revealed in the way they sailed into port. The English had made peace with Portugal and thought themselves to be the owners of the world. Only the Spanish were oppressed and humiliated. That caused us great pain, since it was because of our sins that the Enemies of the Faith had triumphed.

## Chapter VIII
### The Difficulties We Had Disembarking and How It Was Executed

After all the hardships that I have already mentioned, we suffered a new one now that we were in a Catholic port and the Dutch would not let us disembark. Some said that from here they would set sail for Holland; others gave us hope because they told us that once the king of Portugal found out he would not let them do that. The captain and the leading seamen went to and from the city in their launch, but no one was allowed to send a note, even though there were many passengers who had relatives and friends in Lisbon. There being no way to send word of our predicament, everything was in a state of chaos. Some boats kept passing by us, not only fishermen, but others of stature who had heard about the Dutch prisoners and came to see the ships that were so large and beautiful. They lamented that they belonged to heretics, and that they had been so easily captured.

During one of these days it was Our Lord's will that a boat carrying two Jesuit priests and a Genoese captain would come close to ours. Our father confessor was on the main deck and he spoke to them in Latin telling them of the wickedness of these men, especially since it had been four or five days since we had dropped anchor and they had not let anyone go ashore. He also told them that on the aforementioned vessels there were very important people: ninety men from the Company of Jesuits, five Capuchin nuns for the foundation in Lima, the archbishop of that same city, and bishops and *oidores* for various destinations, all whom they had crammed so tightly together that they could hardly breathe. The blessed priests, when they heard this became so inflamed with the zeal of God that they promised to inform the king, the queen, the nuncio, the archbishop, and all the city of Lisbon so that they would save us. The Genoese captain promised the same and they left very quickly. They were our angels, and they informed others of our predicament so well that in a very short time the whole city knew of it. Since they are of pious hearts there was a great uproar in the palace, lamenting the harsh treatment meted out by the Lord's enemies on the wives of Christ.

The Portuguese majesty ordered that the Dutch captains not leave the port without his permission, and he surrounded them with sentries. When the Dutch found out that it was from the cabin that the message had been sent, they also positioned cannons on the cabin's balcony so that no ship could get close. The two priests whom I have already mentioned returned within two days with a special discharge from the king and with a large launch to take away their priests. The Dutch soldiers shouted at them to leave, and seeing that they were being ignored, they fired a musket at one of the priests; it was a miracle that he was not killed. After all this, they allowed the launch to near the ship and they saw the order from His Majesty that they were to hand over all the Jesuit priests who were prisoners.

This was the first comfort we had received, seeing that the Lord had taken pity on us. The same day that the Jesuit priests left, the Dutch captain sent word telling us that the Nuncio Señor Cardenal Conti, (who is now a Pontiff under the name of Inocencio Décimo Tercio) would come for us that very afternoon and that we should be ready.[71] We gave thanks to Our Lord for such mercy, and I told our father confessor to call the captain so that we could say goodbye to him and thank him for everything he had done for us. He came, showing great courtesy, accompanied by Father Arnold (he was the interpreter I have mentioned). The Dutch captain had been our only refuge and defendant because he had a spirit similar to Saint Francis Xavier.[72] It so happened that during our captivity, filled with the zeal of God, he told the Dutch soldiers that they were forewarned that if any of them overstepped the limits with any indecent action, he would tear them to pieces. We have always revered him as a saint because his model life and his wish to do good for everyone won him this respect.

I told this priest [Father Arnold] that he should thank the captain for his kindness and that he should ask him to continue doing the same by allowing us to retrieve our books of the Divine Office, the trunk with the vestments, our humble attire, [a statue of] the baby Jesus with an image of Our Lady and the holy Christ that we always used in our processions. He said yes to everything, assuring us that if it only depended on him all would be done with the utmost gallantry, but the others were watching and he could not give them an occasion to report him to the commander. I respected him greatly and I told him that I was sorry I could not repay his favors because I was only a poor nun. I wanted him to check on our bundle of clothing, but he did not do so. He told the priest that he was amazed to see the happiness we displayed with our poverty and that the Dutch

---

71. Conti later became the Pope: Inocencio Décimo Tercio (Innocent XIII, 1721–24).

72. Saint Francis Xavier (1506–52), born in Spain, one of the first Jesuit missionaries to travel to the Far East.

were never satisfied no matter how much gold and silver they had. The priest told me this and I responded by saying that nothing could satisfy the human heart except God, and therefore those who possessed material goods could never find happiness. To this he movingly replied that not everyone is granted the gift to know and appreciate spiritual things. He was very attentive. I do not know if this was his fault or because he feared the others, but he did not return the vestments. Even our clothes took a very long time to be given back and they were returned only because the Dutch had no use for them. They took anything that had even the slightest use.

The señor cardinal was not able to come that afternoon, but he did come on the morning of Easter Sunday. The captain made sure we were given our breakfast early, but we could hardly eat a bite because we were upset about not having heard Mass nor taken communion in the previous days, along with everything else that weighed heavily on our hearts. Our father confessor was also extremely troubled, not so much because of all he had lost, but because he did not know how he was going to support us and help us continue on our journey. We tried to console him by telling him that we were headed for Catholic territory and that we believed God would rescue us through his divine providence. The captain had told us that he would accompany us when we left the ship, but that neither our father confessor nor any other prisoner would be allowed to leave; this was by order of the commander. I told the captain that this was out of the question, if he [our father confessor] did not leave then we would all stay. Seeing our determination they let our father confessor go with us. Even if they did not want to let him go they could not have kept him because that would have gone against the authority of the señor nuncio. The Dutch plotted so that His Eminence [the nuncio] would not approach our ship. Instead, they made him board the Dutch commander's ship where they fired a volley in his honor and welcomed him. They entertained him, giving him enough time to send his advisor to come and get us. He also sent a Capuchin priest, who was his confessor, and other important persons from his entourage. All this was the reason the Dutch were wary that the other prisoners might take advantage of the nuncio's efforts to get them out of there. Thus, the Dutch did not let His Eminence disembark until they saw us inside the launch.

The comfort we felt when we later saw actual Catholics cannot be described. I asked the nuncio's advisor [*auditor*] to prohibit any of those men [Dutch sailors] from approaching us, and he did exactly as I requested. Thus friars and other religious men were helping my sisters into the launch. I was the last to leave the ship, and when I was saying goodbye to the Dutch captain he took my hand and tried to kiss it, but I took it away. I asked him for some insignificant prints that were on the altar because they would be worth nothing to them. He promptly sent them to us. In this man I observed many good qualities: he was kind, well mannered and not a tyrant like the rest. This was obvious during the time when they robbed the wife of the presiding magistrate of Chile because he then punished the seamen who committed the crime. We always commended him to God and we were told that he was secretly a Catholic. May the Lord let this be true. He left the cabin first and made the sailors take their caps off to us. I felt a great comfort in this, not because they had to honor us, but because we processed with a statue of the holy Christ, and I truly wanted those barbarians to worship His [Divine] Majesty so that in some way they could encourage God to pardon them. We were not allowed to see or say goodbye to any of the other prisoners on the ship. Before we left they had used one of their schemes to trick the prisoners; they fooled them by calling them all together for a meeting or a conference and once they had them together they locked them up. Thus, we did not have the comfort of seeing them, nor were we able to give them hope that we would do everything in our power to set them free. Later when the prisoners finally set foot on land, it was hard for them to express how utterly demoralized this scheme had left them.

We boarded the launch which was very richly adorned since it belonged to the king of Portugal. It was amazing for us to see all those people and sailors who were such devout Catholics. Within a short while we neared the commander's ship (as I have already mentioned) who, because of his evil intentions, had obstructed the señor cardinal [the nuncio] from coming to see us. Later, when His Eminence saw us, he boarded our launch with great pleasantries. He gave us his blessing, but he was saddened that there were only five of us, since he had been told that we were a whole community of nuns who had been saved. The Dutch fired a volley, and we continued until we came to an area of shore where it is very easy to disembark.

The señor nuncio got off first to help us disembark and ordered that no one approach us. One by one, he then led each of us by the hand from the launch to the coach, which was quite tedious because it was a long sandy trek and it was boiling hot. After we had all settled in the coach he stood on the step and spoke to us with such kindness that we lost all the shyness we had felt upon seeing ourselves favored by such a sovereign prince. We were told that he came from one of the most illustrious families in all Italy whence there had been a long line of sovereign pontiffs. We gave him thanks for honoring us, and we asked him to take care of our father confessor. He told us that he would do so, and he asked if we would like for our confessor to ride in the coach with us. We responded that we were happy with whatever His Eminence decided. He called our father confessor saying: "Come take custody of the nuns." His Eminence then shut the running board all by himself and took with him some prayer books so that they would not be in our way. He left in his own carriage, and we continued in such a procession that it felt more like a triumph than a rescue.

We arrived at a convent of Augustinian nuns called Santa Mónica. His Eminence stopped the coaches and told our vicaress [Madre Estefanía] and another nun to get off. I was really surprised to hear this, and it suddenly occurred to me that maybe he was dividing us up to save costs. I implored him for the love of God that he let us stay together. I told him that we were just poor daughters of Our Father Saint Francis and that we would hardly cost them any money; even if we had to sleep under a staircase, we would make do. His Eminence spoke very little Castilian Spanish so his advisor responded for him: "*Madres*, be patient, at the moment this is the only option because since His Eminence had heard from some sources that there were fifteen nuns, and from others that there was a whole community of you, he notified three convents. If there were at least six of you he would be able to show respect to each convent, but now that he cannot do that, His Eminence will keep his word to the two most prestigious ones."

Seeing his determination, I did not think it wise to protest and so I sent the mother vicaress with Madre Gertrudis. They were received by that large community with such open arms and treated with such respect that I am at a loss for words to describe it. The Augustinian nuns were greatly surprised to see them crying as they entered their community, until they realized that we had been split up. They lamented not knowing this beforehand because they would have done everything in their power to keep us together. God did not want it this way, but in His utmost wisdom He saw to it that the kindly inclinations of the souls [nuns] that lived in that community or another would benefit from the positive example set by my saintly sisters.

After having left our nuns there, His Eminence came out of his carriage. He was touched to see us in that state and he said:

"*Filias*[73] I have no excuses." We continued on our way, crossing most of the city, which is quite nice, but since it is built on many hills and also many long stretches of open country, it is difficult to traverse. We traveled with the curtains tightly closed because there were so many people gathered around us that we needed to be very careful to keep ourselves concealed. We felt such anxiety that we preferred not to look outside. However, when we went by the palace we did take a peak; the entrance is very ornate, although it is inferior in every respect to that of our king of Spain.

We arrived at the Convent of our Mother Saint Clare when the community was in the middle of the sermon after the Miserere. His Eminence got down and helped out my two sisters, Madre Bernarda and Madre Josepha Victoria, handing one of them over to his confessor and the other to a priest. As for me, being the most unworthy of all, he deigned to escort me himself, taking me by the hand. There was a big hill and it was very difficult for him to make it to the gatehouse. I dropped a candle from my sleeve, and he quickly bent down to pick it up.[74] I was so confused that I wanted to throw myself at his feet.

As we entered the convent we were welcomed by the mother abbess and by a very large number of nuns. When I heard that this was not the whole community I was truly impressed, because I had never seen so many nuns gathered together. After entering we knelt down to receive the blessing from the señor nuncio, who was waiting for us so he could finish the service in the choir. When he had done so we went to him, and all of a sudden we were surrounded by such a throng of nuns that it seemed to me they were an army of angels, so much affection did they heap on us. I cannot praise them enough, other than saying that this is just the way of the Portuguese nuns. They thanked His Eminence [the nuncio] for bringing us to their convent, and they begged him to bring the other two whom he had left behind. This saddened the saintly prince, but he did say that he would give his word to do whatever possible to reunite us; even with all his power he was never able to do this. Later when the nuns of Santa Mónica found out about this they sent word that if the nuncio wanted to take away the

---

73. In this section of the manuscript she writes "filias" but later in the document she uses "fillas." It is possible that the Nuncio was speaking to them either in Latin (*filia* is the Latin word for daughter) or in his native tongue, Italian (*figlia*).

74. "A mí se me cayó la regla [the Peru transcription says vela] de la manga y a toda prisa se bajó a cogerla." In this case I opted for the Peru version of the transcription, because "regla" does not make sense in the context of the sentence.

treasure [the two nuns] that God had given them, then he could rest assured that there would not be a single one of them left in the cloister. Thus, in order to keep the peace, it was necessary to yield to the devotion of those saintly nuns and all the time (five weeks) that we spent in Lisbon, we suffered the pain of separation from our sisters.

We were amazed to see the convent, especially the choir and the cloister which are a wonder. After a long conversation with the women of that holy community, His Eminence called me aside and asked if we were in need of any material or spiritual goods, because he would see to everything. I thanked him and implored him to take care of our father confessor who was in a foreign land without any protection except for that of His Eminence, now that he had lost all his fortune. He assured me that all his expenses would be covered on his account. He gave us his blessing and instructed the mother abbess to take care of us, as was to be expected of her religious piety, and turning to me he ordered me to obey her every command. Immediately I prostrated myself on the ground as a sign of obedience. I then kissed his hand and with this he said his goodbyes. I was very pleased with the new abbess, who cared for and favored me. She was very discreet, a great servant of God and an advocate for the reformation of her convent.

Later, when we were left with the Portuguese nuns, the hustle and bustle increased greatly. We were dumbstruck by everything there was to see and hear. The choir is extremely beautiful with two sets of stalls where everyone was sitting because it was impossible to get any closer to see us. Although the choir is very large, it did not seem so with everyone in there, or maybe they were just very tightly packed. Everything is decorated with scenes from the life of our Mother Saint Clare, all these on pure leather with gold trim; even the ceiling is decorated in the same way, which is a jewel in itself. Above the grille of the choir is an exquisite altar with silver railings and oil lamps of the same material. The chaplains put the Blessed Sacrament here so that it is on the outside, visible to the choir, but hidden from [the people sitting in] the church. The cloister surpasses all others that I have seen, in both its construction and materials. It has many chapels, all made of marble, that are like little churches in and of themselves. They are all ornately decorated because the nuns of this convent are from noble families of the court and each one is responsible for the care and devotion of a chapel. This amazing church is covered in gold from top to bottom, not only the altars but everything else.

They are devout Catholics in that kingdom and they employ the utmost reverence with anything pertaining to the sacred. It's hard for me to describe the splendor of the interior of the convent, but I suppose it is comparable to the balconies and the doorways of the main square [*plaza mayor*] in Madrid. The cells are extremely beautiful and are richly decorated with every imaginable knick-knack. Each one has its own *quinta* (that's what they call a garden) and the higher rooms have gorgeous views. Our cell had three windows: from one we could see the River Tajo, from the second we had a close-up view of the ocean—so much so that at night we could see the fishermen with the lights on their boats, and from the third we could see a very nice forest. There are more than three hundred nuns to whom nature has given the gift of beauty. In general we observed this gift in the upper class, especially in the women, but the lower classes were dark skinned and ugly. The habits used in these convents are very majestic, and we grew tired of seeing so many daughters of our Mother Saint Clare so ornately dressed. Even though they are pleasing to the eye, this way of dress weighed heavily on our hearts, especially because in all the convents we have visited we have never seen such elegant garb. I have said all this to succinctly document the way things really are.

We were all very pleased with one another. They told us that the night before our arrival His Eminence had written to the mother abbess, telling her that he was going to bring back the Capuchin prisoners. He asked her to take in five because he did not know exactly how many of us there really were, and he wanted to divide us up among different convents in the city. All the Portuguese nuns gathered together and voted unanimously that not only would they take in the five, but every one, even if we were forty nuns. The Portuguese nuns believed this was the right thing to do for a house of our Mother Saint Clare. We already owed them so much even before we had met them.

## Chapter IX
### How the King Sent Us a Visitor
### and All the Things that Happened before We Left

Praise God for letting many things happen to this foundation, because when we had given it up for lost He allowed others who had no special interest in us to lift our spirits. During the time (as I have already mentioned) that we were with those holy nuns in Portugal, a message was sent to the mother abbess saying that we should wait in the convent parlor [*locutorio*] for one of the king's secretaries who had been sent from Castile. He was also accompanied by the señor bishop of Anillo (because the señor archbishop was ill) and also by the mother abbess's brother. The king's messenger first told us that their Majesties were very pleased to have us in their court, even though it was for such a short time. They wanted to know how we had been treated in our prison, and they wanted us to know that they were inclined to grant any of our wishes.

We were very thankful to their Majesties for sending these messengers. This was a great but just favor. The king was frequently kept up to date on the details of our journey, and since these gentlemen were so compassionate I was informed that the king was very sympathetic and inclined to help. If he were not at war with Spain (and for that reason our king did not want his help) he would have provided us a warship to guide us to our new convent in Lima. We asked God to pay back his kindly gesture by rewarding him with wisdom and also by granting him salvation. We asked the same for his subjects, regardless of their rank, because they had given us countless favors.

As these gentlemen bade their farewells, they praised Our Lord for the mercy He had bestowed on us. They then informed the king and queen [of Portugal] of the good treatment we had received from the Dutch, and since their Majesties are such good Catholics they celebrated this news. Once they finished these formalities we were pleased to have a moment to ourselves to dispense with some of the items that the other prisoners had given to us. Since the enemy [the Dutch] had taken away all their possessions, the prisoners feared they would do the same with what they wore on their persons, such as watches, jewels, and ties. As charity we hid all these light items and others so that when these poor gentlemen made it to land they would have something to use as barter so they could eat for at least three or four days.

One of my sisters had a very strange thing happen to her. She was the one carrying a small box of jewels for Don Cipriano of Santa Cruz, and even though it was not that big it still made a large bump on her back. When we entered the convent and took off our veils, it was much more visible. She was the youngest of our group, and the Portuguese nuns felt really bad for her, saying to themselves: "What a shame that this girl is hunchbacked!" We tried to hide our laughter, not wanting to let on because we did not want them to disclose what had happened. As soon as possible we gave the items to our father confessor in the visiting room so that he could return them to their owners. We felt terrible because our confessor had brought many personal items and his brother's suits, all boxed up in the hold, and he was not able to save anything except for a ring devoted to Our Lady of Loreto. He gave it to us to hide, but the Dutch took everything else he had brought, including diamonds and other precious items.

After taking care of this concern the nuns served us lunch, and by this time is was after five o'clock in the afternoon, because it was not possible for us to eat any earlier. Even though we were greatly entertained by the nuns, we just could not relax, worrying about our father confessor and all the new obstacles he was likely to encounter. Although the señor nuncio had told us he would take care of our father, we had not received word as to what had come of this, so I asked and was told that His Eminence had taken our father confessor with him. Later I was summoned to the visiting room where our father was waiting with a document from the señor cardinal to the mother abbess, stating that she should treat our father confessor as a convent chaplain. The saintly lady enacted this at once and provided him a cell in the area where there were four other chaplains, priests of our Father Saint Francis.[75] These men were so comfortable with the new guest that they were upset that it would be for such a short period of time. Considering the grandeur of this convent, these priests are treated with the utmost respect. Likewise they take their privileges very seriously; they do not permit anyone else to administer the sacrament and they do not give out communion more than once a week—inflicting penance on the most devout nuns. They consoled us, however, by giving us communion every day. There are such pure souls among the Portuguese nuns that some of them wanted to accompany us, but we never wanted this. These were not the first nuns to try; there had been

75. Although these were cloistered convents, it was not uncommon for a community to have a few cells—outside the cloistered area—for the chaplains and confessors.

many from other convents, and none of them was given permission.

It was with one of these servants of God that we had a very strange thing happen to us. On the day of our arrival, when we were very teary eyed thinking about our sisters, this particular nun, instead of consoling us, did nothing more than laugh in our faces. Since we did not understand a word of Portuguese, we thought she must be crazy, especially to the extent that she seemed to be rejoicing. Later, when we were able to understand her better, she told us that she was so happy because with our arrival she witnessed the fulfillment of a prophecy from a very saintly priest. On one occasion while he was preaching to them he became lost in his own thoughts and then burst out, saying that some nuns were going to come to this convent. He said that this was not their original destination because they would be set off course and would reach port here. Since he had also predicted the reformation of that convent—I'm not sure if he was referring to this one or another one—she had rejoiced at the possibility that this prophecy had come true. She trusted in the goodness of God and His Divine plan for us to lose our way, because there is nothing new is His power to do great deeds through such insignificant instruments. Praise be to Him for all our confusion, because we have seen wonders in His works.

Let me return to what I was saying about the role the chaplains have in governing this community. They are the only ones permitted to say Mass on the high altar, a privilege they did not give even to our father confessor,[76] nor did they let him go near the ambry. However, they carry out all their duties with such enthusiasm and preciseness that all the nuns admire them for this, even when they denied the nuns communion when they would ask for it. To a certain extent this behavior can be excused because of the complicated apparatus used to set up communion. We have never seen anything like it before. First, they prepare an elevated altar that is then covered with a canopy. After this, the priest puts on a choir robe, and he incenses and lights up the area to make way for His Divine Majesty. We were all greatly relieved to see the reverence with which they treat the Blessed Sacrament in that kingdom. One day when we were in Santa Mónica, it was decided that a sick nun was to receive communion. First they went into the choir to celebrate the sacrament, then all of us processed together as

---

76. The word "padre" is missing in the Madrid manuscript but is present in the Peruvian version: "…que solos son los que dicen misa en el altar mayor, que ni con nuestro [padre] se despensó esto…" I have included it in my translation.

they carried the Blessed Sacrament under a canopy to the sick nun's cell. The celebration of Mass inside the convents is very common. On one occasion when Madre Josepha and I were feeling slightly under the weather, the father chaplain accompanied by our father confessor came into our cell to say Mass and to tell us that the mother abbess would not allow us to get out of bed. I expected this treatment, and so it did not seem out of place.

They had given us a special cell that they had prepared for us. As I have already mentioned before, it was very lovely and bright and also secluded from the hubbub of the convent. Their purpose was to provide us with more tranquility, but actually it did not turn out that way because these affable nuns are so fond of the Castilian nation that they never left us alone, not even to pray the Divine Office. They would just watch us without saying a word. In order to get to the convent parlor we had to cross the whole convent, and they would constantly stop us to visit with them. The same would happen when we would try to go to an area [*tribuna*] that they had set aside for our spiritual exercises. As soon as they would hear us pass by they would open up their cells, inviting us in to entertain us, so that by the time we would make it to our final destination we were exhausted. Although we appreciated their attention, this extreme kindness never stopped bothering us, to such an extent that to this very day Madre Josepha says that she overdosed on sweets and little girls in Portugal.[77]

We witnessed many acts of charity from their beautiful hearts, one in particular that we had never seen before, even though we had visited many convents. One of the nuns, who is quite revered and comes close to perfection, spends all her days crisscrossing the convent with a set of small saddlebags and asking for charity to be given to the poor religious women. Our souls were warmed to see such a beautiful young nun loaded down as if she were a servant. May God make them saints, as we love them and are obliged to them for all that they have done for us.

The señor cardinal was very interested in finding out how we were doing and sent his confessor who, as I have already mentioned, was a very educated and saintly capuchin friar. He asked us how we found the place and said that if we were in need of anything he would speak to His Eminence and it would be granted. I thanked him very much and told him that I only wanted the five of us to be

77. This humorous line in Spanish reads: "hasta hoy dice la Madre Josepha qué de dulces y de criaturas se empalagó en Portugal."

together. He responded that he could do anything except this, that it was impossible. He explained that he felt an obligation to each religious community. He also said that it would be good for us to offer this up as penance in order to avoid ruffled feathers that would later have to be smoothed out.

He was from the Genoese nation and even though he spoke Castilian Spanish he was not able to express himself accurately. In a charming way he said to us: *"Fillas,*[78] why do you cry when you are so highly esteemed? Everyone is fighting over you, they all want you and you are lacking nothing when there are so many other poor people who do not even have a corner to stand in. So many are begging for you to stay with them that I am not sure which sirens from the sea have bewitched all of us, but I am the first to fall under their spell." This really made us laugh. I tried to pay back the charity he showed us, and also that which we received from all the court, by offering them our continued prayers. I told him how we had lost almost all hope of the foundation since our father (the one who had financed the whole trip) had been left penniless. We did not even know how we were going to get back to Castile. When he heard this he became very animated and gave us a speech, telling us to trust in Divine Providence and to gather the courage to continue with the task at hand; God's works always need to pass through the gauntlet of difficulties and contradictions, and we should brace ourselves for even more hardships because they were sure to come, but that the Lord would help us. With an angelic spirit he also told us many other similar things, all of which left us feeling extremely encouraged.

It felt as if our heads were melting due to the change of season and also because we kept our veils on all the time. The heat was so oppressive that it felt like we were suffocating. Our sisters in the Convent of Santa Mónica suffered the same symptoms. Because of this the Portuguese nuns showered us with gifts of all different sorts, especially a copious amount of sweets. They also gave us many large Portuguese oranges, a type that is referred to in Madrid as Chinese oranges. The servants bearing these gifts were not satisfied with just bringing them from their mistresses, so they each gave us as many from their personal share as they were able.

We accepted all these gifts so that we could give them to the male prisoners who often came to visit us. It broke our hearts to see them deprived of everything, even though on a daily basis the pious

---

78. The Peru transcription says "filias."

convent fed twenty or thirty men, while others ate at the hospitals. The convents and hospitals benefited through the charity of helping their fellow man. I do not want to go into greater detail on this matter, but I do want to say that these saintly Portuguese nuns gave general aid to all the calls for help that came to their attention. They gave food and clothing to the men who came to see us, many of whom were in such great need of assistance that they had not eaten for twenty-four hours. Other men were so indecently naked that in order to come in and speak to us they had to be given capes to cover themselves. This is what the malicious enemy inflicted on all the poor lower-class men, since the rest of the gentlemen and upper-class men, although they had also been stripped of all their belongings, at least were left with the clothes on their backs.

Out of the goodness of their hearts the Portuguese nuns hurriedly made a shirt and collar for our father confessor who was also in this same situation. He went many days just with his frock coat because he did not have his frock, but this servant of God did not mind a bit. One day in particular he laughed at the fact that some youngsters had made fun of him on the street. They did not know what to make of a priest in secular clothing. Even though he was dressed in black, this was not the style for priests in Portugal; anywhere else this would not have been unusual. On Palm Sunday it was heartbreaking to see him enter as the chaplain's assistant (as I have already mentioned) because in this convent the priests always use a rochet[79] without any openings other than at the head, and since he did not have the frock over which it should fall, the garb looked so comical that it caused many a chuckle. We did not find it amusing, but to the contrary we felt really sorry for him, especially seeing someone who was accustomed to having so much wealth become so poor and humiliated.

The Portuguese nuns helped him in a thousand ways, and our father told them he never had felt happier because he had always wanted to be poor for the love of God. In memory of this benefit, he was going to always save the shirt and collar they had given to him. The nuns were very embarrassed when they heard this and worshiped him like a saint.

They gave him a tour of the entire convent, in particular a chapel that has a statue of Our Lady of Bethlehem, to which they showed great devotion because she had appeared there before. They told us that a priest had given them this statue. He was a very humble

---

79. A type of white surplice, a robe (*roquete*).

servant of God and told the Lord that he wanted to give that statue to the convent to save many souls. The chapel is uniquely decorated and is so esteemed that they say it was made by angels. Our father could not stay very long; he had to visit the other two nuns who were in Santa Mónica, and one of them was ill (adding even more work for him). The two convents were very far apart, and as I have already mentioned the streets were very rough, and since our father was not used to such climbs it took a lot out of him.

After a few days here we were visited by the señora countess of Santa Cruz who was of very high rank in Castile. She had married in Portugal, but when we met her she was already a widow. This lady lived up to someone of her position: she was very generous, giving us money and also fabric, with which we made wimples and other necessary items. Until that time we eagerly had embraced the shortages of our holy poverty due to the delay of the Dutch in returning our poor wardrobes. Even though the Portuguese nuns had helped us out with their great generosity and love, the clothing was way above the standards of our austerity. She [the countess] often asked about what our father had lost and she documented it in a report. She tried to use her influence through her sons to recover part of his losses, but these good intentions never amounted to anything. She told me that she felt really bad because at that moment she was not as wealthy as usual, but she would like to do a lot more, and when she received her allowance she would send frocks for our father. The humbleness of our holy father was so great that even though in that city he had many siblings and relatives of his brother-in-law—I am referring to Don Antonio Melo who was married in this city of Lima to Doña Josepha Gallegos—he did not tell a soul about his situation. Since all these people were of such high dignity and wealth, when they heard about this by accident they immediately went to look for him, offering him their houses and haciendas. He accepted only a few frocks and there was no talking him out of leaving his cell. His brother, Don Ignacio, the one going to fill the post of *oidor* of Chile, received the majority of their generosity. On many days he went out with them, and they gave him money and all his other necessities, although he did not go to live with them because he was very happy in his present situation (through the generosity of the nuns), spending time with his brother and with us. Everyone who had any relationship with us was well taken care of by the Portuguese nuns, and they also tried their best for all the others they heard about who had traveled on the ships with us.

The person who found himself the most destitute when he stepped on shore was Don Cipriano, but Our Lord saved him by a unique act of Divine Providence. When he found himself on land, without any idea where to go and without any news of our whereabouts, he looked very confused. It was in this state that a friar from the order of our Father Saint Francis bumped into him (Don Cipriano thought that for sure he was Saint Anthony; to whom he is very devoted). This saint or friar told him everything that had happened to us and walked him to the Convent of Santa Mónica where they thought he was our second chaplain. They treated him with incredible care, love and decency, greatly entertaining him with musical performances (which are excellent in both of these convents). When we arrived at our convent they had just finished with the election and we found them preparing for a whole slew of theatrical productions [*comedias*],[80] evening parties with dance and music [*saraos*], and a variety of festivities in honor of the new abbess. They celebrated in the same way when Easter arrived, but we did not want to participate in these festivities even though they begged us to come. They held these events in the lower choir so that they would not be seen by anyone other than the four chaplains and our father. In this matter they always acted with prudence just as they always walked around the convent properly dressed and wearing the wimple so that you would never see them any other way, which would be a scandal since this is a deep tradition in that convent. Another tradition is that they all sleep together in the dormitory. If only they could be so correct in other matters, but one can never expect perfection in such a large community; many of them are quite saintly and for the most part they are very pious. May the Lord help them to be true daughters of my Mother Saint Clare.

All the señoras of the highest class at the court were related to the nuns. They came to visit us with true concern and kindliness, and in private my sisters and I admired their speech and dress.[81]

80. Dramatic productions were quite common in convents in Europe and in the New World. Some convents opted to put on plays written by the nuns themselves. Two of the most famous playwrights from the seventeenth century, one from Spain and the other from Mexico, were Sor Marcela de San Félix and Sor Juana Inés de la Cruz. See Marcela de San Félix, *Los coloquios del Alma: Cuatro dramas alegóricos de Sor Marcela de San Félix, hija de Lope de Vega*, ed. Susan M. Smith and Georgina Sabat de Rivers (Newark, DE: Juan de la Cuesta–Hispanic Monographs, 2006) and Juana Inés de la Cruz, *Obras completas de Sor Juana Inés de la Cruz. IV Comedias, Sainetes y Prosa*, ed. Alberto G. Salceda (Mexico: Instituto Mexiquense de Cultura and Fondo de Cultura Económica, 1994).

81. Although the convents were cloistered, this section shows that there was a certain influx

The first thing I had difficulty with was their language. Even though I had been there listening to them for almost a month and a half, I just could not understand them and for this reason several amusing things happened to me. One incident in particular really embarrassed Madre Josepha, who happened to understand Portuguese. We had stepped into one of their cells and the Portuguese nuns asked us "Do you want to eat here [in the cell]?" As I thought they had asked "Are you going to eat?" I replied yes. This prompted a flurry of motion as they scurried to get everything ready for us to stay there with them. At this point my sisters explained the question to me; I pleaded my ignorance to the Portuguese nuns and did not accept their invitation.

The second thing that was difficult for me (concerning their dress) was that at times they looked like men, because the more noble señoras wore wigs, French dress coats, and ties. It is difficult for me to describe the shock we felt the first night we were in the convent when we saw a certain señora with the Portuguese nuns. She had been a lady in waiting for the queen, but because her hair was tied back and she was wrapped up in a scarlet cloth cape, and because we did not want them to take us for gossipers, we did not have the nerve to ask: "what is a young gentleman doing here?" Finally, when it was time for our goodbyes we heard them call her Señora Doña Felipa. They all made room for her to pass because they admired her nobleness. She also took care to treat us with great love.

In sum, all those people and everyone at court begged us to stay and establish a convent that had already been started, but for circumstances that I never understood, the founders were not happy and had left it. We thanked them for their kindness, but we never had any other wish than to come to Lima or, if this were not possible, to return to our beloved convent. They are so drawn towards Castilians, however, that they openly expressed their great wish for us to follow their proposal. This was taken to such an extreme that since we happened to be with them during Holy Week [Easter] they did not want to start any of the services unless the Castilians were in the church.

They carried out all the ceremonies with great pomp. We witnessed something very unique on Holy Thursday and Good Friday. They do not cover up the Blessed Sacrament as we do in Spain but keep it exposed on the monstrance.[82] They also use the monstrance

---

of secular women who were allowed in and out of the convent. In this case, family members, all nobility, entered the convent.

82. The act of exposing the Blessed Sacrament on the monstrance (an ornate silver vessel)

on Easter Sunday when they have a very solemn procession in honor of this mystery. Before we could start the procession, we waited a long time because they said we were missing King David. I was expecting someone of great authority to perform this role. Instead this person entered with a lot of commotion (he had come from other processions), dressed up as a make-believe king. Actually from his outfit, crown and harp and the faces he was making, he seemed much more appropriate for a short comedy [*entremés*] than for a procession. We could not help but laugh at his rendition, although with everything else we had much for which to praise the Lord, seeing them so Catholic and respectful.

---

is officially called the Exposition of the Blessed Sacrament. It is a very common practice in the Catholic Church (even today). The host is taken out of the tabernacle and is exposed (displayed) in the monstrance so that all can see and adore it. Madre María Rosa made frequent reference to this act; like other devout Catholics, she truly believed that Christ was present in the host.

# Chapter X
## Our Departure from Lisbon
### and Everything that Happened until Our Arrival at Yelbes[83]

The time was nearing when the prisoners would be allowed to return to Castile. Since Portugal was at war with Spain,[84] they were not permitted to stay any longer than absolutely necessary. Before leaving the city they first went to say their goodbyes to their friends and even to people they hardly knew. We felt great pity for the señor bishop of Buenos Aires because he looked so sick and was without any funds. The same was true for the servants of the Señor Don Pedro Levanto, who were left to fend for themselves since their master remained a prisoner on the Dutch ship. Even the Portuguese king's influence could not free that saintly prince. It was a complicated case, enmeshed in international politics, so that no one was able to intervene on his behalf. The Dutch took him to Holland where the terms of his release were later negotiated, and then they let him return home. When his staff sailed for Seville, Our Lord saved them from an attack by Moorish ships. Other poor souls were not so lucky. To everyone's dismay they were taken prisoner; just after they had been freed from one tribulation, they entered a new one. Thank the Lord who saved us from such a tragedy. We later learned from the señor archbishop of Lisbon that if we had continued [at the beginning of our sea journey], and not fallen into the hands of the Dutch, just a short distance beyond them were seven Moorish ships waiting to capture us.

Returning to what I was saying about our journey back to Spain, we asked the king of Portugal to grant us safe passage. With pleasure he conferred it on us, and with his compassion he helped us with a very respectable financial donation. He sent his secretary directly to us to make sure we received it. It saddened the king that he could not be more generous, but because of the war his whole kingdom was under a tight budget. We thanked him for so many honors, and we also thanked Don Diego Mendoza who, as a pious Catholic, arranged a carriage for us. This was a difficult feat since there were so many prisoners and not enough transport.

Before we left that convent, the marquis of Minas and his son came to visit us. I had quite a scare because I remembered hearing

83. Portuguese city close to the border with Spain, approximately fifteen kilometers west of Badajoz. Yelbes (spelled also as Yelves) is known as Elvas in Portuguese.

84. The Spanish War of Succession, 1701–14.

about him and what had happened three or four years earlier. Just before we had left our convent, the archduke [Charles II of Hapsburg] had invaded Madrid, and at that time this gentleman was the general of the Portuguese army. Since the people of Madrid bitterly resented his invasion, they took great offense even at any mention of his name. This also rang true in our convent where we tolerated his name even less because we had professed great loyalty and love to Señor Phillip V [the king] (may God protect him). This whole situation was quite embarrassing for me, especially the thought that he might have heard about our convent's dislike for him, but luckily when I spoke to him I was wearing my veil so that he would not see my face. I pretended that I had never heard of him before. He spoke to us with such politeness and affection that he alleviated all our fears. He offered to help us in many ways and gave us a generous donation which we used to buy some things for our trip. May God repay him, since from that day forward he has been very dear to us.

The mother abbess [of the convent where we were staying] and all her saintly community very much wanted to meet my two sisters. The nuns of Santa Mónica also wanted to meet the three of us. We were not weighed down by these demands, because we were so grateful to each of the communities that we wanted to meet and thank them in person. Yet we did not want to be the ones to ask permission to leave the cloister; our guiding principle was never to leave a convent of our own accord. The convents we visited were at the discretion of the prelates of each city, and the same happened here in Lisbon. The señor nuncio, seeing the proximity of our departure and the longing of the nuns [from both communities], gave a decree to his advisor to ask the mother prioress of Santa Mónica if she would entrust him with the two Capuchin nuns. That saintly prioress promptly agreed, because she was assured that in the afternoon not only would the two be returned, but all five of us would return. She was very satisfied with this promise.

Since the nuns of our Mother Saint Clare had already received this message, the whole community waited at the door from seven until ten in the morning, when the advisor came and handed the two nuns over to the mother abbess. The advisor notified her that he would return for all of us at five in the afternoon. She told him that under no circumstances would she allow this, as she was in charge of her own convent. She also said she would write to His Eminence, asking that he not permit any of the five of us to leave unless it was for our departure. When we did not show up on time, and it was obvious that the agreement had been violated, the nuns of Santa Mónica did everything in their power to have us returned. This was not possible for two days. When we did come back we were so loaded down with food, sweets and other items for our departure that we could only accept a few things from the nuns of Santa Mónica because, as I have already mentioned, there were just not enough carriages and we could only take the absolute necessities.

After two days, when the nuns of Saint Clare least expected it, the señor nuncio cardinal sent an adamant message to the mother abbess mandating that she hand over the five nuns so that they could be brought to Santa Mónica. This news caused much upset and disturbance in the Convent of Saint Clare, but it could have been worse; at that time the majority of the convent was participating in a play [*una comedia*]. Even so, the convent was so large that a sizable number of them did hear the news, causing us great pain to see them so upset.

At last we left and were taken to the Convent of Santa Mónica where we were greeted with incredible festivities. All the servants were staging a type of masquerade [*mojiganga*]. They played small drums, rattles and tambourines, looking as if they were crazy. We then went to their choir which was very beautiful. Afterward we proceeded to the cell they had prepared for our use and many nuns were waiting for us there. They served us dinner and later performed a wonderful concert. They are very talented and passionate about everything concerning Castile, to the extent that they do not even sing in their own language, but in ours. We really enjoyed listening to them, although I was very tired from making arrangements for our trip. Also, I had been in constant poor health, and I found myself falling asleep. My sisters let me know that I was nodding off, but no matter how hard I tried, I just could not keep awake. To be polite I told them that the music was very beautiful even though I never heard anything more than the beginning and end of each hymn. Since it was eleven o'clock at night and they knew I wasn't feeling well, they let us retire. We would not allow anything other than a wooden platform for our bed.

The next morning we went to the choir where they have a crucifix of the Lord hanging over the grille. The workmanship is so breathtaking that it just stole our hearts away. One of the convent's confessors came in to say Mass because he was going to give communion to a sick nun. The confessors have permission to say Mass in the cloistered convent. We took communion, and afterward the nuns lined up in a solemn procession just as when [a statue of] the Lord is carried in the streets. The entire the holy community walked with candles in their hands as they prayed the psalms. This community is very large, much larger than that of our Mother Saint Clare. Within it reside many great servants of God, and with the good example given by my sisters they reformed their ways in many respects. During all our travels we have had many important reasons to praise the Lord for the good intentions he has spread in the hearts of his wives. After this event they showed us all around the convent. It was very large and beautiful; the living quarters were even more so.

While we were there we received the answer to a letter that I had written to the señora abbess of our Mother Saint Clare (her name is Doña Margarita de Santa Isabel). I had thanked her very much and told her how sorry we were to have left her kind company. I assured her that we would be perpetual wards to both her and her holy community. She told me that she had read my letter aloud to all the nuns in the choir and that it had made them all cry, especially those who did not have a chance to bid us farewell. This letter really touched us and so did others we received from several nuns. We spent that day with the Portuguese nuns of Santa Mónica, and our father told us that we should be ready to depart very early the next morning because the king's launches had already been summoned. That is exactly what happened; after communion they came very punctually for us. The Portuguese nuns knew the tide schedule and were very upset, asking, "Why must you leave so suddenly when you do not have to leave until around noon?" The nuncio's advisors, our father confessor, and all the rest of the señor nuncio's entourage told them we were in a great hurry, but all this fell on deaf ears; at that moment they were only interested in giving us many fine things that would be greatly appreciated in Lima. In particular they gave us pitchers, many of which we had to leave behind because we didn't have room to take them with us. At the time of our farewell so many tears were shed that it seemed as if we had lived many years—I mean to say, many years together.

As we were getting into the carriage the nuncio's advisor told the driver to go to the Convent of our Mother Saint Clare. We had no idea that this was the plan, because without our knowledge the nuns of Saint Clare had begged His Eminence to authorize our visit. Their wish had been granted and they were waiting for us at the main door. They showed such incredible joy that it made our first meeting seem dull by comparison. There were so many Portuguese nuns that some of them grabbed us by the arms and others threw their arms around us. It was almost impossible to walk with our own two feet, so much so that we had to be careful not to lose our veils, especially because there were a lot of people from the outside watching us. Each one of them wanted to hug us and tell us how it had crushed them to watch us go. I have to confess that it pulled at my heartstrings, seeing them cry and making a fuss over poor creatures such as us. They showed such care for us that we asked God to save every last one of them; at that moment I was surrounded by more than four hundred Portuguese nuns.

When I looked around to find my sisters I couldn't see any of them. The Portuguese nuns had taken them through the convent to see some sick nuns. I asked the nuns several times to bring my sisters back so that we would be ready to leave with the tide. The convent is so large that it took a very long time to find them. When they finally came back the Portuguese nuns brought us to the Chapel of Our Lady of Bethlehem, which is said to have been made by angels. We said goodbye to Her [Divine] Majesty and sang Her the *Salve Regina*.[85] We were sent word about the tide, but a long time elapsed we could actually take leave because the nuns kept showering us with gifts. The mother abbess was at the door with many lay people who had gathered to accompany us. I remembered the señor nuncio's command to obey the abbess: I told her that she was my superior and asked her to give me her last blessing. I prostrated myself in front of her to receive it and to kiss her hand; shedding many tears she blessed me. We left the cloistered convent accompanied by the nuncio's confessor and advisor. The nuncio had sent them in his place because he wasn't feeling well, and he also sent his blessing.

As Portugal was at war with Castile, a captain had to come get us with his armed soldiers. They kindly asked us to commend their souls to God. They told us that they had to take us as if we were military prisoners, but they also said that their devotion was such that if it were up to them and all the court, they would have done it another way. They brought us to a ship that was decked out as if to honor His Majesty—who favored us in every way. We had such a strong wind that within three hours we dropped anchor in a Galician village.

All the villagers gathered around to see us step onto shore. There are no carriages in that place, so it was necessary to walk in a procession. We were accompanied by two Capuchin fathers, by our

---

85. From Latin, "Hail, Holy Queen," one of the most widely used Catholic prayers in honor of the Virgin Mary even today.

father confessor, Don Cipriano Santa Cruz, and by the rest of the group; I praised God for this procession and told the priests that the world had rarely ever witnessed such a spectacle. Father Fray Antonio (who was His Eminence's confessor)—a very spiritual and cultured man—took me by the hand in order to exalt the works of Our Lord. He assured us that we would see the foundation of the new convent completed, and everything he said has come true. Fray Antonio and his staff said their goodbyes in order to return to Lisbon. We asked them to tell the señor cardinal that we again would like to throw ourselves at his feet in gratitude for all the honors he granted us.

Waiting for us in the village were two gentlemen, cousins of our father confessor, who, having heard of our setback, traveled from the city of Yelbes. They brought with them many provisions, such as food and money, and they came to guide us to the Convent of our Mother Saint Clare in Yelbes (which is twenty leagues from Lisbon). I have already mentioned our father confessor's relatives in Lisbon on the side of his brother-in-law Don Antonio Melo, but these gentlemen to whom I am now referring were from his father's side of the family. All of them were of the nobility and were greatly esteemed in both Lisbon and Yelbes. His relatives were so generous that none of the gifts they lavished on us seemed enough to them.

We spent two days in that Galician village waiting for a carriage. Even though the king [of Portugal] had ordered that we be given a carriage, it took a while for one to arrive. It was Our Lord's wish, although we did not ask for it, that we be given a conduct of safe-passage through Yelbes. It was the best route, and this way we also had the pleasure of meeting all our father's relatives. We were brought three small carriages [*literas*] (which were really more similar to a calash [*calesa*]). In two of the carriages sat my four sisters and I went by myself in the other one. We headed towards Castile, and after a short distance we stopped at a small chapel that has a statue of Our Lady. She had appeared at that spot, and so a chapel had been built to house her image. Her [Divine] Majesty humbly did not permit this, and every time she was placed in her niche she returned to the place where she first appeared. We sang a *Salve Regina* at the hermitage where we saw the product of one of the Virgin's miracles: near the hermitage's doorway was a large stand of very tall pine trees. It just so happened that on one occasion the king of Portugal had ordered these trees to be cut for ships. The caretakers of this area were very upset with this decision: this would be a bad deed for all the people who visited the shrine because the shade from those trees protected them from the sun's harsh rays. The caretakers begged the Virgin to prevent such destruction, because it would hurt those who were devoted to Her [Divine] Majesty. The next morning all the tree trunks were twisted together so that they formed a type of awning. They still look like this today.

We continued the day's journey. The terrain was very rough in that part of the country and our escorts were unfamiliar with the route. I became separated from the others, and within six hours I could not see a soul of our entourage. I was left alone with the Portuguese calash driver who was accompanying me. He never said a word and every once in a while he would yank back on the horses so that the calash would straighten out, scaring the wits out of me. I put myself in God's hands, seeing myself so alone; my only solace was to have a holy Christ [statue] at my side. The sun was starting to set when we came upon a group of travelers on foot. It panicked me to think they were thieves, and I didn't dare look outside. I invoked the mercy of all heaven's saints to save me from this situation. At that moment I saw some outlines of buildings that seemed like our destination, and then I heard our father confessor shouting. He and some others had come out with lanterns looking for the carriages; there had been so many trails that the calashes had gotten separated one from another, but nothing bad had happened because we had all gotten back together. This event served as a lesson: in the future we should all stay together. That same day, however, we got separated again. There was a tremendous storm with thunder and lightning, rain and hail. It was so bad that each calash driver could only take care of himself, without paying attention to whether he got separated from the group. The storm was so loud that it sounded like it was smashing the calashes to bits. I remembered to take out the relic that I carried with me of the holy *Lignum Crucis*,[86] holding it outside the curtains. The honest truth is that the tempest ceased at that very moment. Once it calmed down we stopped at the nearest village. We could not continue any further because everyone was sopping wet and needed rest.

We set out very early the next morning. We were looking forward to taking communion and hearing Mass in a cooler place; it was already very warm and Portugal is a very hot country. We arrived at noon, and since everyone in that kingdom had already received news that we were the prisoners, they came out to welcome us and begged

86. Fragment of the Cross.

us to stop at a noble woman's house. We thanked them for the honor, even though it was not necessary for the owner of that house to provide us with anything because, as I have already mentioned, we were well stocked for the journey.

From there we headed towards Estremoz [Portugal], which is a fortified town with a large fortress. We notified the governor who was shown the conduct of safe-passage. He accepted it and then welcomed us with open arms. We got off at a house owned by a relative of our father confessor. His name is Diego de Lemus. This very wealthy and pious gentleman owns a house that is more like a palace. All the rooms are so richly decorated that we did not know which was the most elegant. He told us to choose a room, and our father confessor picked the most private one. He doted on us and said with great sorrow: "*Madres,* this is more like work than pleasure, because I am only allowed to entertain you for such a short period of time. I would be a lucky man if I could serve you for at least two months. Nonetheless, because you are here for only a short time I have asked all the potters in the area to work all night for you." This is exactly what happened. The next morning he brought us two baskets of exquisite clay pitchers. That village was renowned for this type of work and one can only praise God because the whole countryside shines as if it were one bright red pitcher. I have never seen so many rare items as I did on that occasion. They made stars, rosaries, medallions, earrings, chairs, stools, hearts, amulets; in sum, whatever could be made out of gold they made out of clay. We felt sad that we could not bring it all to Lima, but the little that we did bring was esteemed by us even more than if it had been jewels. As we got ready for the day's journey, they all came out to accompany us to the door of the castle, although they were not permitted to pass through it.

We continued on to the city of Yelbes (which is the last one on the Portuguese side of the border). It was there (as I have already mentioned) that our father confessor also had relatives, and they came out to welcome us with much pomp. It is a beautiful city and everyone was moved to see the novelty of us prisoners. We arrived at the gatehouse of the Convent of our Mother Saint Clare. Our father has two aunts and a niece in this convent. They, along with the mother abbess and the entire community, welcomed us with songs and tears, considering the difficult trials we had endured. They brought us to our hospice—two cells belonging to our father confessor's aunts. They made us feel so welcome that it is difficult for me to put these feelings into words. The whole community entertained us that night with musical instruments and many beautiful hymns. This lasted quite late into the evening, and even though we enjoyed listening to the Portuguese nuns, they left us when they realized that we were exhausted.

Later, when we arrived at the fortress, our father confessor sent a message to the general of the Spanish army (the duke of Vendôme[87]) telling him that we were ready to cross over to Castile. The Spanish general was just outside of Yelbes and quite close to the Portuguese army. He responded by sending a message to the Portuguese general (the count of Villaverde), asking permission to send two squadrons of Castilian soldiers to come and get us. The Portuguese general, a very pious man, was disappointed because he wanted to accompany us with his highest ranking officers, but he gave in to the wishes of our general. The next day before we left we went to take communion and were very moved by the holy tradition they used for this act. After the Eucharist was placed on the monstrance, they sang with gusto the Magnificat.[88] They sang so beautifully, with such devotion and sweetness, that they seemed like angels. We learned a lot from these lovely nuns.

87. Louis Joseph de Bourbon, duc de Vendôme (1654–1712). The Madrid manuscript says the duke of Veé, but I have opted for the Peruvian version. I could not find any historical reference to a duke of Veé, but the duke of Vendôme makes sense because he was a French military commander during the Spanish War of Succession.

88. Named for the opening text in Latin, "Magnificat anima mea Dominum" (My soul doth magnify the Lord) and also known as the Song of Mary, it was a canticle frequently sung (or said) at vespers. The prose version can be found in Luke 1:46–55.

# Chapter XI
## Our Departure from Yelbes and Arrival in Badajoz

As we were preparing to depart the bells began to ring in alarm; the Castilians had made an advance and had come very close to the city's walls. Everyone was extremely alarmed and so were we. We begged Our Lord to cool down the disturbance, for the Portuguese nuns grieved over Castilian persecution. As the commotion was dying down and while we were eating, we received word that the general count of Villaverde was waiting for us. He was accompanied by his highest ranking officers, among them the sons of the señora countess of Santa Cruz. I have already mentioned how she favored us in Lisbon and had told these officers [her sons] to pay us a visit. The nuns were concerned that we had not eaten, but this did not matter to me because I did not want to detain such illustrious persons. However, when the general heard that we had not eaten, in order to give us time to do so he said that he needed to run an errand and would return shortly. We bade our farewells to all those holy nuns. They were extremely affectionate and so generous that they wanted to give us everything they owned. May God bless everyone in that kingdom, both men and women, because they treated us with such kindness that, although we have always been well received on our journey, nothing compares to what we experienced in Portugal.

The general and all his corporals were waiting for us at the convent's gatehouse. As soon as these pious men saw us walking in a procession with [a statue of] the holy Christ they knelt down in two rows so that we could pass between them. They helped us into our small carriages, but they were disappointed that they could not take us all the way to Castile. The duke of Vendôme had ordered that they accompany us with only two squadrons and that His Excellency would also receive us with two. We proceeded in this manner for about one league—there are three leagues between Yelbes and Badajoz (the first city on the Castilian side)—and in between were the two armies. Our Lord wanted us to see the two armies so that we could keep both of them in our prayers. The Portuguese soldiers accompanying us signaled their presence and the Castilian soldiers responded on the third call. The Castilians were on the other side of the river that divides these two kingdoms. Our soldiers were waiting for us there, and they treated the Portuguese soldiers with great civility, as if they were old friends. The Portuguese said goodbye, and we were greeted by the vicar-general and other ecclesiastical authorities who had been sent by the señor bishop [of Badajoz]. The bishop was ill at the time and for that reason could not come himself.

We gave thanks to God to see ourselves among our own people. We headed towards the city which was very beautiful; the walls and the bridge were a wonder. Many curious townspeople came out to see us. Some women arrived in small carriages crying bitterly and cursing the Dutch for having thwarted our foundation of our new convent. We arrived at the Convent of Discalced Franciscans where the Señor Bishop Francisco Valero[89] awaited us and welcomed us with open arms. He gave us his blessing, and then the resident nuns took us with them while singing *Te Deum Laudamus.*

The bishop covered all our expenses while we were in that city. This would have been more than enough but, with an act of great generosity, he also invited our father confessor and all his family to stay with him in his palace.

At the time of the revision of this account, this saintly prince [the bishop] has passed away.[90] The Catholic Church has lost a great soul because his life was a perfect model for ecclesiastical prelates. The way he conducted himself with the members of his staff, the way he acted and the way he observed religious ceremonies made him appear as if he were more a humble friar than a bishop. He would rise to pray every morning at four, inflict penance, eat breakfast in the refectory with all his staff, and also read a spiritual lesson to them. The palace would be closed at eleven in the morning so that everyone could gather together and no one would miss lunch. Before the afternoon prayers he would follow the same routine as mentioned above. His dress was very humble and poor. He never wore anything made of silk, and the lace on his rochet was never worth more that four *reales.*[91] He led a very ascetic life and it overwhelmed us to see him act that way. His whole life revolved around helping others. On holy days he would alternate preaching in one of the six or seven nunneries of that city, reforming them with his pious doctrine.

This señor was a priest before becoming a bishop. He was so content with this position that he showed true disdain when promoted to bishop. A Jesuit priest assured us that during the bishop's or-

89. Francisco Valero Losa (1664–1720), bishop of Badajoz, later archbishop of Toledo.

90. Josepha Victoria is referring to her own revisions from 1722. She does this several times throughout the document.

91. A type of silver coin.

dination in Madrid (to his dismay this function was celebrated under the celestial vault) it looked as if he was about to take his last breath; he truly felt the weight of his new position. His Illustriousness told us himself that during the time he was ordained bishop, our previous father confessor in Madrid, Doctor Don Francisco Barrambio, had passed away, and when he heard this he sincerely wanted to take over the position of confessor. God, however, had destined him for higher glories and did not permit this. After wearing the miter of Badajoz he went on to become the archbishop of Toledo where he spent the rest of his virtuous life. During the time we interacted with him we could see why he had acquired such universal fame for his saintly lifestyle; his actions reminded us of Saint Charles Borromeo.[92] He was a very virtuous and kind man who spoke in such a straightforward manner that even the lowliest sinner felt like they could open up to him. I think I have said enough to show the indescribable good that God granted him and so I will continue with my narration.

The bishop came to say Mass very early and to give us communion. During the thirteen days we spent in that convent, he visited us many times. We enjoyed all his visits and always benefited from his holy teaching. He only spoke about the sins of the world and his assessments of them.

During the time we spent in Portugal, we received no messages from our convent [in Madrid] or from our prelates, although we had written them from Lisbon to keep them informed of our trip's mishaps. We told them about the events that had occurred and we wanted to hear their opinion of our setback. Later, when we had arrived in Badajoz, we received word that very same morning that a letter had come from the señor bishop of Sión in response to the ones we had written. He expressed grave concern at hearing about all our trials. Further, he had decided (if the Portuguese king would permit it) to come and get us. He expressed these feelings and others with so much tenderness and discretion that we were assured by those who had read the letter that it brought tears to many eyes (since we were at war all the letters were circulated and opened). After our general had read this letter he forwarded it to Lisbon. It provided us some solace to hear from our prelate, even though we never actually saw the letter.

92. Saint Charles Borromeo (1535–84), archbishop of Milan who worked on convent reform as part of the Council of Trent. He supported the Capuchin order because of its austerity and he personally planned and built a new convent in Milan. See Iriarte, *Las capuchinas: Pasado y presente*, 32, 33.

We wrote directly to him to tell him that it was not necessary for him to go to Portugal since we were already in Castile.

Shortly thereafter our father confessor gathered us together and asked us about our plans. Did we want to return to Madrid or did we want to continue with the foundation of the convent? I told him my opinion: I was ready (with the grace of God) to give my life for the completion of our mission. I had made this same promise even when I was first nominated for the journey. My beloved sisters also fervently insisted that they were not willing to give up such an important task. Once we had made this decision, our father confessor wrote letters to the king, the presiding magistrate and the Council of the Indies to tell them that we were in good spirits and that we also had the strength and health to continue with the foundation. Our confessor then informed our prelate that he was determined to accompany us to Seville while we waited for a new ship departure date. He also wrote to the archbishop of Seville and the Mother Abbess Sor Josepha, asking them to let us stay in the convent of Capuchin nuns. Our father confessor asked the mother abbess to send a carriage to Badajoz for us since there were none in that city. We promptly heard back from the archbishop that he graciously would give his permission for us to stay in the Capuchin convent. He was very pleased to have the opportunity to provide us a place to stay again in his archbishopric, and we would be welcomed with open arms for as long as we needed to stay. He also would give us a daily allowance of ten *reales* to take care of our needs. May God help him rest in peace, since he has since passed away at the time of writing these revisions [1722]. We are indebted to him as if he were our father confessor.

Madre Palafox also wrote us a very friendly letter. This illustrious and saintly woman has always treated us as daughters of her heart. We shall always be indebted to her because on that visit we spent close to a year and a half in her convent. It is difficult to put into words how well treated we were by those servants of God. It should suffice to say that we never missed our home convent because this one was so similar.

When the carriage came for us we sent word to the bishop [of Badajoz] asking his blessing for our departure and also thanking him for everything he had done for us. He was sorry that we had to leave so soon, but because he was taking a purgative, he would not be able to accompany us. He did not want to add to any of our expenses so he would not detain us any longer. The bishop sent his prelate to take us out of the cloistered convent. This dismayed all those holy nuns who were very gracious company during all the time we had the pleasure of knowing them. They were very [devoted] servants of God.

We spent that night in a *posada*. The next morning Our Lord consoled us by bringing letters from our Capuchin sisters in Madrid. It broke our hearts to read the laments of each nun. Even though all our sisters and everyone at court knew that we had been well cared for as prisoners, they still felt really sorry for us. Nonetheless, our letters eased their grief and had been passed around, serving as a small consolation to our sisters in Madrid.

We continued that day's journey until we arrived at a discalced Carmelite convent in a place called Talavera.[93] The nuns treated us with great kindness, also inviting us to dinner and spending their free time with us until they were called to matins. They then left us in the sacristy where we slept on wooden platforms. We were very tired and had to get up early the next day. The next morning the mother prioress took us to see the beautiful garden. While there, we were called to the convent parlor. To get there we had to pass by a dark stairwell leading down on one side to the convent's crypt. Since I was walking very quickly and did not know my way around the place, I fell down the stairs, rolling right on top of a tomb and its torch stands. I tried to get up as best I could, looking for the light to find the nuns. When they saw me covered in dirt and cobwebs, they felt horrible for having left the door open; it had been just a short time since they had buried a nun there. They treated me on the spot. I asked them not to mention this to our father confessor because he would delay our departure. I was really banged up and so rattled that I thought I was going to faint at any moment. I suffered from bruises and a hurt foot that lasted for more than a month.

We said goodbye to those holy nuns and traveled to another town called Villafranca. We spent that night in a convent of our Mother Saint Clare, and the nuns gave us a warm reception. They had caught wind of all our adventures, but wanted to hear everything with their own ears. We had the pleasure of meeting the mother abbess, who is very humble, and the whole community of nuns. Although they are not a discalced order, they are very pious and wear modest religious garb.

The next morning we left early to avoid the intense heat. We stopped at a tiny little village, but the only place to stay was the

---

93. The Peru transcription says "Talavera." I have opted for this spelling over the Madrid manuscript which reads "Taraveruela."

church. After Mass and communion our father sent a message to the priest asking him to let us stop at his house for one or two hours. For some reason God did not permit him to grant us this small request; he made an excuse saying that he already had guests. We gave thanks to Our Lord remembering when he said: "No prophet is accepted in the prophet's hometown,"[94] because we realized that we had been much better treated by foreigners than in our own country. Even though it was quite late, we still hadn't eaten breakfast and no one had even offered us a pitcher of water. We tried to console our father confessor because he felt horrible any time we were not treated as he deemed proper. This occurred on the eve of Holy Trinity [June 15, 1710] in that ridiculously small village that did not even have a *posada* or a place to eat. Our father confessor's brother, Don Ignacio Gallegos—who, as I have already mentioned, was to be the future *oidor* of Chile—went out into the streets, crying out: "What land is this that no one will give lodging to a group of nuns?" He comically added: "Who would like to give me some eggs for God or for money?" When one good woman heard this, she offered us her house, which was really nothing more than a doorway, but we appreciated her generosity. That day our food was like our lodging in that we were only offered three eggs and some lettuce. We gave thanks to God for everything, for the shortages and for the abundance.

We left the next morning and at eleven o'clock arrived at another tiny village, even smaller than the previous one. We got out of the carriages before we entered it because there were a lot of rocks on the trail. We walked a long way, but since it was so hot and we were very tired we stopped at a *posada*. There were so many people inside that we couldn't take a breather from wearing our veils. Seeing this, our father confessor requested a separate room. They gave us a dirty and tiny room with barely any place to sit. To make matters worse, it was filled with sacks of tobacco, and with the heat they emitted an intense odor. We were dazed by the stench, and we could not stop sneezing. Being Capuchin nuns we do not smoke and we are not accustomed to the smell. I was affected more than anyone since I have never tried to smoke in my whole life. I called our father confessor and asked him to take us out of that dungeon.

We went to hear Mass and Our Lord God (so we would have more to offer up to Him) willed the church to be far away on a very high hill. The sun drained the energy out of us and we were burning

94. Luke 4:42.

up with our veils on. Because we did not want our father confessor to feel guilty (he was already feeling quite sorry for us) we barely dared even to take a breath. We arrived at the church where we hoped to rest, but we found a new reason for self-mortification. Since it was the Solemnity of the Most Holy Trinity [Trinity Sunday: June 15, 1710] the Mass was being sung, the church was packed and the organ was so loud that we were not able to make confession. It seemed like everything was against us. Even though we were all dying of the heat, one of our sisters was worse off than the rest of us. Her head was burning up, causing her to have a terrible nosebleed. We were in a bad way since we only had our wimples to help clean her up. In sum, all this helped us to be prepared to take holy communion. Even though the religious festivities were over, everyone in the church stayed around, curious to see us. Some lively boys made fun, saying that we were Franciscan friars who were just covering up our faces. A lady came up to us and offered her house to us, although she was sorry that she would not be able to provide us with all the proper amenities. We thanked her profusely, especially because her house was very close to the church so that we would avoid having to walk under the heat of the sun. We spent the whole day in that place. There we received news that a man who had been crossing the mountains of the Sierra Morena was killed by bandits. We gave thanks to Our Lord that He saved us from that sort of tragedy. The people of that village are very pious and would not leave us in peace until we had given them religious prints and relics.

The next day we arrived in a town very close to Seville. The mayor welcomed us and offered us a place to stay in his house. We were very well received by him, his wife, and his whole family. From there we sent word to the mother abbess of the Capuchin nuns of Seville that we would be arriving that very day.

The saintly mother abbess sent word to all the convent's benefactors and to all the nuns' relatives so that they could come out to meet us. The señor archbishop, who had other obligations, sent his confessor and the vicar-general in his place. We were accompanied to the gate house by many important persons. The entire saintly community welcomed us and shed a great many tears. We all remembered the first time we were in their gracious company, and now, because of the sad turn of events, we had returned to that saintly house of God. Ever since we had left Badajoz we had been dying of the heat. It had been so hot that even though we had traveled by coach and left really early each day, we were extremely burned by the sun. The nuns cried out when they saw our faces, saying that they looked like pomegranate peals. This all occurred on the twenty fourth [day of June, 1710]. May God praise and bless a gentleman, Don Diego Gil of Cordoba (the father of one of the nuns in the convent), who on that day in Seville sent us a refreshment of iced drinks. We all greatly appreciated this kind and timely gesture.

After enjoying this refreshment, we went to our previous living quarters of the novitiate which had all the amenities within the limits of the Capuchin order. The entire convent has many personal and sumptuous touches since it had been built by the señor archbishop who is the mother abbess's brother. We spent a year and a half waiting in that convent to hear the final verdict on our fleet of ships. The ships had been brought to England and there was a lawsuit that took a long time to sort out. It's impossible to put into words the good treatment we received in that convent. We were never permitted to do any type of work, even though it was our greatest desire to help out; since Capuchin communities have no servants, our presence added even more work for the nuns. The abbess assigned us two nuns to take care of all our daily needs. They flawlessly completed their new duties, in perfect obedience to the wishes of their prelate.

It was good for us to spend time with all those saintly nuns because their kind treatment and soothing conversation helped us bear the trials of having to wait such a long time. Among all the damage wreaked by the Dutch, not the least was their destruction of the official papers we needed for our foundation. Thus it was necessary for our father confessor to return to the court in Madrid to recover these important documents.

We felt terrible about his departure, but since we believed it would only be for a short time we resigned ourselves to his necessary journey. He requested permission for his travels from the señor archbishop, and he also asked him to assign us a temporary confessor. The archbishop assigned us to the convent's auxiliary confessor, Doctor Don Pablo Lamperes, who was the señor canon of that saintly church. He always attended to us with great punctuality and courtesy, at least as much as his devotion to silence and austere lifestyle (which is without comparison) would allow him. I don't have anyone to compare him to except for the servant of God, Gregorio López.[95] Our new

---

95. It is not clear whether she is referring to Gregorio López (1611–91), the first Chinese Catholic priest and bishop, or to Gregorio López de Tovar (1496–1560), president of the Council of Indies and lawyer for the Catholic monarchs.

confessor's silence was so extreme that during the fourteen months he heard our confession, he never spoke a word to us except for what was absolutely necessary in confession. He never asked us about how we were doing, which was very difficult for our broken hearts. God permitted all this for our own good; bless the Lord for all His creatures.

Our father confessor arrived in Madrid with the goal of returning to our side as soon as possible; he rapidly set out to acquire the needed documents for the foundation of the convent. After only a few days we received word from him that everything was going according to plan. The next letter, however, saddened us greatly when he told us that God had only created him to endure tribulations. Even after all he had been through, he could already see more hardships coming, because the Archduke's troops [Charles II of Hapsburg] neared the city and would enter the court within two days.

## Chapter XII
### All that Happened before We Returned to the Port of Santa María and We Set Sail for a Second Time

We held onto that letter with much worry and sorrow, imagining all that could happen. We already had experience in this matter because the archduke had once before entered our convent. We felt indescribable pain when we were told of all the horrible sins the soldiers had committed in offense to our holy faith and of how they had destroyed the possessions of the people in that whole region. Now that the soldiers were even more irritated with the Spanish people, we could only imagine what would happen to our holy mothers as well as our father confessor.

We heard nothing for three months because the mail had been cut off completely. We waited and endured a torturous silence; we were far from our home convent, without hope of starting the new foundation, and without our father confessor. The whole world was in a turbulent storm.

Throughout this whole ordeal we never stopped praying or conducting spiritual exercises. We were aided by everyone in that saintly community; they were the only solace the Lord had left us. But God did want to give us relief from our afflicted state, and after three months (as I have already mentioned) on the birthday of the Virgin Mary [September 8, 1710] we received several letters from our father confessor and convent in Madrid. They gave us an account of how the enemies of our faith had committed atrocities on all the sacred places. The soldiers did not even respect the cloistered convent of our Capuchin sisters. They tried to enter the convent after they had first sacked our father confessor's house. He, like the nuns, was a great follower of our King Philip V.

Seeing that those soulless men wanted to enter and search our convent, the nuns had the novitiates call for help from the outside windows that look out onto the neighborhood. This attracted many people who were devoted to our holy institution. The soldiers said that they had come to get the count of Pinto whom the nuns had hidden behind the cloistered walls. This was just an excuse to steal all the things that they had heard were hidden in the convent; they had received a tip that some of the convent's benefactors had hidden trunks there for safekeeping. In fact, the mother abbess had hidden the trunks in the dome ceilings of the church, but our Lord did not permit the soldiers to see the trunks when they searched the church, even though they were right under their noses. Our Father Saint Francis had kept them well hidden for his devout followers.

The abominable excesses they committed against the Blessed Sacrament and the sacred images are impossible to describe. Their crimes were notorious in all Spain and all Christendom. Thus I will stop here because I do not want to stir up the bitterness in my heart. Their destruction had left people in such dire straits that even our father confessor who is a person of means, could not obtain anything else to eat but bread made out of barley. He told us later that it really hurt him not to be able to help so many poor people whom he saw fainting from hunger. Our sisters [in Madrid] wrote to us that with the departure of the king, his advisors and all the rest of the court, they were left in a shocking state. For three weeks they survived only on peas which were the only provisions left in the larder.

Once all this trouble had cleared up and our king and queen had returned to the court, our father confessor returned to his goal of acquiring the necessary documents for our journey. This time everything was much more complicated. It took a long time for everything to return to normal, but his great virtue and patience helped him persevere without stopping until he obtained everything he needed. He spent fourteen months in Madrid when he thought he would be there for only one or two.

During this time our beloved father and prelate, Señor Don Pedro Levanto, returned from England where he had experienced many hardships. Yet we were so overjoyed to see him, and so many good things were happening at once, that all the suffering was soon forgotten. Our ships—the ones used to hold us prisoner—had arrived at the same time as our prelate and they were now free and ready to set sail. We were delighted to have our prelate and ships and now we were just waiting for our father confessor. Our Lord, however, permitted this saintly prince [Don Pedro Levanto] to have second thoughts about the upcoming journey, especially because he felt as if his sins had caused all the previous calamities. He was swayed by these concerns and by all the advice he received on the matter, particularly from many close friends in Spain who did not want to see him go. He was famous for helping the poor, especially in Seville. In one year when bread was scarce for everyone, he gave out more alms than the archbishop. Although he had to tighten his budget, his staff was amazed to see how his assets just kept multiplying, and this was due to God's grace towards this liberal and charitable man. As such we were not deserving of him as our prelate. It must have been the Lord's Will for Don Levanto to stay in Spain, because He allowed him to give up his future position as archbishop [of Lima]. However this did not come easily because Don Levanto had to ask the king of Spain three times before he accepted his resignation—all to our dismay.

Our father confessor arrived in Seville on the eve of the day of my father, Saint Francis [October 3, 1711]. On that day we felt such relief to have him back with us because of our love for him and especially all that we owed him. Soon thereafter he began to organize all the necessary items for the second sea voyage, which would be leaving from the Port of Santa María. Due to several obstacles we would not stop in Cadiz, which made us feel awful, because the discalced nuns of that city wanted to see us again and we wanted to see them. This was impossible, however, because of some political issues between various prelates.

Our great benefactor, the Señor Archbishop of Seville, Don Manuel Arias—who later became a cardinal, but has since passed away—told us to choose from any of the convents in the Port of Santa María. May God bless this man who did so much for us; he will always be in our thoughts and prayers. We chose the Convent of the Purísima Concepción where we had spent a night when we had traveled to Cadiz before we set sail the first time. Once everything was ready to go, he came to give us his blessing and to say goodbye, showering us with a thousand gifts.

The day of our departure arrived, the ninth day of November in the year 1711. We said our farewells to our Capuchin sisters with much emotion on both sides. We felt really close to one another after living together for almost a year and a half. Those holy nuns had treated us really well, especially our beloved Mother Abbess, Josepha de Palafox. We owed her so much (as I have already said) for making us feel as if we were in our home convent. May the Lord grant her a long life so that she may continue to lead her convent with the same perfection with which she established it. This convent is one of the best we have seen in all aspects, both spiritual and material.

We went to the gatehouse of the convent where Señor Don Pedro Levanto was waiting for us. Although he had already renounced his position as the archbishop of Lima, he paid attention to every detail in order to honor us. His Illustriousness, along with many other gentlemen, accompanied us a long way. We then prostrated ourselves on the ground in front of him and he gave us his heartfelt blessing. We also embraced him and kissed his hand with the same tenderness. He took off his ring and placed it on a statue of the Virgin Mary that we had brought with us. He told us that since God had not destined him to travel with us, he wanted us to carry a token of his.

We arrived that night in Utrera where for a second time the same service [for the redemption of souls from purgatory] was conducted for Madre Gertrudis's father. From there we traveled to Jerez to the same convent of discalced nuns of our Mother Saint Clare that we had visited before. We were welcomed, just as we had been in all the convents, with many tears; they were reminded of all the things that had happened in the close to two years since we had left our home convent. Now it was as if we were at the beginning of our journey again.

We continued on to the convent in the Port of Santa María that I have already mentioned. Everyone in the city did everything possible to attend to us during the forty-six days we spent there. The holy Abbess, Doña Bárbara Escobar put us up in her cell. She is from one of the noblest families in all Andalusia and she continuously lavished gifts on us. Now as I rewrite this account for the second time, she has since passed away. It breaks my heart to think about how sorely she will be missed in her community, especially since an incursion from Spain's enemies on that city has left the convent in ruins. This holy lady, through her many deeds, good judgment and connection to the highest members of society, did much for the well-being of that convent during her two terms of three years as the mother abbess. May God grant her eternal rest for all the good things she did for us; with her grace and skill she helped us sew new vestments to replace the ones that the Dutch had stolen. During our time in that city our father confessor acquired all the provisions for the sea voyage. He set about obtaining many necessary items for our daily needs, but also many niceties, to such an extent that we had to remind him that we were just poor nuns and at this rate he would not let us offer anything up to God. May he be rewarded by Him many times over.

Our departure was set for Saint Stephen's Day [December 26, 1711]. That day we were given breakfast very early, but it was almost impossible to eat, let alone leave, because everyone was crying: the nuns, many laywomen, and in particular a few of the young novice girls who were relatives of the mother abbess. They were all wailing, crying out that they wished they had never met us. We thanked them profusely, but we felt horrible to see them sobbing so. In order to help calm them down we excused ourselves by going to the choir. There we sang a *Salve Regina* to their patroness: the most holy Mary of the Immaculate Conception. We waited in the choir until they informed us that the señor vicar and everyone else had come to get us (we just didn't have the heart to pass through the convent and see such weeping). May God make them all saints, because I do not think I shall ever again witness such affection. The time for our departure had arrived, and we went to the gatehouse accompanied by all the holy community. We were then escorted by the city's vicar, many noblemen, and countless other people. We arrived at the beach (which is very beautiful) where a chair had been prepared to transport us to the ship. We sat down one by one and the sailors carried us to the ship. There they had another chair rigged up to a piece of machinery in order to hoist us up. This way we did not have to climb the ladder. They had thought of everything so that we would not be inconvenienced in any way.

We gave thanks to God for seeing us aboard ship for the second time and for permitting us soon to continue with the new foundation. Until this moment we still could not believe it was happening. Many people did not want us to take this risk again: the nuns of our mother convent told us many times that we should return home to them and the señor bishop of Sión also tried to take us to Toledo. Since we knew that all these demands stemmed from their love for us and that we were not required by obedience to accept them, we thanked them as best we could, but at the same time we remained steadfast in our commitment to the Lord who always helped us remember our promise not to abandon this journey even if it meant that we had to die for it. May the Lord be praised in everything He does.

We set sail on the Day of Saint John the Evangelist [December 27, 1711]. After two days, God willing, we arrived at almost the exact same place where we had been taken prisoner the first time. In some ways we felt much more nervous and worried this time because during the previous journey we felt secure with the safe-passage and we did not really experience any fear until we were already in the hands of the Dutch. Now that we had learned from that lesson, we were very frightened when we saw a British warship headed at top speed directly towards us. Although our ships were bigger, they were so loaded down with cargo that they could not ready their artillery as fast as the British ships. As soon as the British ships got within shooting distance they fired a cannon, sending a ball which struck the gallery right next to where we were standing. I can't believe we didn't die. Everyone on the ship was visibly shaken as they prepared for battle.

We were taken out of our cabin and led down to the [chaplain's cabin above the] magazine [*santabárbara*].[96] We were so scared and seasick that we could hardly walk. When we passed by the passengers and people we knew, they said goodbye to us as if this were the end. The contrast between light and dark was so great that we could not see a thing when we entered that area. It was also filled with Jesuit missionaries, who like us, were also seasick and stumbling about so that we all kept getting tangled up, sometimes stepping on each others feet, at other times knocking our heads together. It was very disorienting until all identified themselves according to where they had been hurt. Everyone felt flustered and scared in this confusing situation. Those saintly and virtuous missionaries helped us into their bunks where we stayed for over an hour, fearing for our lives. Everything was made worse by the updates: some said that it was a losing battle; others said we could not defend ourselves because of the heavy cargo on board; and others came to put mattresses behind us as a shield against the cannonballs. We were in such a state that we could not even bring ourselves to say confession before dying. Our father confessor was mortified to see our suffering, so much so that he didn't dare leave our side to go above and find out for himself what was happening.

In the end Our Lord willed that after all this horrible fright everything would work out. We were told that a delegate from our ship had taken the conduct of safe passage over to the enemy ship which had accepted it. However, the safe passage did not mention a small boat that was traveling with us and so they took it with them. Nevertheless, that boat would be really needed on our arrival at the River Platte because it would be used to lighten the load of the other ships and thus some of our sailors went to rescue it. They gave the enemy an official document so that in Cadiz they could be reimbursed for its value which was 2,500 pesos, subtracting what they had already taken off the aforementioned boat.

96. The Spanish name *santabárbara*, or a ship's magazine, takes its name from Saint Barbara, the patron saint of gunners. In addition to the traditional definition of the room used to hold the ship's ammunition, or ship's magazine, the *santabárbara* can also refer to the chaplain's cabin above the magazine. This latter definition seems more appropriate for this passage of the manuscript, although in this case it was filled with Jesuit missionaries. See *Enciclopedia General del Mar*, ed. José María Martínez (Madrid: Ediciones Garriga, 1957), s.v. *santabárbara*.

It was around sunset, when we were all recovering from this scare, that we had a new concern: three sailing ships were spotted in the distance. The Spaniards asked the British ship if it would escort us past the Canary Islands, but they had no interest in helping us and continued on their way. The next morning the ships were much closer and everyone thought they were Moors. The fear that this news caused cannot be described. I for one can say that I thought my heart would burst out of my chest and even more so when I saw my three sisters half dead from seasickness on the floor. They looked really pitiful. Madre Gertrudis and I (as we were not as seasick) kept crying out to God, reciting litanies and psalms so that He, the Lord, would free us from such a frightful situation. Our intense emotion was augmented when we saw our neighbors, the leading Jesuit missionaries (the ones who were in the other half of our cabin) all alone as they tried to nail everything down. Each blow of the hammer sounded like a musket shot. I couldn't do anything else but beseech Our Lord by saying (as if He didn't already know) that although for His love He had put us back in harms way, for the same reason He should save us. During that whole day we could see the ships, but after a while when we saw that they did not make any advances toward us, we found out that they were mercantile ships sailing to Cadiz. This news calmed everyone down.

We continued on for three days with a good wind at our backs. We then arrived at a place called the Golfo de las Yeguas [the Gulf of Mares]. This is a difficult place because the seas are very choppy. Living up to its name, every wave seemed like a mountain. These rough seas began to stir up during the morning of the eve of Epiphany [January 6, 1712], and they continued until the first light of the next day. The seas were so powerful that while one wave would wash up over the prow, another would come over the stern, both meeting in the middle of the ship. This would cause such a crash that it seemed like the sea was going to swallow us every time it happened. Throughout that whole day it was impossible to cook or do anything. With the onset of dusk, the darkness made us and everyone else even more fearful. No one could remain calm. They[97] tried to mitigate our fear, but it was only possible in between the crash of the waves. The swells were so frequent, however, that we only had time to say five or six creeds during the longest interval between waves. At times the waves swelled with such violence that

---

97. It is unclear who "they" are: the crew or the priests.

they would fill our cabin with water. Fearing the worst, I would reach down with my hand to feel whether the water had started to touch the bunks. The sailors came in to save us, breaking down the gallery wall so that the water that came in would be able to flow out again. They assured us that the ship would not suffer any grave detriment. It was new and very strong, but because the gallery was part of the freeboard deck it was at risk. When Madre Josepha heard this—her bunk was closest to the gallery—she suffered great distress. She already thought she was going to drown, but just in case, she secured herself next to the person who had the bunk closest to her side, tying herself with her cord to Madre Estefanía (may she rest in peace). It was such an amusing sight to see what happened to Madre Estefanía who had no idea what her companion had done. When she tried to get up the cord kept on pulling, and Madre Estefanía did not know what was holding her back. She asked Madre Josepha what she was doing, and she answered with a witty reply: "In case I had to swim I just did not have the courage to go by myself." All the passengers got a good laugh out of this scene. They also laughed when they heard about her antics from another night. On that occasion the wind was blowing so hard, causing the ship to roll about, that Madre Josepha tied herself to her bunk with some metal rings lying nearby. She wanted to make sure she didn't fall out.

Another amusing event happened with Madre Josepha. One of the Jesuit priests had passed away and there was nothing but a boarded wall separating him from her. Madre Josepha was very frightened and in that state fell asleep, but all of a sudden she started to shout: "Nobody sees what I'm seeing." Since it was pitch black and she spoke so clearly, we all thought she was awake, until we realized that she was dreaming about the deceased. The next morning after the funeral service, such as would have been performed on land, the priest was thrown overboard. We all put our heads out to see that spectacle, except for my frightened sister who tried to hide her horror by praying and lying prone with her arms out in the sign of the cross. She joked about her timid nature, saying: "It's possible that you all won't believe that I am doing this for virtue and mortification and not fear!" We all had a good laugh over these things. Returning to my narration of the storm, on the night of Epiphany [January 6, 1712], after the water had come on board the ship, there came such a torrential rain that it even poured down on us. Everything got soaked, including our habits, the bedding, and the floor. There was absolutely nothing we could do except to recognize that we had a lot to offer up to God. Everything was left in such a bad state that we could not even hear Mass that day. We arrived at the Canary Islands and were told that from that point on we had nothing to fear because we had left enemy territory.

## Chapter XIII
## Our Arrival in Buenos Aires and Other Things that Happened in that City

Our Lord always had a new trial prepared for us, and hence we learned that our vicaress [Madre Estefanía] (may she rest in peace), suffered from a cancerous tumor [*zaratán*]. She had hidden this serious illness from everyone until finally one of our sisters found out about it and her conscience made her tell me. Madre Estefanía was given every possible remedy because the ships were very well stocked. None of us was ever in want of anything, and they treated the sick nun with many special touches and great care. It's impossible to describe the great devotion shown to us by the captains and chaplains and everyone else traveling with us. The same was true for the representatives from the ships' owner, Don Andrés Martínez de Murguía. He was such a saintly gentleman and very special person, a true follower of our Father Saint Francis, that he swore to us that even if the foundation of our new convent was the only reason for him to charter his fleet that was enough for him to take up this venture. May God bring him good fortune and shower him with blessings for the charity he showed us.

In between the worries and concerns one suffers on a ship, we did have some moments of pleasure. We had occasion to thank God for the variety of fish we spotted in different areas. Sometimes we would see whales, which was always a good sign because it meant that there was wind. To the contrary, on calm days the sharks would appear. The sailors loved fishing for these animals that were about the same size as rams. Although they are not edible, they fished them just for fun. It was a pleasure to watch how easily the men would trick them. To give us a show they would rig up a cord on the galley and then tie to it an iron hook, dangling a piece of meat from it. The sharks would bite the meat and get snared by the hook. The sailors would then hoist them out of the water. This was very entertaining, particularly to see their two rows of teeth and huge mouths that could fit a small child inside.

One day during the siesta hour a gigantic fish appeared. Although the sailors all had much experience with the different creatures of the sea, no one had any idea what this could be. It seemed to me to be a type of shark because of the shape of its head. I believed that it must have been quite old to have grown to that proportion. It calmly swam under the ship and did not cause us any problems or fear. It appeared to be about ten *varas*[98] long and six wide. The head was so large that two or three bodies could fit in its mouth. A whole school of small fish was playing on top of it. In conclusion, everyone who saw it was truly amazed; praised be He who creates such marvels.

After this enjoyable activity we had a very worrisome experience. On the Day of Saint Frances of Rome [March 9, 1712], a man fell overboard. In our eyes there was no saving him. All the friars and priests gave him absolution by shouting it out to him. The man cried out to Jesus and the Virgin Mary to stop the ship, but it was moving so fast that the sailors could not stop it to effect a rescue. We were wrought with grief to see before our very eyes such a fatal situation and we did not cease to entreat God to save him. Everything was already planned out by His Divine Majesty, because earlier that day the crew had readied a type of buoy (a huge piece of wood) attached to a very long rope that is used when a ship nears land. The sailors believed we were nearing land so they unwound a cable, which they assured us had taken a lot of work and time. Because the man overboard was a sailor he knew how to swim and was able to tread water for a long time. Finally [as he clutched the buoy], the other sailors readied the launch and went to rescue him. It is true that his ability to swim helped him, but more importantly the grace of God saved him from that imminent danger and also us from seeing him die. We suffered deeply (although from natural causes) the death of the other Jesuit priest [mentioned earlier]. He had been a very saintly man and very useful as a missionary; even on the ship his pious soul and religious conviction shone as he preached and taught Christian doctrine to everyone on board. At first he began to cough up blood, but then he suffered from a high fever, causing him to lose even more blood, eventually costing him his life. During his illness we were physically so close to him [separated by only a thin wall] that we could hear all his moans and his requests for us to commend his soul to God. We did this with great love, but his fate was not to live and thus he died, giving us all a perfect example of acceptance and patience. The Jesuit priests provided him all the proper funeral rites and brought his prepared cadaver outside our cabin. During the morning, apart from the sung Mass, the priests offered many prayers for his soul. We were able to hear most of this because on a daily basis one of the leading Jesuits would come to say Mass for us. God always provided us the solace of having such kind companions.

---

98. A *vara* is a measurement of length of approximately thirty-three inches.

After we saw what happened to this saintly priest, we begged the Lord to save our vicaress. His [Divine] Majesty wished to console us, and she rallied for a while but died after we arrived in Buenos Aires (as I have already mentioned at the beginning of this account). I forgot to mention something that happened to her that provides specific proof of her innocence and saintly life. Her spiritual father was convinced that she had never lost the innocence of her baptism, and all of us who had spent time with her believed this. Her virtuous nature was particularly evident on one occasion when our confessor from Madrid could not attend to us. He was replaced (as is the custom) by the convent's auxiliary confessor, whom we called the pilgrim. After hearing Madre Estefanía's confession and not finding a thing for which to absolve her (because of her saintly and spiritual soul), he asked her to tell him about four lies or any other sins that she had committed during her lifetime; this type of request was customary in such cases. She replied, very distressed: "Father, I do not remember ever lying in my whole life or ever having done anything else that would warrant absolution, but absolve me as you wish." The father insisted that she specify something and the poor penitent nun became so upset that it was necessary to take her out of the confessional. The abbess told the priest about her way of life, about her candid innocence, and also about her very simple nature. From that moment forward he treated her differently and did not question her further. In all the convents we visited, we were given reason to praise God seeing her speak to the young children. It seemed as if they knew her, especially because all the girls would gather around her. She would proudly tell us all about the young ladies and everything they had told her. In addition to her innocence, she exercised such great penance that it seemed as if she were waging a constant battle against any bodily comforts. After a lifetime of suffering, she endured even more during the last two years of her life. When she was mortally ill, she was made to eat poultry, an act which caused her many more tears than her sins. She only gave in to this when she was required by obedience to do so.

As the ship neared the equator the temperature became so hot that many of the secular people on board took off as much clothing as possible and some of them even cut their hair. We, however, did not alter our wardrobe in any way. We continued to wear our habits and even to sleep in them. Everyone admired us because the heat caused a lot of suffering, so much so that we were sweating profusely and some of us had open sores from the rough sackcloth rubbing against our waists. Unlike our saintly patient [Madre Estefanía], at least the four of us were able to walk out onto the gallery for a breath of fresh air. She was confined day and night to her bunk, although she did not complain about the heat or anything else. She did not want to take off her habit, even though it is permitted when we are in the infirmary. In such cases we are allowed to wear just our tunic. She would have died wearing her habit if it had not been for one of her sisters who tricked her by saying that she needed to take it off so she could go shake it out. When she did not return it, Madre Estefanía cried out for her habit. She calmed down only after she was ordered by her vow of obedience to keep it off. The tumor on the patient's chest had grown so large that her habit barely fit over it, but she kept her suffering a secret so that we would leave her to bear this mortification. Blessed be the Lord who brought her into this world.

We continued on our journey and on the eve of our Father Saint Joseph's Day [March 19, 1712] we spotted land. Everyone was delighted since it had been three months since we had that comfort. On the Feast Day of Señor Saint Joachim [March 20, 1712] we dropped anchor in the River Platte. The river is so large that it feels more like a wide sea; the only noticeable difference is in the color of the water. It is shallow in some sections, forcing the pilots to creep along with great care so as not to breach the ships on the sand bars. Thus, we ended up spending many days on this river, because it was necessary to unload a large quantity of iron and other heavy things. Everything was left in Montevideo, and once the ships were much lighter we continued at a crawl. The pilot steered the ship using a sounding line[99] and would stop where we would least expect it. All this was a very good exercise in patience for those who were anxious to arrive at port.

On the twelfth day of April [1712] we arrived at the port that is three leagues away from the city of Buenos Aires, although the river later runs by the city. Once the word of our arrival had spread, we were visited by a representative from the ecclesiastical part of the city council (the seat of the bishop was vacant). The señor bishop who had traveled with us on our first sea voyage had been so traumatized by all the misfortunes that had befallen him and by other things that had occurred in Spain, that he had renounced the bishopric of Buenos Aires. Nevertheless, he later accepted it, and now that we are in this convent [in Lima] he has come to visit us. We were very pleased to see him because he is a very kind and saintly prince. May

99. A type of depth finder.

His Divine Majesty bless him with much success. Also, the city sent representatives to welcome us and they brought us fresh meat, bread and fruit. Although we had always been well cared for on the ship, one could only get hard tack and no bread, so this was a great treat for us. They told us all about the house where we were going to stay. It was one of the best in the city and also the residence of some religious women who lived there in a type of *beaterio*.[100] Their chapel looked out onto a beautiful garden where we spent a lot of memorable moments during the time that we lived there, especially because it was quite secluded from the rest of the neighborhood and free from disturbances.

When the time came for us to get off the ship, and with the possibility of leaving that same afternoon, we sent ahead all the blankets and other things we used for sleeping. As soon as the boat left with our things, a tremendous wind began to blow so that there was no way we could get off the ship, and we had to spend the night without our bedding. The chaplain, the captain and the ship's master quickly sent us elegant bedspreads and pillows with lace covers. We laughed out loud when we saw such inappropriate things for our use. We only accepted two blankets and the prayer books for our pillow, and that is how we spent the night. The next morning when they came to our cabin to help us board the launch, they first gave us a tour around parts of the ship that we had never seen before; this was despite the fact that we had spent a long time on that vessel. The seamen fired a great volley when we left the ship; we will always be indebted and truly grateful to them for all their kind treatment. Later the launch arrived, and we boarded it with the general of the South Sea [*Mar del Sur*[101]], his wife and family (who were traveling with us).

That gentleman, along with the dean and many other clergy accompanied us to the house where we were to stay. The dean lamented the fact that he had not earlier received word of the exact time of our arrival. Originally he had planned to greet us with all the city's different communities, but instead he gave the order to ring all the city's church bells. He then took us to the cathedral where he sang *Te Deum Laudamus* accompanied by music. He exposed the Blessed Sacrament and after the service showed us around. I can't even attempt to guess the number of people who came out to see us. It did not bother them a bit that it was during the time of their midday meal; we were told that they left their meal to come see us.

100. A house for pious lay women.

101. That is, the Pacific Ocean.

They had never seen nuns in that city and they all wanted a convent. As a form of solace for everyone, we left the carriage curtains open so they could see us. This meant that we had to go to the trouble of keeping our veils on to keep them happy.

We were very distressed when we arrived at the residence, because our patient [Madre Estefanía] had become very seasick from the launch's rough journey, causing her to cough up blood. She was in so much pain that it was all we could do to find a place for her to lie down. We owe much kindness and affection to everyone there. They are very pious people and truly wanted their own convent. I must confess that had it been God's Will I would happily have established a monastic community, as all those young women I saw were very virtuous. Everyday they cried more tears of frustration because they wanted to convert their *beaterio* into a military hospital, but no steps had been taken. Those angelic women were extremely dejected, with no hope of becoming nuns.

The woman in charge of the *beaterio* told us an amusing story. She related that before our arrival they had some hope of becoming nuns, although later they discovered the truth. It all began when a saintly priest who attended them told her in secret that he had seen [in a revelation] a ship so light that it appeared to be flying. The ship was traveling to that city [of Buenos Aires] with five nuns on board, and they were carrying a decree from the king to found a new convent. She was very excited by the news; this priest was very virtuous and she had no doubt that it was a premonition. Moreover, it all made sense because they had already asked the king for a license to establish a convent.

This was not the only time God had made manifest the revelation that five nuns would be traveling on a very swift sailing ship. The same happened to Francisco Araujo, one of the gentlemen traveling with us on our ship. At first, he had been undecided as to whether he should go back to Spain to wrap up some business. A priest of unquestionable virtue had told him that he should go back to Spain where he would obtain his wealth. The priest said that he would return a happy man, traveling on a swift ship, where there would also be five nuns accompanied by a very saintly man. Francisco Araujo told this story during our ship voyage. Every detail of the prophecy had come true to such an extent that it was necessary to stop our vessel so as not to lose the flagship, which we referred to as "the infirmary" because it was so slow.

I have already related some of the details of the illness and the other circumstances surrounding the death of our beloved sister and vicaress so I will not repeat them again here. I will say, however, that we stayed in Buenos Aires from April 13 until September 27 or 28. At that time we were taken to a hacienda or *chácara*[102] (that's the term used in the Indies) owned by Don Joseph Arregui, a very noble gentleman from Buenos Aires. It was four leagues from the city and all the land and livestock were truly magnificent. Moreover, he used the wealth of the *chácara* to help fund many acts charitable in the eyes of God.

When we arrived at the aforementioned *chácara* there were close to one hundred Indians living there. The majority were very young. There were also a few old women who were completely unable to grasp anything pertaining to our holy faith. It was pitiful to see them in this state. That fine gentleman had the utmost concern that both the old women and the children be taught and instructed in Christian doctrine. For this purpose he had assigned a friar from the order of our Father Saint Francis. It was wonderful to see how he instructed all these barbarians. During the fifteen days we spent on the hacienda many other poor little Indians came to the ranch. The Spaniards had killed their fathers in warfare, and they brought all the women and children to the hacienda. The little ones quickly soaked up all the Christian ways. We were very joyful, praising the Lord that He had brought the knowledge of the true faith to those poor creatures and that He had used this gentleman [Don Joseph] to that end.

Don Joseph Arregui was extremely generous and treated us like royalty during the time we spent in his house. As I am now writing this narration, he has passed on to a better place and his saintly wife has withdrawn to a convent. I have since heard that the Indians got smallpox and more than eighty have died, although they were already baptized; blessed be the Lord that did good unto them.

The reverend father, Fray Juan de Arregui, visited us many times at the hacienda. He always treated us with kindness and generosity. He had such a tender heart that he would always get teary on his visits (as I have already mentioned during the funeral of our vicaress). On one occasion, when we left the city we passed by the Convent of our Father Saint Francis where she was buried, and we stopped in to pay our last respects. We said a prayer for the dead and kissed the tombstone that covered her venerable body. It's true

102. The Peru transcription says "chakra."

that everyone was greatly moved by her passing, but that saintly friar seemed to be especially affected.

While at the hacienda we also had the pleasure of meeting the greatly respected friar, (that was his title at the time) Gabriel de Arregui, Commissioner General of the Order of our Father Saint Francis. He later became the bishop of Buenos Aires and is now the bishop of Cuzco. When this illustrious man heard about our arrival in the Port of Buenos Aires, he left the city of Cordoba (over two hundred leagues away) because he wanted to meet us. Our Lord God granted us the pleasure of speaking with him, although we were worthy of only three days to get to know him. Nonetheless, in that short time the Lord bestowed onto us the opportunity to learn many of the good things that He had done for His servant. May His Divine Majesty grant him a long life so that through his example and doctrine he may convert many souls.

I know it's not fair for me to tread on his modesty, but I will only say one thing that I observed during the Mass of Saint Peter of Alcántara. One of the prayers for the dead praises the saint with these words: "Our Father Saint Francis is already dead, but it is as if he never died because he left in Saint Peter a son who followed the rules of his saintly father to such a degree that he never wavered to the right nor to the left." I'm saying this because our venerable father, the illustrious Señor Don Fray Gabriel de Arregui, fit this description perfectly. His appearance, his pious conversation, his continuous penitence and his thoughtful meditation on all things are a mirror image of my Father Saint Francis. All his words are arrows that ignite hearts in their love of God. God has bestowed on him, among many other gifts, the ability to touch the most intimate side of the human spirit. We as poor souls all grasped at his words of advice and felt ratified (confiding in the grace of God) in our goal to establish and found this saintly house with as much perfection as possible. Shedding many a tear, he asked us to continue with our task and we also cried at having to leave his benevolent company.

Unfortunately we had to leave his company because it was getting late in the season and we still had to travel 300 leagues by land to Mendoza. From there we would cross the mountain range of Chile that—due to very high levels of snow—is only passable during the hottest time of the year, obliging us to wait in Buenos Aires. Our Lord did not wish the illness of our vicaress to detain our journey (as I have already mentioned). Whenever she heard mention of the trip she assured us that she would not be a hindrance. This is exactly what happened because she died soon thereafter, giving us enough time to get everything ready. The preparations were extensive since those deserted lands are completely forsaken, as I shall describe in the next chapter.

## Chapter XIV
## The Departure from the Chácara and Everything that Happened on Our Way to Mendoza and then on to the Mountain Range

There are 300 leagues between Buenos Aires and Mendoza. In order to travel that distance with any bit of ease, the same amount of provisions are required as if it were a ship journey. That stretch of land is so deserted of inhabitants that one cannot find any drinking water. In some areas the situation becomes so extreme that many oxen and horses die of thirst, and for this reason it is necessary to travel with a large number of livestock. There are so many herds in that area that they roam free without any owners.

We left the aforementioned hacienda on the tenth day of October [1712]. We were accompanied by the señor bishop [Gabriel de Arregui] whom I have already mentioned; his brother [Fray Juan de Arregui], who at that time was the custodian of the Franciscan convent and is now the provincial minister; his other brother [Don Joseph Arregui], owner of the hacienda; and his wife, Doña María Castellanos. All of them competed to help us and treated us like royalty. We were also accompanied by the captains and the chaplains of our ships, the latter of whom escorted us during sixteen leagues of the journey; it was so hard for them to see us off that they didn't know when to turn around. We had been in contact with them for close to a year and held these upstanding gentlemen in very high regard. They were greatly honored by our attention and had always made a point of visiting us on the ship and later in the city. The chaplains said Mass for us on a daily basis, and because on Feast Days they were obligated to say Mass on the ships, they sent other friars in their place so that we would not miss our chapel.

When it came time to bid our farewells there was a lot of sadness from all parties. Yet they said they were happy to endure this pain, because of their devotion to us and because they had the opportunity to serve us. May God in his infinite generosity bequeath on these men spiritual goods in return for all that they have done for His poor wives. One of the priests was a Basque named Don Domingo de Ornazabal and the other one, Don Juan de Vidaurre, was from Navarra. The two captains from the fleet were Don Joseph de Ibarra who was the commander and the second was Don Joaquín de

Triviño. These men, along with Don Miguel de Subiegui,[103] who was the ship's master, supplied everything onboard ship that we needed to set up house when we arrived in Buenos Aires. At the time of our departure they did the same thing for our [land] journey by giving us tablecloths, pewter dishware, spices, and anything else available to them. May the Lord reward them by making them saints and grant us the consolation that we all will rejoice together for all eternity.

We used a large convoy of carts for this section of the journey because our father confessor already had knowledge of these solitary lands. He had brought eleven people with him from Spain, all of whom came in the hope of making their fortunes in the Indies, and our confessor paid for their ship passage and everything else. Those men made us feel much better because all of them were very honorable persons. Furthermore, they would defend us if we were attacked by heathen Indians. We traveled with twelve carts: one for hard tack, another for bread and chickens, others with lots of firewood, and others filled with even more boxes. These twelve carts were owned just by our father confessor. In addition to these, the general of the South Sea and the viscount of Miraflores brought their own supplies. There were also many oxen so that the drivers would always have fresh ones on hand, numerous cows to use as food and a whole herd of horses. It took many people to tend to all these animals, so much so that when we all gathered together it was like a small city.

We sat in an oxcart assigned to the four of us. This mode of transportation is extremely tedious because the oxen walk very slowly, but since they are very hardy they are ideal for this task. The trip lasted forty-one days. We practically slept sitting up the whole way because even though there was enough room for the four of us, we could not stretch out our legs. Moreover, in that whole region there were no lodgings or country inns other than our oxcart. We accommodated to this situation.

Every morning, our father confessor would say Mass and give us communion. He would conduct the service under a tent and leave it up every night. At midday the entourage would stop. We would get down from the cart and go into the tent to get out of the sun. We would pray there because it was impossible to do so in the cart with its constant jarring. During this time the workers would rush around to prepare lunch and there never seemed like enough time to eat it. Within two or three hours they would kill the cows and chickens and

103. The Peru transcription spells his name "Suborregui."

then cook them. In that rustic environment, there was no time for any other conveniences. In the evenings they would do a little less, but everything was done with a lot of vigor for the love of God.

Along this entire route there were no trees or villages, and we would only come across a ranch every thirty or forty leagues. The inhabitants, knowing that we were passing by, would come out to see us. They reminded me of the shepherds of the nativity, each one with a small offering. They all had a great longing to hear Mass; it had been years since some of them had had this opportunity. It's a great pity to see these poor people because, even though they are Christians, they live and die as if they were not; years can go by without them ever saying confession or taking communion. When they die, they do so without any spiritual assistance and are then buried in that countryside. For this reason there are many crosses scattered all over the place. The worst is that their children are brought up without any knowledge of Christian doctrine and completely ignorant of its virtues.

On this route there were many poisonous snakes, but God saved us from them and also from jaguars that we were told roamed the countryside. One day something happened that really touched my heart. We were told that a poor man from one of those ranches was on his deathbed from a snakebite and that there was no possibility of curing his soul or body. We were all very saddened by this news; our father confessor tried to get everyone to leave early so that we might offer (if at all possible) some solace to that poor man. When we arrived we were told that a friar from the order of my Father Saint Francis, who had been brought from twenty leagues away, was already at his side. He had already heard his confession and shortly thereafter our father confessor and the priest celebrated Mass for us. They brought the sick man communion and were accompanied by such an entourage of people that it was an amazing sight. There were so many candles carried by gentlemen that they looked like a small town. The sick man was consoled and his spirit soothed, so much so that within a few days we were told that he was out of danger. Later, the working hands brought us a jaguar paw (they actually had been able to kill it), which was a terrifying sight. The shape was just like that of a cat, but each claw looked like a knife. Thanks be to God who kept us out of harm's way.

There were many very large ostriches [*avestruces*][104] and boys brought us their eggs so that we could see their size. I estimate that each one weighed somewhere between a pound and a half and two pounds. They also brought us partridge eggs. There was a great abundance of them all along the route from Buenos Aires. Many of the partridge eggs are so large that they look like hen's eggs, although there are also small ones like those in Spain.

Everywhere we went we received the good will of Jesuit priests. On one occasion in particular we seemed to be blessed by Divine Providence. This happened towards the end of our trip when two carts were sent to us from a ranch owned by Jesuits. The ranch manager brought with him new supplies of wine, sheep and firewood. We were especially thankful for the wood since our stock was exhausted. The saintly priest told us that he also had run out of firewood, and when he heard that we were passing through he figured that we would need some. As a result he decided to knock down a corral and load up a cart for us. May God bless this very saintly man. He was inspired by Our Lord who has always taken care of us without our deserving it. The same happened with water because we were always well provided for by the Jesuit priests. Praise be to His [Divine] Majesty, since the Jesuits said that they had never before experienced such abundance of water.

Everyday we came across many savage Indians on horseback (in that region it is very easy for them to obtain horses). The Indians were so ugly looking that, had we not been heavily guarded, we would have been absolutely terrified. Most were naked, giving them the appearance of devils. Our father confessor had the working hands offer them something to eat and in particular he gave them bread or biscuits, which was the most coveted item for them. Even the Spaniards who lived on the ranches only eat meat; they never have their daily bread.

We arrived at a place that at one time was a city called La Punta, but now, even though it still has the same name, it seemed more like a hamlet [*arrabal*] with only four to six insignificant houses. Given that there was no lodging for us, we just stayed in the cart. The local priest, a very devoted servant of God, lamented that he could not celebrate our visit the way he would have wished. He brought us to the church where he exposed the Blessed Sacrament and sang Mass. Everyone sang a few verses, accompanied by a guitar. We had to remember the situation in which we found ourselves so that we would not laugh too much and

---

104. These could have been any number of birds that are indigenous to South America and look a bit like ostriches. Some examples are the rhea, ñandú, and nandow.

because that saintly priest tried to offer us the best that he could. May God forgive him as I have since heard that he died suddenly.

We continued on to Mendoza where we were welcomed by the Señor Vicar Don Antonio Sepúlveda y Leyva, a person of great virtue, letters, and nobility. He acted accordingly, and because of his generosity he never gave us a chance to feel any of the shortages that the Jesuit missionaries had told us they experienced; they could not even get enough bread. This saintly and generous gentleman made it his business to insure that we never went without bread during all the time we spent in that city. The first day he treated us to a splendid lunch, and we were treated to lunch the second day by the governor's wife, Señora Doña Luisa Pedraza. Those two people were very supportive, and we are very thankful for their generosity, no small feat in such a poor land. For instance, the houses are very rustic and the one in which we stayed was without bricks or whitewash. Furthermore, the adobe walls were infested with creatures quite similar to bedbugs, but they are much larger; each bug is four to six times the size of the ones in Spain. You don't see them at all during the day, but every morning we would awake covered in bumps. At first we did not know what was causing the bumps, and we just thought we were swelling up. Later, when we were better accustomed to that land, we learned the cause and started to look for them. Also, mice were as abundant as a fall harvest. It's hard to imagine, but without exaggerating they were like rabbits, and they created such a ruckus in the rafters that they tormented us on many occasions.

The weather during our time in Mendoza was already extremely hot. We were also visited by crowds of people, and it was very draining. Unlike a visit to a convent where we could be separated by a curtain in the convent parlor—and where we did not have to worry about our veils—here we had to receive people throughout the whole day with our faces covered up. God saw to it that we spent only seventeen or eighteen days in that place while our father confessor sent to Chile for saddles and mules for us to cross the mountain range.[105] The distance from Mendoza to the city of Santiago is over seventy leagues. That route was to be the most arduous for us, especially for me since I had never mounted a horse or mule, let alone seen a woman undertake such a feat. I had much to offer up to God. Better said, I was fortunate to be able to sacrifice myself up to the Lord.

---

105. The author never uses the term "the Andes," but only refers this mountain range as *la cordillera*.

At the hour of our departure our father confessor had devised a small type of platform for us to use to mount the mules. This way the men would not have to carry us, instead they lifted us on the platform between two poles and we were easily able to settle onto the mules. They did the same thing to help us get down.

We began our trek accompanied by the viscount of Miraflores who had been our companion since Spain. He was a very humble and saintly gentleman, traveling to take the position of the *corregidor* of Guamanga, where he then lived for a few years. About two years ago, after having been married for only several days, he suddenly died in the city of Cuzco. I hope to God that he is safe, because I always observed great virtue in him. We were also accompanied by two Jesuit priests who, along with our father confessor, said Mass for us. Although we encountered many adverse conditions, we always tried to attend Mass and to take communion.

As we were not at all accustomed to riding mules or being exposed to the sun we suffered greatly. This was all so new to us that the first day when we stopped at a hermitage or small house at the foot of the steep ascent into the jagged peaks, we were in horrible shape. One could see nothing else but those towering peaks from all the leagues that we had already covered.

We stopped for one day in that place to help relieve two of my sisters: one suffered from a high fever and the other's face had completely swollen up. We spent the whole day trying to cure them with wet rags and other measures. We continued onward in the name of God as if we were marching through purgatory, because although that region is extremely cold, we could only cross the passes during the hottest time of the year; otherwise the passes are completely blocked with snow. All the sharp vertical peaks closed in around us, exposing us to such extreme sunrays that I don't even have words to describe it. Only for the love of God is one able to traverse these mountains. One minute we would find ourselves frozen to the bone on a mountain top, and the next we were deep in a valley drenched in sweat. These drastic changes in conditions caused our hands and faces to peal as if we had suffered severe burns. The constant river crossings were so frightening that I don't have words to describe them; only one who has had such an experience can give it credit. The whole day one is so continuously surrounded by cliffs that you need to offer up your soul to God. It's a miracle that we made it safely because we saw with our own eyes many horrible mishaps. With one slip of the hoof, horses and mules would fall headlong into the river, which runs below the trail, giving it the appearance of being decorated on either side by the cliffs.

Among my sisters, Madre Bernarda and I were the most burdensome for everyone. We were both poor riders and I had the additional problem of being quite fat, causing the mules to tire easily. Moreover, the mules could sense that I was a poor rider, and on several occasions I was scared out of my wits, especially when I saw myself at death's doorstep. Once my mule balked by the edge of a cliff, and it would have rolled on top of me, crushing me to pieces had not God allowed our father confessor to come to me just in the nick of time. On another occasion I fell off with such force that I bruised my entire body, especially my feet and knees, because I landed on some very large rocks. There would never be enough time for me to tell all that I suffered on that route. May the Lord receive my pain for His mercy.

We encountered a multitude of crosses all along the route. There were markings of the sites where many had succumbed to the bitter cold. We arrived at a site where three men recently had frozen to death and we even saw the remnants of the clothing they had worn. With this apprehension and also because they were well aware of our own vulnerability, many learned and pious people tried to convince us to put on stockings and some type of warm clothes. They reminded us that many secular people, even with all their precautions, had suffered countless misfortunes: those people did not realize that the freezing cold had seeped into their bones to such an extent that they had been left frozen stiff. Since we confided in the Lord's Will and did not want to change our dress, we did not take their advice. We trekked through such deep snow that it almost touched our feet while we were mounted on the mules, although it never harmed us.

The hardest day was a climb of a league and a half over the last peak. The pack animals were exhausted as they neared the crest; their stumbling caused many books and other items to fall and be lost forever. Our Lord God granted us the solace that no one was hurt, considering all the cargo that had fallen. This climb was extremely arduous. Throughout the whole ascent we beseeched Our Lord [for mercy], not daring to look down for fear of fainting. The trail was made up of switchbacks, but the mules were so well trained that we did not have to guide them at all. It's as if they were rational creatures; they would stop at every corner to rest, and then they would continue on their way.

On that day, when we found ourselves on the summit of the peak, which is the highest of any within a seventy league radius, I asked one of the mule drivers if we could take a short rest. The drivers were amused by my request, telling me: "*Madre*, you have no idea where you are. It's very common for wind and snow storms to whip up suddenly and there could be so much snow that we would be trapped here." Thus, they had no wish to delay our departure any longer. And exactly what the mule driver described to me happened to another group behind us.

We came across some chests in a place where the wife of the general of the South Sea also left a note (for when we would pass by) describing everything that had happened to her. On the one hand, that señora was generally very brave, but on the other she was very cowardly; in this case, on account of the mice and critters in Mendoza she wanted to get out of there as soon as possible. Consequently, she found herself stuck under a tent in the middle of the mountain range; they waited out the weather for a few days until they were able to hurry on to Santiago, Chile. Returning to what I was saying about the chests, I was very impressed that they were left in that spot without any owner. I was told that the penalty for theft was excommunication so that no one would take anything. If a group of travelers were caught by a severe storm, and could only hope to save themselves, they would have to leave their cargo for a whole year because once the mountain passes were closed with snow (as I have already mentioned) they are not passable until the next year.

Many of those mountain passes are so dangerous that we had to cross them on foot, always with a prayer on our lips. It's wonderful to think that there are people who would put themselves in harm's way for no other bodily reason than for the glory of God. We crossed many rivers and climbed so many slopes that there must have been at least twenty or thirty times a day when we could have perished. Blessed be the goodness of the Lord that allowed our journey to go so smoothly. The mule drivers were shocked at our luck, because they said that they had never traveled that harsh route under such mild weather conditions.

Just before the birthday of the Lord, we spent Christmas Eve in a forsaken place similar to Bethlehem. That afternoon we found ourselves on the edge of a cliff called the Salto del Soldado. The mountainside is extremely treacherous, and even though the drivers told us to look down at the river, we didn't dare glance at it, for fear that we would fall headlong into it. The name, Salto del Soldado [Soldier's Leap], stems from a situation that happened to a soldier. After deserting his company, his officer in command had followed him in hot pursuit. When the soldier saw that he was about to be overtaken, he was more worried about his commander's wrath than he was for his own life and so he leapt from one cliff to the other. To think that he crossed right over the deep and mighty river terrified us to hear about it. It's astonishing to think that one man, without the aid of any special miracle, could do such a shocking thing; it has never been forgotten.

After taking a whole day to traverse that dangerous pass we came to a small clearing called los Duraznos and camp was set up there. Since in our [Capuchin] order we have the custom of observing the mystery of the Nativity with many celebrations, we thanked the Lord for letting us celebrate this service in such a lifelike setting. We set up an altar with [the figurines of] Jesus, Mary, and Joseph and as many candles as possible. Several campfires were lit, and the young gentlemen who were traveling with us played the guitar and serenaded the Christ Child. That whole night was spent in great joy. The next morning our father confessor said three Masses for us as if we were back in our convent. Many of those present took communion, making it the main part of the celebration.

## Chapter XV
### Our Arrival in Santiago, Chile;
### The Many Favors Given to Us by the Señor Bishop Don Luis Francisco Romero and by the Whole City; and Our Arrival in Callao

After leaving the mountain range and entering the territory of Chile, we stopped at a place called Concagua.[106] It was so pleasant that it seemed to us as if we had just risen up out of purgatory and entered heaven. The priest of that valley had received an order from the señor bishop to provide us lodging, and that's exactly what he did. We rested for two days at his house, and all his servants took great pains to look after us. They were quite distressed to see our severe sunburns: we looked like monsters, covered in fish scales.

After we left that place and traveled a very long distance, the mule drivers lost the trail. We were extremely late in our arrival at another accommodation arranged for us by the valley's priest. If he had not sent out a search party (since he knew we were coming), we would have been in deep trouble because we were completely disoriented. That priest showered us with hospitality and assured us that he would have done so without the urging of the señor bishop. He was very devoted to our Father Saint Francis and he felt honored to have the daughters of that saint at his house.

Because it had been ordered by His Illustriousness, we were shown the same excellent treatment by all the parishes we visited before we arrived in the city [Santiago]. The bishop had also given the order to have a feast—as abundant as his great generosity— waiting for us in a country manor three leagues from Santiago. He had already shown proof of his generosity because we were later told at the [Santiago] convent, where we were lodged, that ever since the bishop had received news of our departure from Madrid he had planned many things for our comfort. After we had eaten and rested at that country manor, we received word from the Señor Presiding Magistrate, Don Juan Andrés de Ustaríz that he was sending a carriage for us. We used his carriage and thanked him for granting us many favors. From that point on the route was filled with so many

---

106. The Peru transcription uses the name Aconcagua, which is the highest peak in the Andes (6962 m). It is found in present day Argentina, but only a few kilometers from the border with Chile. The term *Concagua* is the archaic form of Aconcagua and refers to the valley on the Chilean side of the peak (it is currently referred to as the Valley of Aconcagua).

people, and our arrival stirred up so much commotion that it seemed like we were going to found a new convent in that city.

As we neared the city we received a message from His Illustriousness that we should use the calash he had sent for us. We immediately obeyed his wishes, and we were also accompanied by countless other calashes as we arrived at the Convent of our Mother Saint Clare de la Cañada. The nuns were well prepared for our arrival. They had the Blessed Sacrament exposed and some young girls sang beautifully.

Once this was finished, we were told that His Illustriousness was waiting for us in the cloister. He blessed us and received us so warmly that we felt as if he had always been in contact with us. He told us that due to some unforeseen circumstances he had not been able to meet us on the trail. We thanked him for his kindness and were taken to the cell that had been set aside for our stay. It had very fine beds with canopies and other things that go against our religious order. We begged the bishop to have such ostentatious items taken away and to allow us to sleep on our accustomed bed, which is a wooden platform with two blankets. As he is very kind, he agreed to our request. He then sent for refreshment. He pretended that he was very thirsty so that we would not feel inhibited—something we realized later on. He acted as if he were dying of thirst, but we never saw him touch a drop. Delicious iced drinks were brought out, and the bishop served us with his own two hands. He engaged us in a long conversation about happenings in Spain and about his relatives who lived there. He then blessed us and left until the next day when he visited us again, just as he was to do on numerous other occasions. Before leaving, he asked the nuns to entertain us. The young girls who lived there immediately jumped up and graced us with a wonderful performance of music, song and dance. On another day they performed a well choreographed dance that we enjoyed even more.

We spent twelve days in Santiago, wooed by the order of that saintly prince [the bishop] who took great care with every detail. We also received great favors from the presiding magistrate, the *oidores*, other gentlemen, and friars.[107] All of them lamented the fact that we would not be staying longer! The bishop in particular was very upset that we did not wait for a ship so that we could travel more comfortably. Although we appreciated all these gestures of kindness and devotion, we felt we would be tormented by any more delays. We thanked them

---

107. The Madrid manuscript reads "religiones," but I have opted for the Peru version which reads "religiosos" (friars) and makes more sense in the context of the sentence.

sincerely, especially the presiding magistrate who had given an order so that a ship (that was ready to leave) should wait for us while we finished up matters in Santiago. In that ship they prepared a cabin for us that really had no amenities, but we were grateful for them being so quick to accommodate us, something that we truly appreciated.

Returning to what I was saying about the kindness of His Illustriousness, he arranged for us to visit three other convents in that city. We first went to the Augustinian convent, which has as many nuns as that of our Mother Saint Clare. They welcomed us with such enthusiasm that when the bishop came for us that evening, they would hear nothing of it; he finally gave in to their demands, letting us stay until the next day. I do not have words to describe how well those nuns treated us. It was very difficult to get them to retire for the evening, and so we did not go to bed until midnight. They were up again at four in the morning when we heard them singing outside our door. Their angelic voices and ballads could ignite even the most indifferent heart to the love of God. We went to the choir and for the next three or four hours we listened to a splendid harpist; this was all because they had heard that we liked that instrument. The whole day they entertained us, and that evening they performed a play [*una comedia*], but they ended it in tears when they heard that the bishop had sent for us. He decided it was better not to come in person because of what had happened the night before. We really loved that community and their pious mother abbess, whose great attributes I shall forgo describing, so as not to offend her humility. It suffices to say that her name is Señora Doña Augustina Hurtado de Mendoza. She lived in that convent with her five sisters (who are also nuns) and with her pious mother. They are beloved in that convent by all the nuns and venerated by the whole city because they come from an illustrious and pious family. We received many favors from them especially because of her brother, Señor Don Jerónimo Hurtado.[108] He gave us a much needed donation, and her other sister, a secular woman named Doña Rosa, was very kind to accompany us to all the functions around the city. May God make them all very saintly.

When we returned to the Convent of our Mother Saint Clare, we found the nuns very upset and hurt as if we had been absent a whole year. They even got the bishop to agree not to let us spend any night in the other convents that we had yet to visit.

108. The Peru transcription cites his name as "Gregorio" instead of Jerónimo.

Next, we visited the Carmelite nuns, who for some reason always have been very supportive of the Capuchin order; throughout all our travels whenever we have had the pleasure of meeting them, they have provided us with indescribable support. Those saintly nuns welcomed us with open arms but were very disappointed that our visit would be short. They treated us extremely well, and in the evening His Illustriousness sent for us.

The following day the bishop took us to another convent of our Mother Saint Clare (there are two in this city). The nuns affectionately treated us like sisters, and we also held them in very high regard. In the afternoon the secular girls in the convent presented a play [*una comedia*] and afterwards they served us all refreshments. After saying our goodbyes to those saintly nuns, we returned to our convent accompanied by the señor bishop, where everything was being quickly prepared for our departure to Valparaiso.

If it had not been for the need to continue our trip, we would have been very content to stay in Santiago, since both the people and the climate are very similar to that of Spain. On the day of our departure to Valparaiso, we said goodbye to the señor bishop, thanking him for the indescribable gifts and favors he had lavished on us. With great kindness and affection His Illustriousness gave us his blessing. The emotions displayed by the mother abbess and all her saintly community are beyond words, as is our ability to thank all those who favored us. Lastly, we were escorted out of the cloister by many ladies and gentlemen.

The Augustinian nuns had asked His Illustriousness to let us pass by the door to their garden so that they could hug us goodbye. Upon our arrival the whole saintly community had lined up, causing them to seem like Seraphim because their dress was very venerable and religious. When we entered the vegetable garden, we saw that they had set up a canopy and tables filled with delicious iced drinks and other refreshments to which they treated us. Because we were pressed for time and all the nuns wanted to speak to us, it was impossible to make all of them happy. We suffered terribly that we were not able to spend enough time to enjoy their great devotion and affection. Our gentlemen escorts kept urging us to leave, but this was beyond our control. The men did not stop hurrying us until Don Jerónimo Hurtado, the mother abbess's brother, got angry, and told them to leave us alone because no one was benefiting from this. We then said goodbye to those pious señoras. We will never forget them for their kindness.

From there we went to a *chácara* owned by a gentleman named Pedro Espejo. He took very good care of us that night. The next morning the mules were saddled up, because from that point on it was necessary to ride them again. Even though the trail was not as bad as in the mountains, we were told that it was much longer and it would be very difficult to ride in the calash. Since we wanted to continue as fast as possible, we didn't mind giving up the comfort [of the carriage].

That section of the journey was thirty leagues long, and every one of them was covered with hawthorns [*espinos*]. We needed to take great care to protect our faces because many times the thorns tore our veils to shreds. The lodging on the plain was under a tent. On one of the travel days we had a horrible fright: there were various paths leading off the trail, and when we stopped by a stream to rest, we realized that our father confessor, a young boy, and Madre Bernarda were all missing. Members of the party went searching for them all over the place and after two hours they were still nowhere to be found. Our Lord, however, saw to it that they were found before dark, as it upset them greatly not knowing how to find their way back to us; with them the young page was carrying the holy Christ [statue]. The three of them had lost sight of everyone else and had lost the trail at the beginning of the day. That stretch of land was just monstrous; it was very hilly, and had we not already passed over the mountain range, we would have found it very challenging.

We stopped at a place very close to the port [of Valparaiso] where we were met by the governor. We gave many thanks to God for letting us lay our eyes on the sea again; thus, we could ratify giving up our lives for His love. You cannot see that spot until you almost enter it—it looks like a nativity scene at the foot of the mountain—and the descent into it is very difficult. I must confess that I was terrified (later I found out that my sisters also felt the same way, but I did not tell them at the time). I started to shake all over when I saw the sea (the water was extremely deep in that port). My heart wanted to burst out of my chest; in all our travels we had never seen a port as menacing as that one. We stopped at a church where a priest was in charge of providing us lodging. His name was Juan de Covarrubias and he was a very honorable person. He gave the order to ring the church bells, and many people came out to see us. While still mounted on our mules, our faces covered by our veils, we said a prayer to the Blessed Sacrament. Afterwards we went into his house (it was very close by), which was well adorned.

We spent three nights at his house where we received several visitors, including three French captains. As compatriots of our Mother Saint Colette they offered us the service of their crew and ships. One captain in particular admired us greatly, saying he last saw us when we left the Port of Cadiz. He could not say enough about the grief that everyone in the kingdom had felt when they had heard about our mishap with the Dutch. They were, however, very happy when they heard that we had been well treated. Don Fernando Vicente, the name of this captain, was always a very pious man. In fact, when he returned to Lima with his ship he gave us several donations. On this particular occasion he provided his launch to take all our things to the ship. He also hoisted us up in the launch so that we could easily board the ship. In the days we spent there we were just waiting for wind. The señor vicar exposed the Blessed Sacrament, sang Mass, and prayed for our safe passage.

On Jesus' sweet name day, January, 14 [1713] we boarded ship; even though there was no wind, the crew wanted us to wait aboard so as not to miss a chance to set sail. It was amazing because a good wind picked up as the ship came in to get us and then it changed directions on our way out. This happened so quickly that they [the sailors] told the men who accompanied us that they had to get off the ship right away since we were starting to pick up a fast clip. It is very dangerous to get out of that port because there is rarely enough wind, forcing many people to board and then disembark their ships between six and eight times. Our Lord, however, favored us and we didn't have to wait, not even an instant, which was our fervent wish.

Nothing out of the ordinary happened to us on this ship. It only had to travel the short distance of 500 leagues. The sea was very calm throughout the whole trip and it was amusing when the pilot said: "I already had an idea that by taking your reverences with us the waters would be like a lagoon. I really don't like such delicate ripples; I would prefer a robust wind that would put us in the port in fifteen days." We took nineteen.

On the first day of February we set anchor in Callao. Some of the gentlemen who accompanied us went ashore so that they could notify the señor viceroy, the high court and the city council of our arrival. The viceroy was the esteemed Señor Don Diego Ladrón de Guevara, also the Bishop of Quito. He treated us like a father confessor as I later will explain. We also had the opportunity, by way of our father confessor's nephew, to send word to our beloved *colegialas*. This upstanding gentleman, Doctor Don Joseph Bucaro, is both learned and virtuous and although he is very young he shows the maturity of an older man. He had left Chile (where he was living) to meet up with us in the mountain range. He became so attached to us during this time that it kindled his aspiration to become ordained.

When my *colegialas* met him they did not know how to entertain him. They received him warmly and showered attention on him. They constantly wanted to hear about us and our way of life. He told them everything he had observed with his own two eyes. He said to them that he had never seen us use tobacco and that they should give it up. He later assured us, when he returned to our ship, that with his slight urging all of them were giving up this small pleasure. Further, they were excited and prepared to give up even bigger things in order to become Capuchins.

It is difficult to put into words the atmosphere of excitement that the people of Lima were feeling when they later heard about our imminent arrival. Everyone had loved the pious house for its virtuous practices and now they happily saw themselves as participants in this new foundation. Many different gentlemen from various administrative bodies came out to the ship to welcome us and to accompany us on shore. In particular, the Señor General Don Jorge de Villalonga,[109] also known as the count of la Cueva and currently the viceroy of Santa Fe, came to welcome us. This gentleman (by order of the señor viceroy) had prepared accommodation for us in His Excellency's palace in Callao. Also some of the city's noblest women accompanied us in the launch to shore. The ships then fired a great volley and all of them displayed their pennants; they showed the maximum demonstration of joy that is possible in such a situation.

When we arrived at the dock we were met by the Señor Doctor Don Manuel Antonio Gómez de Silva, the vicar-general of this house. He was accompanied by that presidio's Señor Vicar, *Maestro* [Teacher] Don Dionisio Granados, who was wearing a choir robe with a white cross, and by many clergy and countless others. We all walked in a procession to the church where they exposed the Blessed Sacrament. After saying a prayer and closing up His Majesty [in the monstrance], they brought us to a palace where the Señora Doña Rosa Urdánegui had set out refreshments. She was in charge of our lodging and took great care with all the details. This lady treated us with a thousand favors (she was the first woman we met in Lima)—she had

109. Jorge de Villalonga was the first official viceroy of New Granada (1719–24).

come out to our ship to accompany us to shore and then she became our inseparable companion for the two days we spent in the Port of Callao. We still owe her so much for her extraordinary care. We were visited by many people and the señor vicar treated us with great generosity; may God reward him for this.

Our sisters, the *colegialas*, were not satisfied with the fact that the chaplains and the assistants of the house had gone to visit us; they wanted to share the good news with everyone possible. We were very eager to meet them and to show them the true love that God had instilled in us by all the trials we had endured. We truly appreciated any token from them; in this case our only consolation was a letter with a small gift that had made its way to us in Mendoza. We handed out the sweets and chocolates they had sent us as if they were relics.

The first night after we arrived in Callao there were so many functions and courtesy visits that we did not finish until very late. Also, the veils covering our faces were suffocating us, but with the pleasant thought of the closeness to our beloved Lima, all was made sweet. The next morning the sisters and nieces of our father confessor came to visit us at the palace. We were very pleased to meet them, as they were related to a person to whom we felt a great obligation and appreciation. Since there is no perfect pleasure, however, we saw the counterbalance because they were in mourning for the death of their pious father.[110] We felt terrible about this because we had wanted to meet their father and thank him for being instrumental, by way of his fortune in establishing this foundation so to the liking of God.

While we spoke to these ladies along with many other upstanding people, the Señor General Villalonga came in to tell us that the townspeople had lined up to welcome us. Many came in, but the highest ranking man, called Salvador (he was their brigadier general), spoke to us with the utmost politeness. All of them were well dressed and adorned. It was a great pleasure to see them and to hear them. Likewise, they were overwhelmed by our presence; with our arrival they thought that we would be able to speed up the process of beatification of their countryman Nicolás de Dios.[111] I told them that I would do everything in my power to help this process and anything else that they would like to ask of me. They were very thankful, and from that

---

110. It is not clear to whom they were referring. Perhaps it was the father of Joseph Gallegos or perhaps the confessor of the *colegio* at the time.

111. See the introduction for more information on Nicolás de Dios, also known as Nicolás de Ayllón.

point on we became close friends. Later when we were staying with the Trinitarian nuns they would come to visit us, bringing small gifts.

That afternoon the vicar-general [Antonio Gómez de Silva] and the general [Jorge de Villalonga] arranged for us to see all the presidio's churches. They are all beautiful, especially the Jesuit's church, which is a precious gem. They showed us inside to see the boys who were studying there. I asked the priest's permission to let them go after they prayed a Hail Mary. We all had a good laugh because as soon as they were excused they raced out, tripping over one another, making it impossible for them all to fit through the door at once. They also showed us the Hospital of San Juan de Dios. Its cleanliness and charity were very impressive. In all the churches we visited we were either received with a *Te Deum Laudamus* or with the exposition of the Blessed Sacrament. May His Divine Majesty fill all of them with His love for the many ways in which they always honored us.

## Chapter XVI
### Our Departure from Callao and Arrival in the City of Lima

Our departure from Callao was arranged for February 4, [1713]. There were many discussions regarding which convent would take us in. We were to be housed for an indefinite period of time while we waited for our convent to be completed according to the standards of our Capuchin order. We wished (since it seemed just and reasonable) to be taken in by the nuns of the Convent of our Mother Saint Clare; they were also hoping for the same. Our Lord, however, chose the Convent of the Discalced Trinitarian nuns. Those nuns, who were very close to the señor viceroy, had also known our father confessor for many years. They made a great effort to favor us, pleading with the authorities to take us to their blessed company, where we stayed for a very pleasant three and a half months.

When it was time for us to leave the palace [in Callao], there was more discussion, this time regarding the señoras who were going to accompany us. Each señora obstinately wanted us to ride in her own carriage. So as not to hurt anyone's feelings it was decided that we would separate: Madre Bernarda and I went with Señora Doña Rosa Urdánegui, her sister and both daughters of the marquis of Villafuerte; Madre Gertrudis and Madre Josepha Victoria went with Señora Doña Rosa Luján, wife of General Don Antonio Mari who was the alms collector [síndico] for this blessed convent; at that time he had graciously sent us a very generous donation to help us buy supplies. May the Lord already have rewarded him because he was taken by His [Divine] Majesty during our first year in Lima. To this day and always in the future we will be grateful to him.

Once we had settled in our carriage, and all the other ladies and gentlemen did the same, we left together in a great procession. Lieutenant General Don Francisco de Castañeda, who was the father of one of our *colegialas* and a very considerate man, ordered the cannons to fire a royal volley and all the soldiers to fire their weapons. We continued in a procession together and there was such a large crowd that it seemed more like a village than the countryside.

When we arrived at a place that is half a day's journey, called La legua [The League], many other people whom we had met in Spain and on the ship came out to accompany us. The *compañía de los naturales*[112] also came out to escort us and after them the city council, both

112. I am not sure to whom she is referring; perhaps this was a delegation of Indian chiefs

secular and religious, welcoming us from each branch of the state. There were countless coaches and carriages and many people on foot on the roadside. I couldn't do anything else but ask God to let everything go smoothly; it was a long route of two leagues and with so many people they were trampling each other.

About a half league from the city the señor viceroy's cavalry arrived to inform us on behalf of His Excellency that we should enter the city of Lima in his coach. We were very happy to accept his order because all four of us could travel together. The very kind ladies did not feel the same way, however, and they were upset to have us leave their company.

After this we saw Brother Juan Benites in one of the calashes. This man was venerated by all since he was the most beloved and oldest brother of this blessed house, to which, from a young age, he had offered his service and fortune, promising to be its lifelong slave. He had always carried out his service with the utmost perfection, setting an example for everyone, especially in the area of penance. Nothing seemed too difficult for the *colegialas*. This was true even when he was very ill; when we saw him he looked like Saint Francis of Paula, in both his dress and physical appearance. He was very handsome, but pale, indicating his penance and lack of health. He used to be very robust, having been brought up in Spain whence he came with the same thirst for riches as others. Yet he changed his mind and traded these earthly desires for greater ends and benefits, as if he were a prince. The whole of Lima was witness to this truth, and we were as well after we saw everyone's devotion, from both the young and old alike, during his funeral. We took three whole days to bury him because nothing was enough to satisfy the great devotion of all the people who lined up to see him. Many assured us that he was responsible for several miracles. He died four or five years after the convent's foundation. When Brother Juan Benites saw us on the day of our arrival, he spoke to us as if he were Simon, saying: *Nunc dimitis servum tuum Domine secundum verbum tuum im pace.*[113] He spoke these words with such fervor that he then fell to the ground as if he had fainted. I must confess that even though I had already heard about him, he seemed to me even more virtuous than his reputation. As soon as he was able he climbed

---

from local tribes or maybe it was a military company made up of local soldiers.

113. "Now you dismiss your servant, O Lord, according to your word in peace," is a slightly altered form of the line from Luke 2:29: Nunc dimittis servum tuum, Domine, secundum verbum tuum in pace.

down from his calash to welcome us. When I heard him saying that he was so wanting to die, I told him that I was now his abbess and that I mandated he not ask God to take him away, but only let Divine Will be fulfilled. He accepted this with great humility, and during the time he served us he did so with the same goodwill he had always had.

From the moment we stepped into His Excellency's coach his guards escorted us. This was a good precaution because we were surrounded by a multitude of people, causing a lot of confusion. In addition, all the church bells were ringing, and there were bonfires and *luminarias*[114] in the streets. We were embarrassed to see the reception that this illustrious city had prepared for us. Everyone clamored to see us, and we entered the city with the curtains open and with [a statue] of the holy Christ between us. Nonetheless, the people were not satisfied with only seeing covered bundles, and some of them (if they had not been stopped by the guards) were determined to lift up our veils.

We entered the street of San Juan de Dios that is very close to this blessed house, where our little sisters, believing that we would be permitted to stop in, even if for just a minute, were waiting for us with music, the exposition of the Blessed Sacrament, and a thousand other little details. There were many priests dressed in white surplices, and when they saw us pass by our future convent without pausing at all they walked right between the mules, trying to stop us, and saying that our little sisters would be very upset if we did not pay them a visit. We felt horrible about this, but there was nothing we could do because the distinguished canons, seeing the masses of people, were afraid that we might get trampled. They also believed it was best to continue on since it was already quite late. In fact, they even had to use twelve torches to light our way. For these reasons it was impossible to give this consolation to those *señoras*, and we offered up our inability to see them to Our Lord, which was quite a penance.

As we continued along there was so much clapping, applause and noise that we had never seen anything like it before. When we finally arrived at the Convent of the Discalced Trinitarian nuns, we did not go into the church due to the same throngs of people. These blessed sisters welcomed us by singing *Te Deum Laudamus*. We went to choir to show reverence to the Blessed Sacrament exposed on the monstrance. After the nuns finished singing they closed up His Majesty and took us to a room they had made up for

114. Candles placed on windows, balconies, towers, or streets during public festivities and celebrations.

us. They entertained us with much discretion and provided us with refreshments. Although it was very late, we were really thankful for this because we were feeling very overheated.

The next day we received several notes from our *colegialas* who complained bitterly that we had not stopped in to visit them. After they received my reply they understood the reasons and actually I think we even felt worse about it than they did. We promised that we would pay them a visit, something we did on several occasions before the foundation. We needed to instruct them on several details concerning cloistered life, for although they were already very virtuous, living as if they were cloistered, there were still things regarding religion that they had not yet learned.

For this reason, and because we needed to redeem some annuities that were owed on this house we were delayed for three and a half months. During this time the señor viceroy, all the high court and especially the illustrious university, generously gave us four grades of *indulto*[115] (which were worth eight thousand pesos). With this extra funding and other sources, we were able to pay the annuity and to start the plumbing: both of which cost seventeen thousand pesos. These were the types of things they did for us as soon as we arrived. May the generous hand of the Lord repay them as we are also doing by being the perpetual wards of this city.

Once we were settled in the [Trinitarian] convent some benefactors sent alms, causing us great joy because we did not want to be such a burden to those servants of God. Since they have a very generous spirit, they felt bad that their finances did not allow them to give as much as they would have wished.

The day after our arrival the señor viceroy came to visit us, something he did many times because he was partial to nuns. We thanked him for honoring us with so many details he had arranged, many of which he had carried out himself. Since it was during his term [as viceroy] that God had looked kindly on this new foundation—a task that had not been achieved for many years—we asked His Excellency, with all his authority and affection, to be the father and caretaker of our new foundation. He gave me his word, and by putting his hand on my head he said: "Mother abbess, do not despair, because

---

115. In addition to the more common meaning of indult—"a faculty granted by the pope to deviate from the common law of the Church"—the word *indult* can also mean "gift," which makes sense in the context of this sentence. See *The American Heritage Dictionary* (4th ed. 2000), s.v. "indult."

I am here with you and I will always support you in times of need." That is exactly what he did. It was through his efforts, and because there is a vein of charity in the hearts of those at court, that everything I have already mentioned was accomplished. Also there was a lot of construction on the upper portion of the convent to prevent neighbors from seeing inside. Two distinguished *oidores* of the high court were able to collect enough alms, in addition to the eight thousand pesos in indults, to cover all these costs. One of these men was our brother and alms collector [*síndico*], Don Gonzalo Baquedano of the Order of Santiago, who is now in Madrid and a member of the Council of Indies; the other was Don Pedro de Echabes of the Order of Alcántara: together they collected four thousand pesos. They also gave us some of their own funds, and His Excellency, at the last minute, gave two thousand pesos. He also wrote to some of the most powerful people in this kingdom, asking them to give us alms. Blessed be the Lord who had arranged for this saintly prince to come to our aid. I hope that his good deeds have served him well in the presence of God who took him away from us three years ago when he was traveling through Mexico on his way to Spain.

The first day that we visited our blessed convent its inhabitants greeted us with such strong displays of affection that words cannot describe how they welcomed us. We were consoled by the fact that our main aspiration [the foundation] would soon be fulfilled. They [the future nuns] seemed so lovely to us, and in addition not one of them was elderly, indeed most were of a very lovely age, very capable and from well-known families. All this, along with their many other attributes, more than helped us instruct them in the tasks of convent life.

Concerning the status of our convent, much had already been done: the cloister is very beautiful and according to the standards of our constitution; there are sixteen cells which are larger than is customary in our communities, but this could not be remedied because they [the builders] constructed them thinking that we would use them in the style of the Carmelites so it was not their fault at all; if anything, it was a lack of foresight not to have sent our requirements from Spain. The choir is very beautiful, but since the grille was too large, the inside had to be modified by making it smaller according to the correct size. We were not permitted to modify the outside of the choir so as not to alter the beauty of the arch. We also found that there was already a finished antechoir, sacristy, workroom, laundry room, kitchen, and refectory—although the latter needs to be lengthened because we are now double our original number [of nuns]. Though not totally completed, the majority of the church was finished. It is very beautiful.

Since experience has taught me what is necessary for a community, I informed His Excellency that what we needed most were the following: running water, some cells, and above all, a covered roof that did not need to be totally completed, but just enough so that we would be protected from the elements. All this was done. Moreover, since the day of the foundation, with all the charitable donations, construction has never been halted on the convent. The first things constructed were the novice quarters, the pantry, the plumbing, two cisterns, and stone washing basins. The kitchen was constructed with the convenience of running water (without our having to carry it) so that it flows directly into the same vessels that are then used to wash dishes. The water also flows out of these vessels; the same system was set up for the washing basins, making everything so much easier. Sixteen cells were also constructed and now at the time of the revision of this account the infirmary has been built. For seven years we have had to make do with just a large cell, and now (blessed be the Lord) it is the most comfortable workplace in the convent. Because it was constructed with our input, every last detail was added, not only to care for the ill sisters, but also for the nurses. It has a very beautiful main room with an altar on the main façade. There are patient rooms off to one side, a cell for the nurse on the other side, and another small room for the unmentionable needs. In each small patient room there is a little wall cupboard so that the ill sisters can store their things. The refectory has a table with sturdy benches and each seat has its own little storage box. It also has two armoires, a pantry, a small patio, a cabinet to store large earthenware jars, a fully equipped kitchen, and everything possible that is allowed by the Capuchin order. Last year, in 1721, the church was finished and it was inaugurated for the *septena*[116] of our Father Saint Joseph which is our great feast day.

It is not right to keep secret the names of those who have sponsored the building of this convent. The infirmary was built by our benefactor Señor General Don Joseph de Angulo, Knight of the Order of Santiago, who also built us a room with views of the sea that is used to hang clothes; and last but not least, the basin next to the turn is very useful for that spot. When we arrived we found that he had built a very fine entranceway for the turn. The viceroy, the university, and other benefactors saw to the cells, the running water, and all the

116. A series of seven prayers.

other things that I have already mentioned. As for the church, (after what had already been constructed), our father confessor along with the alms collector [*síndico*] at the time, Señor count of las Torres Don Juan Calderón de la Barca, who was the *oidor* of the Royal High Court of the Order of Santiago, went out asking for alms. May he rest in God's grace—which I hope he does, because he was a very great supporter of our order. He proved this even after his death when he left us ten thousand pesos: eight thousand for a chaplaincy and the remaining two thousand to help offset the costs of his funeral, since he had asked us to bury him in our church. I trust in the Lord's kindness that He will have rewarded his good deeds and accepted our repeated prayers and good works for his soul in purgatory. Returning to what I was saying, they went out asking for alms for the completion of the church, and three or four thousand pesos were collected. That money, along with Don Joseph de Angulo's contribution, was used to erect many beams for the church's walls that were still missing.

This was all that was done to the church until the beginning of the year 1720. At that time Our Lord decided to use a señorita as His instrument to provide a joyous finish to His holy temple. She was from one of the most noble families of this city: the daughter of General Don Pedro de Azaña and of Señora Doña Juana de Llanos.[117] His [Divine] Majesty had inspired in her a great wish to become a Capuchin nun ever since she had heard that we were coming. Earlier she had wanted to become a Carmelite because she believed them to be the strictest order, but when she heard that the Capuchin order was even more rigorous, she was determined to become one of us. Her parents never were in accord with her wish to become a nun, especially a Capuchin. They had other children, but she was the only girl and the most beloved for the virtuous nature the Lord had bestowed on her. This señorita avoided discussing the subject of becoming a nun with her parents since, as a loving and obedient daughter, she saw that it caused them such distress. Nonetheless, this did not stop her from secretly arranging the steps to realizing her vocation. For six years she struggled with her own calling and her respect for her parents. After the first three years of her struggle Our Lord took the afore-mentioned Don Pedro de Azaña [her father]. His passing rendered

117. The Madrid manuscript never mentions her actual name, but Rubén Vargas Ugarte tells us in a footnote in his Spanish edition of the text that she was Sor Juana de Azaña, *Relaciones de viajes* (*Siglo XVI, XVII y XVIII*), 373. He has edited several of her religious poems and a biography of her in volume 4 of the series *Biblioteca Histórica Peruana*.

it impossible for her to fulfill her calling because she did not want to leave her mother alone at this time of grief. Moreover, the eldest son of the family, Don Miguel de Azaña—who today is the *regidor*[118] of this city—had left town to see to the administration of his hacienda. It was God's Will to strengthen her desire and will to become a nun, because her brother made her wait another three years while he was busy at the hacienda. When the time came our aspirant readied herself to put into effect the wish she had so carefully planned, and even moreso when she saw the various steps that were being discussed to arrange a marriage for her. She came up against many obstacles and knew that her mother would never back down, but she saw herself compelled by a divine calling. Furthermore, her soul was filled with such religious fervor[119] that she could only find bitterness in the outside world and its pleasures. She could wait no longer. One day when she went with her mother to give confession at the Convent of Nuestra Señora de las Mercedes she made her move. At the moment when her mother was bowed before her confessor, she jumped into her calash, raced to our convent and entered it as a fugitive. We had been informed of her plans, but had not expected her to come until Purification Day which was to fall on January 19, [1720]. Soon thereafter when the blessed señora realized that her daughter was missing, she frantically rushed to the turn, shouting for us to hand her over, claiming that her daughter was of fragile health and not fit for such a rigorous lifestyle. The señor archbishop was informed and sent his vicar-general to take her out of the cloister and test her to see if she really had a true religious calling. She more than met all the requirements, but it was impossible for him to take her back to the outside world as she would not go. She said that she was not there under duress, that she had entered the cloister of her own free will, and that her action could only be considered a true part of her calling.

We had a very difficult day because her mother entered the convent through the construction site, saying that we should hand over her daughter. Her daughter was so determined in her intentions that we could not get her to budge an inch. When the señor vicar-general saw the state of things, he tried his best to appease everyone, letting them know that we did not have a hand in any of this. He decided to let her brother enter the cloister so that he could speak to her alone

118. The community representative before the municipal government.

119. The Madrid manuscript uses the word "fiscal." The Peru transcription uses "fervor," which makes more sense in the context of the sentence.

and try to convince her to go home. This was done, but all in vain because nothing was accomplished. It was impossible to calm down her mother, who gave many convincing arguments to be allowed to see her daughter, believing that her presence would sway her daughter's determination. Seeing the mother's tenacity, she was given license to enter the cloister where we left her alone with her daughter, but this was a terrible scene that the daughter dreaded because of the great love and respect she had for her mother. She feared that she would be unable to console her mother by returning to her side because it was God's Will for her to become His [Divine] Wife. They had a heated argument: first with promises and kind words, then with anger and threats, but she would not change her mind. This meeting took place in the interior convent parlor where there was a statue of the most holy Christ. Her mother implored the Christ figure not to leave her alone to die of a broken heart. To which her daughter replied: "Señora, if your grace is going to die, then I am already dead to the world. It is the same Christ [you speak of] who has asked me to leave it and it is for Him that I cannot leave [the cloister]." Defeated by her daughter's resolution, she returned to us consumed by the utmost grief imaginable. We had to hold her in our arms as she was half dead; we felt truly sorry that we were unable to console her. Everyone left and His Illustriousness [the archbishop] did not give permission for the daughter to receive a habit that day, so that she had to wait in her secular garb until the next day. At our aspirant's insistence, and since by this time no one had any doubts about her religious calling, she was given the habit on January 20, 1720. Once she saw her dream come true it was impossible to describe the happiness and comfort experienced by both this little angel and the blessed community. Before taking her vows—and because the Lord allowed it—she decided to make an offering to his [Divine] Majesty by using her share of her father's inheritance (of fifteen thousand pesos) to complete the church. She enacted the necessary paperwork; all the while hoping that God would bless her taking of vows. We are not permitted, however, to speak with novices of financial matters in our order, so we excused ourselves from getting involved until she assured us that no one had convinced her to make the donation. She never asked our advice except to receive permission to set everything in motion. After the donation, construction of the church was very rapid, so that by the time of her profession, the church, although not perfect, was nearly finished. Several people tried to convince her that she should postpone her taking of vows so that it would coincide with the day of the inauguration of the church, but she would hear nothing of it. She did not want to wait a day longer, and also she did not want that event to outshine her taking of vows. All her happiness rested in becoming a nun and everything else was of little importance to her. I have said all this in order to document the steps involved in completing the church. May the Lord be praised for all of it, and I hope that through His mercy He will make of her soul another temple pleasing to His divine eyes.

## Chapter XVII
### All that Took Place until the Day of the Foundation

We continue narrating the events of our foundation. While we were staying (as I have already mentioned) with the Trinitarian nuns, the two señores, the dean and the head of the city council took us to see all the convents in the city before we entered our cloistered convent. The nuns of those convents were very anxious to meet us because they greatly admire all things from Spain. There are twelve convents [in Lima] and all of them showered us with such indescribable favors, music, presents and attention that we did not know how to thank them for their generosity. In most of the convents there were sisters and other relatives of our *colegialas*, and this caused an increase in their love and graciousness towards us. In the Convent of our Mother Saint Clare was a sister of our father confessor, who, along with the mother abbess, treated us with great generosity. The last convent [we visited] was the Real de Santa Rosa, where the mother abbess was Señora Doña Josepha Portocarrero. She is the daughter of His Excellency señor count of Monclova.[120] He was the former viceroy of Lima, where he reigned for many years. This illustrious señora took great pains to honor us in accordance with her noble status. She was very famous both in Spain and throughout the Indies for the many trials she had to endure in order to become a nun. For this reason, along with the fact that I do not want to affront her great humility nor offend her modesty, I shall stop speaking of this matter. I shall only say that after meeting and speaking with her we were very impressed with her great virtue and with her wise resolution to become a nun. The Lord had blessed her with such high virtues that there were no other options for her except to serve her creator.

In all the convents we visited, the señor viceroy honored us by paying a visit every afternoon. In this one he made a special effort to visit because of the great veneration everyone showed this señora [Josepha Portocarrero]. As she was trying to shower us with even more favors, she asked His Excellency to let us stay with her for a longer period of time. She wanted to have us at her side for eight days, but the Trinitarian nuns protested so strongly that she humbly acceded to their demands, and thus we only spent two days visiting that convent.

---

120. Melchor Antonio Portocarrero and Lasso de la Vega (Count of Monclova) was first viceroy of New Spain and then of Peru. He reigned in Peru from 1689 until his death in 1705.

Every night when we returned to the [Trinitarian] convent it seemed like springtime. They would always celebrate our arrival with fireworks and other festivities, which they readied for us inside the cloister.

One day the señor viceroy decided to take us to a chapel he had built and dedicated to Saint Liberata[121]—his great place of devotion on the *Alameda*.[122] This was the same spot where sacred species[123] had been found on the ground. All this occurred because a poor wretch of a man (I believe it was due to his complete ignorance) had committed a sacrilege. He carried out—what I mean to say is that he stole a chalice containing the Blessed Sacrament.[124] Nonetheless, His [Divine] Majesty wanted him to be caught. During the days he was in hiding (I think it was four or five) the whole city was thrust into a terrible time of sorrow with demonstrations of mourning and other expressions of true Christianity. His Excellency, since he is such a pious man, participated fully in these acts of faith and religion. Later when he received news of the whereabouts [of the sacred species], (he found out through a young boy who had seen a mysterious thing being wrapped in paper in the countryside), he left on foot, and although His Excellency could hardly walk, he traveled a very long distance in search of the sacred species. They were found in a very damp place and were taken back in an extremely solemn procession. To eternally remember this occurrence, His Excellency built the aforementioned chapel on that very spot. It is very well taken care of. Here [at the chapel] he favored us and treated us with much kindness. We worshiped the ground where His Divine Majesty had rested, which is below the saint's altar. The statue of Saint Liberata is a beautifully crafted representation depicting her martyrdom by crucifixion. This man honored us in every way he could. After all these events, our convent was finally ready and the day of our foundation was set for the fourteenth day of May in the year 1713.

121. Saint Marina of Aguas Santas (Marina of Orense) (119–139 AD), often confused with the popular figure of Wilgefortis (known as Liberata in Italy and France, and Librada in Spain), is sometimes represented as martyred on a cross. This makes sense because later in the paragraph the author refers to her martyrdom. For more information on the events regarding the chapel, see Ricardo Palma, "La fundación de Santa Liberata: Crónica de la época del vigésimo quinto virrey del Perú," in *Tradiciones peruanas completas* (Madrid: Aguilar, 1964), 519–22.

122. Paseo de la Alameda is a popular tree-lined promenade in Lima.

123. In the Catholic faith the sacred species are the bread and wine that have been changed into the body and blood of Christ after the consecration, retaining only the appearances of what they were formerly.

124. The author corrects herself.

His Excellency made grander arrangements for our special day than had ever been seen before in any previous convent's foundation. All Lima's communities set up altars along the way from the holy cathedral to our holy convent. Each religious order processed with [a statue] of its founder or patron, and the floats [carrying the statues] were just as richly adorned as their altars.

On the eve of the foundation all the church bells were ringing and there were so many bonfires and luminarias that one could only praise God. Actually it seemed as if God had come down from heaven to join in the celebrations that were taking place on earth, because from about four o'clock in the afternoon until eight o'clock in the evening there appeared a stunning palm tree in the sky. Its trunk sprouted out of a small cloud—the color of our habit—next to which was a cross made of stars. The Trinitarian nuns called us so that we could see it. Everyone was amazed, and they pointed out to us that there were five beautiful shoots coming out of the trunk and that their fronds were extended outward in a remarkable display of splendor and variety; everyone said that heaven had also set out *luminarias*. I was really confused when I heard this. The señor viceroy was notified of the palm tree and he joyously responded: "Do not be afraid, because it is a sign of triumph. It shows that God has defeated the Devil, who had relentlessly tried to foil this foundation."

The day of our foundation finally arrived, and I do not have the words to express our sorrow at having to leave our blessed Trinitarian nuns from whom we had received such kindness that we never will be able to repay them. We had lived together in such harmony that it was as if we were of the same order. At least we had the consolation of mixing this sad moment with the great joy of entering our new blessed convent; otherwise the pain would have been unbearable.

These blessed [Trinitarian] nuns had spent many days in preparation for our foundation. They gathered together many jewels and pearls in order to adorn five girls and one boy, all nieces and nephews of our father confessor. The patron saint of their convent is Saint Michael, and so they dressed up the little boy to represent the saint. They used the boy to recite a *loa*[125] during our goodbyes. The piece was so touching that we could hardly bear to listen to it. They dressed up one of the girls as Jesus of Nazareth and she walked in front of us, adorned in all her regalia, during the procession to our new convent. They dressed up the other four girls as little Trinitarian

---

125. Short dedicatory poem of praise (sometimes acted out).

nuns and all five of them recited the *loas* in several parts. Most notably the next day they recited them in our church during the Thanksgiving Mass. The four little nuns walked on either side of us.

All the other convents also gracefully represented themselves. Each one of them dressed up two little girls to represent their prelates, one as the abbess and the other as the vicaress. All of them had prepared *loas* which some of them recited in the cathedral, others in [the Convent of] the Merced, others at the Trinitarian [Convent], and some in our convent. It was such a precious sight to see so many little abbesses and vicaresses, each with her staff. These girls, along with servants, were singing and acting with such confidence and grace that it was as if they had all been chosen and dressed up together as a matching group.

Madre Isabel, who had previously been the superior of this house when it was still a school, dressed up three very lovely little girls to represent the patrons of our convent: Jesus, Mary, and Joseph. We were followed very closely by the little girls, and when we arrived at the convent one of them gave me the keys, the other a cross and the third a staff.

I have already mentioned how His Excellency had instructed the religious orders to set out altars between the cathedral and our convent. The distance is five blocks, a stretch we walked on foot. However, from the Trinitarian convent to the cathedral we traveled by carriage. Two of us went with the señora countess of las Torres and the other two with Señora Doña Magdalena Vilela. Both of them were wives of judges [*oidoras*] and they served as our patronesses [*madrinas*]. It was impossible to have four *madrinas* due to the objections of their husbands regarding the rank of the other candidates, and even though there were many señoras who were of equal status and longed to serve in this capacity, this was not to be because of the etiquette that governs this world. Thus, it was decided that one *madrina* would accompany every two nuns in the ceremony.

We arrived at the cathedral accompanied by a countless multitude of people drawn to the event: everyone in Lima, both healthy and infirm, came out to see us; the route was so filled with people that they could not all fit in the streets. We prayed, giving the distinguished canons time to put on their vestments.

At this point we were not able to see a thing because of our veils and the great multitude of people. Thus we cannot give any details regarding the decorations or adornments along this portion of the route. The throngs of people barely let us squeeze by, even though it was a very orderly procession. Each religious community was lined up according to seniority, and all of them processed with the founder of their order. Also the common people of Lima took part, considering it as their own because it related to the house that had belonged to Nicolás de Dios. The señores from the city council and the secular gentlemen along with the señor viceroy brought up the rear of the procession.

As we passed the Convent of the Merced, we entered the church that had been decorated for this occasion. As we looked in the door a cloud of many little birds and doves were let loose into the air. The main chapel was set up with a majestic table with the exposition of the Blessed Sacrament. The music was beautiful. [The monstrance holding] His Divine Majesty was then closed up and we continued our procession until reaching our house of Jesus, Mary, and Joseph. Our street resembled paradise because it had been set up with many flowers which were tossed at us as we passed by.

We entered our church which was ornately decorated, and the Blessed Sacrament was exposed. It had not been part of the procession, as it had already been set up in the church many years earlier. Instead, the *preste*[126] carried the holy cross, and from that day it has become a tradition to pray the dedicatory prayer of our church.

We had been praying for a while when the señor viceroy walked towards us. He took me by the hand and said: "Mother abbess, let me see you all off into the cloister." His Excellency was followed by the *oidores*, high officials from both the religious and secular city council, and many of the leading señoras of this city.

At the convent's gate the *colegialas* awaited us, holding candles and singing *Te Deum Laudamus*. Thus we went in a procession together to the choir, and music was played in the church. When that was finished and the Blessed Sacrament was closed up, everyone congratulated us and then the majority of people said their goodbyes. Others did not leave until after prayers had been completed.

At this time the Señor Vicar-General Manuel Gómez de Silva had everyone leave except the first four [*colegialas*] who were already there and who would spend that night with us, receiving the habit the next day. After this he prepared the cloistering of the convent, by inspecting first the whole house and then the area of his domain. Our father confessor, the notary, the fiscal magistrate and the witnesses who had remained behind, all left through the area outside of the

126. Priest who celebrates Mass.

convent's gate. The señor vicar-general gave me the keys so I could lock the door. Once he had followed these steps he knocked on the door and I responded: "Who is it?" He told me he was the vicar-general, and with this I opened the door. These are all ceremonies to turn this house into a pious convent. May the Lord be blessed for this benefit.

By the time we finished the ceremony and everyone had left, it was eight o'clock in the evening. One can imagine our state: we had left the Trinitarian nuns at three in the afternoon, we had spent all that time with our faces covered by our veils, and our heads were pounding. We had not been able to say vespers[127] and we didn't say compline until ten o'clock at night.

May God be blessed, because the next day was just as grand as the first. The Thanksgiving Mass and sermon were attended by all the high class of Lima. In addition to this there were many visitors and much paperwork, and in the afternoon four habits were given to the ones [colegialas] who had stayed with us. At the designated time they went into the church and then returned in the required manner as we were waiting to receive them.

This ritual was very long, because each colegiala was treated to her own individual ceremony as if she were all by herself. The first was Madre Isabel who was given the new name of María Francisca. The second was her [biological] sister, Sister Rosa Teresa who was given the new name of Sor María Coleta. The third was Sister Estefanía who was left with the same name because she received the habit only with the hope of her professing at the time of her death. She was so ill at the time that it appeared that God had only kept her alive for that exact length of time so that she could achieve the joy of religion. Seven months after receiving her habit, she was struck by a mortal illness and taken away by His Divine Majesty. Before our arrival she had also been gravely ill, but this time there was no saving her. She had lived for many years in this pious house, always providing a perfect example of humility as she never tired in her work, especially in her religious worship. The fourth was Estefanía's [biological] sister, Sister Paula, who was given the new name of Sor María Carlota (in honor of her señora *madrina* and benefactor of this convent). She has also since passed away. She lived as a devout and very observant nun for close to five years. These two sisters, who were the most senior of the house,

---

127. Vespers (the evening service, said around 6:00 p.m. or sunset) is part of a series of prayers said at fixed hours throughout the day, otherwise known as the Divine Office. See introduction.

lived a very religious lifestyle in every possible way. Our Lord wanted to take them away to rest and to reward them for all the love and hard work they had given to Him. That day we also finished very late, but this did not stop us from getting up at midnight to say our matins, which were the first ones we said in our convent.

The next day everything was prepared so that four more *colegialas* could receive their habits. The first was Sister Rosa Josepha, who was given the new name of Sor María Michaela. The second was Sister Ann de la Trinidad, who was given the new name of Sor María Gabriela. The third was Sister Sebastiana de San Joseph, who was given the new name of Sor María Serafina. The fourth was Sister María de Loreto, who was given the new name of Sor María Ana. After five days another *colegiala* entered our order, but as a white veiled nun [*velo blanco*].[128] She had previously been known as Sister Catalina, but was given the new name of Sister María Nicolasa.

The *colegialas* remaining in the school did not enter right away due to illness, but they were given their habits within a few days. The first of that group, who had been second in charge, was Madre Ana de Agustín and she was given the new name of Sor María Clara. The other was Sister Andrea de Jesús who was given the name of Sor María Margarita. The third was Sister María Teresa del Santísimo Sacramento who was given the name of Sor María Buenaventura. The fourth was Sister Ana de Jesús, who was given the name of Sor María Ignacia. These are the thirteen *colegialas* who were given habits, and even though there were originally sixteen, three of them lacked both strength and health to follow such an austere lifestyle. They are currently all living very virtuous lives in the outside world.

Our Lord with His great plans assisted all these women, even those who were ill, to have enough strength to complete the year required of the novitiates and then to profess as nuns, all of which brought us great pleasure. On the one hand we were very happy because they were very deserving of this honor, and on the other because they proved wrong all the wise men from the outside world who

---

128. Although this was a strict discalced order of Capuchin nuns, there still existed a hierarchical system. White-veiled nuns (as opposed to black-veiled nuns) normally came from poorer families, or in the New World were often *mestizas* (of mixed race). This meant that they took secondary vows and could not hold office in the convent. They entered the order as a type of servant class—most often they would clean, cook, and help out in the infirmary. There were some convents, however, that did accept *mestizas* as black-veiled nuns. See Fernández García, *Perú Cristiano*, 162.

thought the observance of our [strict] order was impossible; as if the power of God were limited.

No doubt the Enemy [the Devil] had infused in them [the wise men] a sense of great fear regarding our lifestyle. We suffered these ill effects for the first two or three years because they arbitrated all the dispensations with only a semblance of charity. We have proved them wrong, relying on His Divine Power and remaining firm in our observance. We knew from experience that not only are the Capuchins no less healthy than the nuns of other orders, but in fact we are the most robust. Little by little they have accepted this aspect of our lifestyle, but in other ways the common Enemy, with false pretexts of saintliness, has tried to introduce things that are very much in contradiction to our religious constitution and the general practice of our order. Through the charity of the Lord, however, we have harvested the fruits of his [the Devil's] snares and have only become more determined to follow the merits of our strict lifestyle, and so he has been run off. May His Divine Majesty (and this is what I wish) always frustrate the plots of the Devil that he shall try to maliciously hatch against this house of Jesus, Mary, and Joseph. With such patrons and namesakes, and with the intercession from our angelic Father Saint Francis and our glorious Mother Saint Clare, we will be victorious (if we know how to be God's faithful wives) in all the battles this life can offer us.

After the initial taking of vows of the aforementioned young women, our convent began to fill up with even more novices, until we finally reached our capacity of thirty-three.[129] If it weren't for this limitation, judging by the number of women who have wanted to join us and still ask to do so we would be the largest convent [in Lima]. At the time of the revision of this account our convent is filled to capacity without one novice. Blessed be the Lord for His mercy for He has granted us the opportunity to see this convent spiritually filled with very special souls and governed by two servants of His [Divine] Majesty.

The first is our father Don Joseph Fausto Gallegos (who is our permanent confessor) and who after all the expense, work, and care he has sacrificed for this foundation, has dedicated himself to our assistance. This has all been with such great resolve and care that we have never seen anything like it. He devotes his entire day to our care except for the time he spends in the cathedral. May God give him

---

129. During this time it was believed that Jesus Christ died at the age of thirty-three. This was also the space limit for many discalced orders, including the Capuchins.

much strength, health, and a long life, as he is most deserving.

The other is the most reverend Father Alonso Messía, who, since the convent's foundation nine year's ago, has served as our auxiliary confessor. He has executed his duties with great charity and with a prudence very well known throughout the city, serving as its prophet. I will not say another word lest I tread on his modesty and humility.

A blessed priest by the name of Don Andrés de Ayala has also equally attended to us; for the past fourteen years he has been in charge of asking for alms for our convent. We are very grateful to him not only because he has taken on this task, so contrary to human nature, serving as a perfect example for Lima's population, but also because he serves the parishioners who come to the church by hearing their confession and by singing the Mass and proclaiming the Holy Gospel. He is always willing to lend a hand, and he has so much spirit and grace that I hope the Lord will only increase these gifts and keep him with us for many more years.

Here ends this account, which has provided information on the beginning, the middle, and the final stages of [the foundation of] this blessed house. Some details have been added to the version written by our blessed Madre Rosa (may she rest in peace). May His Divine Majesty be eternally praised for His works and particularly for this foundation, which has overcome indescribable difficulties and hardships, all of which are but nothing in comparison to what our great Lord deserves. Hopefully He will allow all of us to die filled with His love. Amen.

*Finis Coronat Opus*[130]

---

130. "The end crowns the work." This is not in the Peru transcription.

**Audiencia** — High Court in the Spanish territories, composed of presidents (the presiding magistrates), judges, and fiscal officers. The High Court had administrative as well as judicial functions.

**auditor** — A nuncio's advisor, can also mean the judge advocate.

**beata** — Third order religious lay women.

**beaterio** — House for *beatas*.

**calzada** — Calced (shod) nuns, a less strict monastic order than its counterpart the dicalced nuns. Black-veiled nuns needed a dowry to enter this type of convent. They could also have servants and slaves. These orders lent themselves to more of a hierarchical system.

**calesa** — Calash, type of carriage; the narrator also uses the terms *carruaje* and *literas*.

**colegio** — School.

**canónigo** — Canon, title used to refer to a member of a chapter of priests serving in a cathedral.

**capellanas** — Ward, literally this word means "female chaplain" in English.

**chácara** — Ranch, term commonly used in the Southern Cone of South America. The narrator also calls it an hacienda.

**colegialas** — Literally means female students and in this text it refers to the young women who were to be the future novices of the new convent in Lima.

**comedia** — A theatrical play.

**coro** — Choir, a separate room with stalls on one side of the church for use by the cloistered nuns. The choir was separated from the church by a grille. The nuns could see the altar, but were hidden from the parishioners seated in the congregation.

**corredor** — Gallery of a ship; platform or balcony at the stern or quarters of some early sailing ships.

**corregidor** — Justice of the peace; can also be a mayor.

**criollo/a** — White man or woman of Spanish ancestry born in the New World.

**custodia** — Monstrance, a large ornate silver vessel used to expose the Blessed Sacrament (the Catholic Church refers to this as the Exposition of the Blessed Sacrament).

**deán** — Dean, a senior member of the clergy (after the bishop), holds an administrative position in the cathedral and is the head of the chapter of canons.

**descalza** — Discalced (barefoot) nuns were much stricter than the calced orders. The Capuchins were a discalced community. Novices did not need a dowry to enter the convent and were generally not permitted servants or slaves.

**descubrir el santísimo** — To expose the Blessed Sacrament on display in the monstrance for public adoration.

**filia** — The Latin word for daughter. The narrator also uses *fillas*, which could be her spelling of the Italian word (*figlia*) for daughter. She is quoting the Italian nuncio when she uses these two words.

**fray** — Friar.

**legua** — League, distance equivalent to about three miles.

**locutorio** — Convent parlor used as a visiting room.

**luminarias** — Candles placed on windows, balconies, towers, or streets during public festivities and celebrations.

**madre** — Mother.

**madrina** — Patroness of a convent.

**Majestad** — His Majesty [God].

**Mar del Sur** — The South Sea, the Pacific Ocean below Panama.

**mestizo/a** — Person of mixed Spanish and indigenous descent.

**nuncio** — Direct representative of the Pope in a foreign state.

**Oficio Divino** — The Divine Office is a strict prayer schedule. Nuns would pray seven Hours in a twenty-four hour day: a typical day would be marked by matins and lauds (considered as a single hour), prime, terce, sext, nones, vespers, and compline.

**oidor** — Judge of the high court of Indies.

**oidora** — Wife of an oidor.

**posada** — Rustic country inn.

**postrar** — To prostrate: to kneel down or lie face down, as in submission or prayer; to throw yourself at someone's feet.

**prebendado** — Prebendary or Canon, a member of the clergy of a cathedral or collegiate church. María Rosa also uses the term *canónigos* interchangeably with *prebendados*.

**presidente** — Presiding magistrate of the Audiencia (High Court), often times was the viceroy himself.

**presidenta** — The wife of the president (presiding magistrate) of the Audiencia (High Court).

**provisor** — Vicar-general.

**reales** — Monetary unit: silver coins.

**roquete** — Rochet: white ceremonial vestment.

**santabárbara** — Magazine on a ship.

**salve** — Salve Regina: one of the prayers to the Virgin Mary.

**síndico** — Alms collector; convent administrator.

**sobrepelliz** A surplice is a white liturgical vestment; a white tunic of cotton or linen with wide sleeves worn by priests.

**sufragio** — A short intercessory prayer.

**tornera** — The turn keeper; office held by a nun who was in charge of controlling the schedule of the turn.

**torno** — The turn is the revolving window in a convent that shielded the nuns from the outside world, but they could speak to visitors and even pass notes or small objects through the revolving window. It could also refer to the room that housed the turn.

**vara** — A measurement of length of approximately thirty-three inches.

**venta** — Country inn, even more rustic than a posada.

**vicaria** — Vicaress, the nun second in charge after the mother abbess.

**vida** — Spiritual autobiography.

**zaratán** — Breast cancer.

# Bibliography: Works Cited

**Primary Sources**

Acosta, José de. *Natural and Moral History of the Indies.* Ed. Jane E. Mangan, trans. Frances M. López Morillas. Durham, NC: Duke University Press, 2002.

Arenal, Electa, and Stacey Schlau, eds. *Untold Sisters: Hispanic Nuns in Their Own Works.* Trans. Amanda Powell. Albuquerque: University of New Mexico Press, 1989.

*Canons and Decrees of the Council of Trent.* Ed. Rev. H. J. Schroeder. London and St. Louis, MO: B. Herder Book Co., 1941, 1960.

Cartas y expedientes: personas eclesiásticas (1704–15), Signatura, Lima, 536, Archive of the Indies.

Clare, Saint. *Saint Clare's Plan for Gospel Living: The Rule and Constitutions of the Capuchin Poor Clares.* Wilmington, DE: Poor Clares, 1989.

Covarrubias Orozco, Sebastián de. *Tesoro de la lengua castellana o española.* Ed. Martín de Riquer. Barcelona: Alta Pulla, 2003.

"Fundación del Monasterio de Capuchinas de Jesús, María y José de Lima." Ms. 9509. Biblioteca Nacional, Madrid.

Guaman Poma de Ayala, Felipe. *The First New Chronicle and Good Government.* Trans. and ed. David Frye. Indianapolis, IN: Hackett Publishing Company, 2006.

Juana Inés de la Cruz. *The Answer/La Respuesta Including a Selection of Poems.* Ed. and trans. Electa Arenal and Amanda Powell. New York: Feminist Press at City University of New York, 1994.

_____. *Obras completas de Sor Juana Inés de la Cruz. IV Comedias, Sainetes y Prosa.* Ed. Alberto G. Salceda. Mexico: Instituto Mexiquense de Cultura and Fondo de Cultura Económica, 1994.

*Madres del Verbo. Mothers of the Word: Early Spanish American Women Writers, A Bilingual Anthology.* Ed. and trans. Nina M. Scott. Albuquerque: University of New Mexico Press, 1999.

Marcela de San Félix. *Los coloquios del Alma: Cuatro dramas alegóricos de Sor Marcela de San Félix, hija de Lope de Vega.* Ed. Susan M. Smith and Georgina Sabat de Rivers. Newark, DE: Juan de la Cuesta–Hispanic Monographs, 2006.

Salazar, María de San José. *Book for the Hour of Recreation*. Ed. Alison Weber, trans. Amanda Powell. The Other Voice in Early Modern Europe. Chicago, IL: University of Chicago Press, 2002.

San José, María de. *A Wild Country Out in the Garden: The Spiritual Journals of a Colonial Mexican Nun*. Ed. and trans. Kathleen A. Myers and Amanda Powell. Bloomington, IN: Indiana University Press, 1999.

Teresa de Jesús, Saint. *The Way of Perfection*. Trans. and ed. Henry L. Carrigan. Brewster, MA: Paraclete Press, 2000.

Wray, Grady C. *The Devotional Exercises/Los Ejercicios Devotos of Sor Juana Inés de la Cruz, Mexico's Prodigious Nun (1648/51–1695)*. Ed. and trans. Grady C. Wray. Lewiston, NY: The Edwin Mellen Press, 2005.

**Secondary Sources**

Adorno, Rolena. *Guaman Poma: Writing and Resistance in Colonial Peru*. Austin: University of Texas Press, 2007.

_____ and Ivan Boserup. *New Studies of the Autograph Manuscript of Felipe Guaman Poma de Ayala's Nueva corónica y buen gobierno*. Copenhagen: Museum Tusculanum Press, 2003.

Ahlgren, Gillian. "Introduction." In *The Inquisition of Francisca: A Sixteenth-Century Visionary on Trial*. By Francisca de los Apóstoles. Ed. and trans. Gillian Ahlgren. The Other Voice in Early Modern Europe, 1–36. Chicago: University of Chicago Press, 2005.

Alba González, Emilia. *Fundación del Convento de San Felipe de Jesús de Clarisas Capuchinas en Nueva España*. Mexico City: Ediciones Dabar, 2002.

Alvarez de Baena, José Antonio. *Hijos de Madrid, Ilustres en Santidad, Dignidades, Armas, Ciencias y Artes*. Tomo IV. Madrid: Cano, 1791.

Amerlinck de Corsi, María Concepción, and Manuel Ramos Medina. *Conventos de monjas. Fundaciones en el México virreinal* Mexico City: Grupo Condumex, 1995.

Arenal, Electa. "Monjas chocolateras: contextualizaciones agridulces." In *Nictimene...sacrílega: Estudios coloniales en homenaje a Georgina Sabat-Rivers*, ed. Mabel Moraña and Yolanda Martínez San-Miguel, 135–55. Mexico: Universidad del Claustro de Sor Juana, 2003.

Bailyn, Bernard. *Atlantic History: Concept and Contours.* Cambridge, MA: Harvard University Press, 2005.

Bristol, Joan Cameron. *Christians, Blasphemers, and Witches.* Albuquerque: University of New Mexico Press, 2007.

Burkholder, Mark A., and Lyman L. Johnson. *Colonial Latin America.* New York: Oxford University Press, 2004.

Burns, Kathryn. *Colonial Habits: Convents and the Spiritual Economy of Cuzco, Peru.* Durham, NC: Duke University Press, 1999.

Cañizares-Esguerra, Jorge. *Puritan Conquistadors: Iberianizing the Atlantic, 1550–1700.* Stanford, CA: Stanford University Press, 2006.

Colahan, Clarke. *The Visions of Sor María de Agreda.* Tucson: University of Arizona Press, 1994.

Connor, Carolyn L. *Women of Byzantium.* New Haven, CT: Yale University Press, 2004.

Cook, Alexandra Parma, and Noble David Cook. "Introduction." In *The Discovery and Conquest of Peru: Chronicles of the New World Encounter* by Pedro de Cieza de León, ed. and trans. Alexandra Parma Cook and Noble David Cook, 5–35. Durham, NC: Duke University Press, 1998.

Elliott, J. H. *Empires of the Atlantic World: Britain and Spain in America 1492–1830.* New Haven, CT: Yale University Press, 2006.

*Enciclopedia General del Mar.* Ed. José María Martinez. Madrid: Ediciones Garriga, 1957.

Estenssoro Fuchs, Juan Carlos. *Del paganismo a la santidad: La incorporación de los indios del Perú al Catolicismo.* Trans. Gabriela Ramos. Lima: Instituto Francés de Estudios Andinos, 2003.

Fernández Fernández, Amaya, et al. *La mujer en la conquista y la evangelización en el Perú.* Lima: Fondo Editorial de la Pontificia Universidad Católica del Perú, 1997.

Fernández García, Enrique. *Perú Cristiano.* Lima: Pontifica Universidad Católica del Perú Fondo Editorial, 2000.

Franco, Jean. *An Introduction to Spanish-American Literature.* Cambridge: Cambridge University Press, 1994.

Gabaccia, Donna. "A Long Atlantic in a Wider World." *Atlantic Studies* 1, no. 1 (2004): 1–27.

Gerbi, Antonello. *Nature in the New World: From Christopher Columbus to Gonzalo Fernández de Oviedo.* Trans. Jeremy Moyle. Pittsburgh, PA: University of Pittsburgh Press, 1986.

Guaderman, Kimberly. *Women's Lives in Colonial Quito: Gender, Law and Economy in Spanish America*. Austin: University of Texas Press, 2003.

Haliczer, Stephen. *Female Mystics in the Golden Age of Spain*. Oxford: Oxford University Press, 2002.

Holler, Jacqueline. *Escogidas Plantas: Nuns and Beatas in Mexico City, 1531–1601*. http://www.gutenberg-e.org, 2002.

Hsia, Ronnie Po-chia. *The World of Catholic Renewal, 1540–1770*. Cambridge: Cambridge University Press, 2005.

Iriarte, Lázaro. *Las capuchinas: Pasado y presente*. Seville: El Adalid Seráfico, 1996.

Jaffary, Nora. *False Mystics: Deviant Orthodoxy in Colonial Mexico*. Lincoln: University of Nebraska Press, 2004.

Kamen, Henry. *Philip V of Spain: The King Who Reigned Twice*. New Haven, CT: Yale University Press, 2001.

Kessell, John L. *Kiva, Cross, and Crown: The Pecos Indians and New Mexico, 1540–1840*. Washington, DC: National Park Service, 1979.

Kirk, Stephanie L. *Convent Life in Colonial Mexico: A Tale of Two Communities*. Gainesville: University Press of Florida, 2007.

Klapisch-Zuber, Christiane. *Women, Family and Ritual in Renaissance Italy*. Trans. Lydia Cochrane. Chicago: University of Chicago Press, 1985.

Kooi, Christine. "Popish Impudence: The Perseverance of the Roman Catholic Faithful in Calvinist Holland, 1572–1620." *Sixteenth Century Journal* 26, no. 1 (1995): 75–85.

Kostroun, Daniella, and Lisa Vollendorf. "Introduction." *Women, Religion, and the Atlantic World*. Ed. Daniella Kostroun and Lisa Vollendorf. University of Toronto Press, forthcoming.

Lane, Kris E. *Pillaging the Empire: Piracy in the Americas 1500–1750*. Armonk, NY: M. E. Sharpe, 1998.

Latassa y Ortiz, Félix de. *Biblioteca Nueva de los Escritores Aragoneses*. Tomo IV. Pamplona: Domingo, 1800.

Lavrin, Asunción. *Brides of Christ*. Stanford, CA: Stanford University Press, 2008.

_____."Unlike Sor Juana? The Model Nun in the Religious Literature of Colonial Mexico." In *Feminist Perspectives on Sor Juana Inés de la Cruz*, ed. Stephanie Merrim, 61–85. Detroit, MI: Wayne State University Press, 1991.

Lehfeldt, Elizabeth A. *Religious Women in Golden Age Spain: The Permeable Cloister.* Burlington, VT: Ashgate, 2005.

Lejarza, Fidel de. "Expansión de las clarisas en América y extremo oriente," *Archivo Ibero-americano* 55 (July–Sept, 1954): 296–310.

Luján Muñoz, Jorge. *Guía del convento de capuchinas de Antigua Guatemala.* Antigua, Guatemala: Editorial José de Pineda Ibarra, 1977.

Lynch, John. *Bourbon Spain: 1700–1808.* Oxford: Basil Blackwell, 1989.

Matute y Gaviria, Justino. *Hijos de Sevilla señalados en Santidad, Letras, Armas, Artes o Dignidad.* Tomo II. Seville: Oficina de El Orden, 1887.

Mendiburu, Manuel de. *Diccionario Histórico Biográfico del Perú Tomo I.* Lima: Solis, 1874.

Mendoza Muñoz, Jesús. *El convento de San José de Gracia de pobres monjas capuchinas de la Ciudad de Querétaro, un espacio para la pobreza y la contemplación femenina durante el virreinato.* Querétaro, Mexico: Cadereyta, 2005.

Mignolo, Walter. "Introduction." In *Natural and Moral History of the Indies* by José de Acosta, ed. Jane E. Mangan, trans. Frances M. López Morillas, xvii–xxviii. Durham, NC: Duke University Press, 2002.

Molina Arrotea, Carlos. "Juan de Armasa y Arregui." In *Diccionario Biográfico Nacional,* ed. Carlos Molina Arrotea, et al. Tomo I, 336–37. Buenos Aires: Rivadavia, 1877.

Montero Alarcón, Alma. *Monjas Coronadas.* Mexico City: Círculo de Arte, 1999.

Muriel, Josefina. "Cincuenta años escribiendo historia de las mujeres." In *El Monacato Femenino en el Imperio Español,* ed. Manuel Ramos Medina, 19–32. Mexico: Condumex, 1995.

_____. *La sociedad novohispana y sus colegios de niñas: Fundaciones de los siglos XVII y XVIII.* Mexico City: UNAM, 2004.

_____ and Anne Sofie Sifvert. *Crónica del Convento de Nuestra Señora de las Nieves, Santa Brígida de México.* Mexico City: UNAM, 2001.

Myers, Kathleen Ann. *Neither Saints Nor Sinners.* Oxford: Oxford University Press, 2003.

_____. "Introduction." In *Fernández de Oviedo's Chronicle of America: A New History for a New World* by Fernández de Oviedo, trans. Nina M. Scott, 1–11. Austin: University of Texas Press, 2007.

Olson, James S. *Bathsheba's Breast: Women, Cancer & History.* Baltimore, MD: Johns Hopkins University Press, 2002.

Owens, Sarah E. "Journeys to Dark Lands: Francisca de los Angeles' Bilocations to Remote Provinces of New Spain." *Colonial Latin American Historical Review* 12, no. 2 (2003): 151–71.

Palma, Ricardo. *Tradiciones peruanas completas.* Madrid: Aguilar, 1964.

Paravisini-Gebert, Lizabeth, and Ivette Romero-Cesareo. "Introduction." In *Women at Sea: Travel Writing and the Margins of Caribbean Discourse,* ed. Lizabeth Paravisini-Bebert and Ivette Romero-Cesareo, 1–7. New York: Palgrove, 2001.

Poska, Allyson. *Women and Authority in Early Modern Spain: The Peasants of Galicia.* Oxford: Oxford University Press, 2005.

Pratt, Mary Louise. *Imperial Eyes: Travel Writing and Transculturation.* London: Routledge, 1994.

Premo, Bianca. *Children of the Father King: Youth, Authority & Legal Minority in Colonial Lima.* Chapel Hill: University of North Carolina Press, 2005.

Prescott, Anne Lake. "Introduction." In *Crossing Boundaries: Attending to Early Modern Women,* ed. Jane Donawerth and Adele Seeff, 11–24. Newark: University of Delaware Press, 2000.

Prieto del Río, Luis Francisco. *Crónica del monasterio de capuchinas.* Santiago, Chile: Imprenta de San José, 1911.

Putnam, Lara. "To Study the Fragments/Whole: Microhistory and the Atlantic World." *Journal of Social History* 39, no. 3 (Spring 2006): 615–30.

Rabassa, José. *Inventing America: Spanish Historiography and the Formation of Eurocentrism.* Norman: University of Oklahoma Press, 1993.

Robinson, Jane. *Wayward Women.* Oxford: Oxford University Press, 1990.

Romero-Díaz, Nieves. "Introduction." In *Warnings to the Kings and Advice on Restoring Spain.* By María de Guevara. Ed. and trans. Nieves Romero-Díaz. The Other Voice in Early Modern Europe, 1–45. Chicago: University of Chicago Press, 2007.

Sampson Vera Tudela, Elisa. *Colonial Angels: Narratives of Gender and Spirituality in Mexico, 1580–1750.* Austin: University of Texas Press, 2000.

Sartolo, Bernardo. *Vida admirable y muerte prodigiosa de Nicolás de Ayllon y con renombre más glorioso Nicolás de Dios, Natural de Chiclayo en las Indias del Perú.* Madrid: García Infancon, 1684.

Schlau, Stacey. "Angela Carranza: El género sexual, la comercializa-ción religiosa y la subversión de la jerarquía eclesiástica en el Perú colonial." In *Nictimene...sacrílega: Estudios coloniales en homenaje a Georgina Sabat-Rivers*, ed. Mabel Moraña and Yolanda Martínez San-Miguel, 111–33. Mexico: Universidad del Claustro de Sor Juana, 2003.

Sifvert, Anne Sofie. "Crónica de las monjas Brígidas de la Cuidad de México." Ph.D. diss., University of Stockholm, 1992.

Strasser, Ulrike. *State of Virginity: Gender, Religion, and Politics in an Early Modern Catholic State*. Ann Arbor: University of Michigan Press, 2004.

Tar, Jane. "Flying Through the Empire: The Visionary Journeys of Early Modern Nuns." In *Women's Voices and the Politics of the Spanish Empire*, ed. Jennifer Eich and Jeanne Gillespie, 263–302. New Orleans, LA: University Press of the South, 2008.

Toppi, Francisco Javier. *María Lorenza Longo Mujer del Nápoles de 1500*. Mexico City: Confederación "Nuestra Señora de Guadalupe" Hermanas Clarisas Capuchinas en América, 2006.

Toribio Medina, José. *Diccionario Biográfico Colonial de Chile*. Santiago: Elzeviriana, 1906.

Turner Bushnell, Amy, and Jack P. Green. "Introduction." In *Negotiated Empire: Centers and Peripheries in the Americas, 1500–1820*, ed. Christine Daniels and Michael V. Kennedy, 1–14. New York: Routledge, 2002.

Vargas Ugarte, Rubén. *Historia de la iglesia en el Perú Tomo II (1570–1640)*. Burgos: Imprenta de Aldecoa, 1959.

_____. *Relaciones de viajes (Siglo XVI, XVII y XVIII)*. Lima: Biblioteca Histórica Peruana, 1947.

Weber, Alison. "Saint Teresa, Demonologist." In *Culture and Control in Counter-Reformation Spain*, ed. Anne J. Cruz and Mary Elizabeth Perry, 171–95. Minneapolis: University of Minnesota Press, 1992.

_____. "Saint Teresa's Problematic Patrons," *Journal of Medieval and Early Modern Studies* 29, no. 2 (Spring 1999): 357–79.

_____. *Teresa of Avila and the Rhetoric of Femininity*. Princeton, NJ: Princeton University Press, 1990.

Wiesner-Hanks, Merry. "The Voyages of Christine Columbus," *World History Connected*, July 2006. <http://worldhistoryconnected. press.uiuc.edu/3.3/wiesner-hanks. html> (9 May 2008).

Wybourne, Catherine. "Seafarers and Stay-At-Homes: Anglo-Saxon Nuns and Mission." *The Downside Review* 114, no. 397 (1996): 247–48.